# US+THEM

# LEADERSHIP FOR THE COMMON GOOD

**HARVARD BUSINESS PRESS**

**CENTER FOR PUBLIC LEADERSHIP**
JOHN F. KENNEDY SCHOOL OF GOVERNMENT
HARVARD UNIVERSITY

The Leadership for the Common Good series represents a partnership between Harvard Business School Press and the Center for Public Leadership at Harvard University's Kennedy School. Books in the series aim to provoke conversations about the role of leaders in business, government, and society, to enrich leadership theory and enhance leadership practice, and to set the agenda for defining effective leadership in the future.

OTHER BOOKS IN THE SERIES

*Changing Minds*
by Howard Gardner

*Predictable Surprises*
by Max H. Bazerman and
Michael D. Watkins

*Bad Leadership*
by Barbara Kellerman

*Many Unhappy Returns*
by Charles O. Rossotti

*Leading Through Conflict*
by Mark Gerzon

*Senior Leadership Teams*
by Ruth Wageman,
Debra A. Nunes,
James A. Burruss, and
J. Richard Hackman

*Five Minds for the Future*
by Howard Gardner

*The Leaders We Need*
by Michael Maccoby

*Through the Labyrinth*
by Alice H. Eagly and
Linda L. Carli

*The Power of
Unreasonable People*
by John Elkington and
Pamela Hartigan

*Followership*
by Barbara Kellerman

*Immunity to Change*
by Robert Kegan and
Lisa Laskow Lahey

*Crossing the Divide*
edited by Todd L. Pittinsky

*The Power of Positive Deviance*
by Richard Pascale, Jerry Sternin,
and Monique Sternin

# US+THEM

Tapping the **POSITIVE POWER** of Difference

**TODD L. PITTINSKY**

Harvard Business Review Press

*Boston, Massachusetts*

No part of this publication may be reproduced, stored in or introduced into a retrieval system, or transmitted, in any form, or by any means (electronic, mechanical, photocopying, recording, or otherwise), without the prior permission of the publisher. Requests for permission should be directed to permissions@hbsp.harvard.edu, or mailed to Permissions, Harvard Business School Publishing, 60 Harvard Way, Boston, Massachusetts 02163.

**Library of Congress Catalog-in-Publication Data**

Pittinsky, Todd L.

   Us plus them : tapping the positive power of difference / Todd L. Pittinsky.

    p. cm.

   ISBN 978-1-4221-7777-8 (alk. paper)

  1. Leadership.  2. Interpersonal relations.  3. Positive psychology.  I. Title.

   HM1261.P58 2012

   303.3'4—dc23

                                             2012010781

The paper used in this publication meets the requirements of the American National Standard for Permanence of Paper for Publications and Documents in Libraries and Archives Z39.48-1992.

*Dedication:*

*Tyrell Harris*

*1988–2008*

# CONTENTS

# ACKNOWLEDGMENTS

This book has been a journey in two parts, first conducting the primary and secondary research to understand what positive attitudes toward "others" are and why they matter, and then crafting a book to share what I had learned. In both stages, I had the generous and talented help of many wonderful people and institutions.

First, I acknowledge and thank those who have worked with me over the years on the Allophilia Project (www.allophilia.org): part-time research assistants Randall Adams, Jane Brinkley, Anna Chen, Theresa Cheng, Kasia Chmielinski, Christine Donehue, Jeremiah Johnson, Diana Lee, Gokul Madhavan, Samita Mannapperuma, Hillary McManama, Justin Ng, Jeong Oh, Evgenia Peeva, Max Ritvo, Altaf Saadi, Jennifer Saura, Ashley Siler, Jill Smith, K. Sloan Strike, Sarah Usmani, Chris Wang, Winmar Way, Ayelet Weiss, and Katie Wheeler; full-time research assistants Laura Bacon, Laura Maruskin, and Stefanie Simon; and postdocs Connie Hadley, R. Matthew Montoya, Jennifer Ratcliff, Seth A. Rosenthal, and Brian Welle.

Laura Bacon brought to the research her most unusual and simply wonderful mix of intellect, passion, and humor. She also is one of the most enjoyable embodiments of allophilia, never passing up an opportunity to learn about—and from—an "other." I owe Seth Rosenthal a particular debt of gratitude for bringing his deep intellect to our collaborative work and for his painstaking attention to detail as well as his incredible skill in navigating the challenges of applied research projects. Seth, a collaborator from the beginning, was instrumental in working on the measurement of allophilia. Seth is great because he is precise—indeed, exacting—but never narrow and never dull. R. Matthew Montoya was the formidable and insightful collaborator (and at times critic) any researcher is lucky to find, never letting me off easy. He also convinced me of the power of looking at normative accounts for explaining and predicting intergroup relations. Connie Hadley reminded me to keep on the most ambitious and positive trajectory and to do so with a sense of humor. During the period when the allophilia research came to a head, Connie somehow kept other projects in the lab working like clockwork and seemed to do it effortlessly. How she did it remains a mystery, but her intelligence, stamina, and good cheer had something to do with it. Finally, I thank Jennifer Ratcliff for collaborating on early work on pride and its effects on allophilia and prejudice.

Across oceans, I thank Sammy Smooha and his diverse and skilled research team at the University of Haifa for the eye-opening research we conducted together in Israel.

The Center for Public Leadership at the Harvard Kennedy School provided seed funding for some of the research on allophilia and leadership reported herein. The Center's emphasis on leadership for the common good made it a perfect place from which to begin to branch out from the laboratory into the world in order to understand what allophilia looks like in real social and political life. Executive Director David Gergen, Director Donna Kalikow, Associate Director Loren Gary, and Research Manager Owen Andrews offered both enthusiasm and early support for my effort to look at "us-and-them leadership" in a new way. I am also very grateful to the Ash Institute for Democratic Governance and Innovation at the Harvard Kennedy School for several research grants to study coexistence in pluralistic countries.

A research grant from the Alan B. Slifka Foundation made possible much of my own research reported in this book, but the foundation's support was far more than financial. Chairman Alan B. Slifka was an inspiring model of passion for coexistence. His community work was a vivid demonstration that any progress on coexistence will require great commitment. At the foundation, board member Riva "Ari" Ritvo provided keen insights. She and Alan further made a generous effort to connect me with others in the coexistence community, from whom I learned a great deal that enhanced the emerging work on allophilia. Foundation Executive Director Sarah Silver asked many good questions; answering them enriched the work.

Several faculty colleagues have been invaluable coaches, providing well-timed ideas and strategies. Perhaps their most profound contribution was their encouragement as I tried to come at the well-established, venerated, and often excellent body of research and writing on us-and-them relations from a very different angle.

Of these colleagues, I thank Richard Hackman first and foremost. He has consistently believed that his students are capable of doing important work, has continuously exhibited confidence that they would, and has provided invaluable help at critical junctures to do such work. I, like many others, have benefited greatly from his expectations and coaching. Barbara Kellerman has been an irreplaceable presence, checking in regularly about the progress of this book and serving at important junctures as a sounding board. I thank Barbara not only for her reminders to work on the book, but also for her well-timed distractions from that work—distractions that only the good friend she has become could provide. Rod Kramer stepped up to provide perspectives on the allophilia and leadership work along with shot-in-the-arm encouragements exactly during that "messy middle" stage of the work when such encouragement was most needed. Joseph Nye, though coming at the topic from a very different discipline, sensed that there is valuable work to be done and offered encouragement and support as my colleagues and I were bringing a picture of allophilia into sharper focus. Nalini Ambady helped me develop my skills as a researcher and, ever since, has been supportive and encouraging of my efforts to do work that is both of interest to the academy and of use in the world. I hope that this book, and what-ever impact it has, are worthy of the investments these colleagues have made.

More recently, the Department of Technology and Society at Stony Brook University has provided a fertile environment in which to con-tinue my work. In particular, the interdisciplinary and goal-inspired perspectives of the applied sciences have sharpened my understand-ing of and commitment to *what-if* and *what can be* science.

I wish to thank the researchers whose own work has inspired me to study positive us-and-them relations and/or who have expressed an interest in the allophilia work. I so hope our combined work continues to grow, challenging and redirecting the pursuit of us-and-them schol-arship in the academy and the improvement of us-and-them relations in the world.

After all the research and discussion and theorizing, one has still to write the book. It was a lot of work, and I benefited from a lot of help. I thank Harvard Business Review Press and, in particular, sen-ior editor Jeff Kehoe. Many years ago, when I was in the early stages of the allophilia work, Jeff was convinced that it had a message for a broad audience and encouraged my efforts. It was natural, then, that when the time came, we would work together on the book. John Elder lent his sharp eye and skill at refining ideas to give the book's profusion of thoughts a richer and clearer form. He also provided many challenges and laughs, making the work not only richer, but much more fun. Three anonymous reviewers of the penultimate draft made suggestions that have improved the book's clarity and enlarged its content.

I turn now to friends. Jim Levine, of Levine-Greenberg, is an old friend and his ongoing interest, support, and involvement in my research and writing have been invaluable not only in giving this book its particular shape, but more generally in getting me out of the lab and "into the world." All academics should have a friend like Jim.

Katherine Chen, Margaret Desharnais-Sarro, Sandy Freiberg, Cheryl Green, Barbara Kellerman, Yuka Kiyota, Tracy Pasfield, Michelangelo Sabatino, Margaret Shih, and Karen Sobel-Lojeski have all given me, among so many other gifts, their excellent ideas, their sharp thinking, and—perhaps most powerfully—the confidence that can come from the support and encouragement of good people. Cheryl Green, whom you will meet in this book, has been my dear friend since college. We agree constantly, we disagree constantly, we're very different, and we very often feel like twins. Katherine and Margaret are both friends and colleagues. Katherine has been a constant comrade—encouraging, challenging, and inspiring me with her own tenacity. She also gave the book its title, after a well-timed prod from Mahzarin Banaji to think more about it. Margaret Shih and I met at a graduate school orientation session. Since then, we have sometimes formally collaborated professionally, continuously informally collaborated, and have always been friends. She has helped me navigate every professional and personal challenge I have faced over the years and, for every accomplishment, she has been there to celebrate. Indeed, it is often Margaret who pulls me aside to make sure I do celebrate.

I was lucky to make two friends in elementary school to whom I still owe thanks. For over three decades, Margaret Desharnais-Sarro has always been ready to help me dissect an idea or figure out a little more about how this world works. I suspect she has more confidence in my abilities than I do and her generous expectations have always helped me move ahead. Since Sandy Freiberg and I met, he has watched me work on homework, then reports, later term papers, and now books. Today he is a teacher and principal whose students now gain as much from his mix of warmth, humor, dedication, and excellence as his friends always have.

Beyond all thanks are my family, the people who have always showed me the way and cheered me on in life, teaching me by their love and their actions what is most important about community: Janet and Bernard; Matthew, Julie, Marin, and Luke; Scott; Larry, Jill, Harris, Marc, and Lauren.

Finally, I thank Vladi for being both dearest friend and family and for blessing me with the incitement and companionship of both. And for showing me empathic joy is real.

# US+THEM

# ONE

# US AND THEM

*Where Is the Leadership?*

**A** CHANCE VISIT to my nephew's middle school brought me face-to-face with the leadership gap at the heart of this book. Not that there was a riot going on or kids selling drugs in the hallways. Things were peaceful in this ordinary suburban school, and I had time to check out the bulletin board, where I found this:

> I pledge from this day onward to challenge prejudice and to stop those who, because of hate, would hurt, harass or violate the civil rights of anyone. I will be aware of my own biases against people who are different from me . . .

In fact, I found nearly a hundred of them. All carefully penned and decorated by young hands. They were not the words of repentant hate-crime perpetrators. They were copies of the school's Pledge to

Combat Prejudice, each signed by a third- or fourth-grade schoolmate of my nephew, and one signed by Marc himself.

But who says Marc and his classmates have any such prejudices and hatreds? This pledge had not been a response to an ugly incident at the school or in the community. However, there was diversity in the school's student body, and it appears that the school's leadership—well-intentioned teachers and administrators—wanted to make sure they were dealing with it. Recognizing and seeking to minimize negative prejudice is what came first and foremost to their minds, and their instinct was, as we will see, quite typical. Parents, too, are leaders, and it seems that no parents had objected to the exercise—to their kids being handled as potential if not latent haters. This too, is quite typical.

Typical, but does it make sense? Why were all the kids being branded with some original sin of hate? At the very least, why were they not also credited with an original virtue—perhaps curiosity, open-heartedness, or enthusiasm for others? Cultural differences and even physical differences are often a source of delight and attraction rather than repulsion. Teachers tell me that it is common for children to get excited about a different culture once they've gotten a glimpse of it—the very difference seems to be what appeals to them. I have seen it myself. Years ago, when I worked at a child-care center, my group included a white girl and an African American girl who, whenever they got the chance, would be touching and rearranging each other's hair. These girls did not "see past their differences," as many would be tempted to say. Rather, they found the difference between themselves so much fun that it became the basis of a friendship: "You're not like me, and what fun it is!"[1] So why weren't Marc and his classmates asked to pledge "from this day onward to get a kick out of those who are different from me, get to know them, and be thankful for what they have to offer"? As I see it, the school's leadership was leading *away* from something, but not *toward* something.

## Leading Away, but Not Toward

One can see the same pattern in many other realms of leadership, from business to religion to government. What we so often see is that a leader, recognizing a situation with an "us" and a "them," pursues what seems like a reasonable action to forestall negative relations between "us" and "them." What we can only see indirectly is that the leader has an underlying presumption that the most natural thing for an "us" and a "them" is to slip into a state of conflict, of "us *versus* them." The leader's job, therefore, is to reduce or eradicate the hatred and prejudice that will otherwise lead to that state of conflict. This is leadership that does not acknowledge a very different set of possibilities for an "us" and a "them," also part of our human repertoire and worthy of nurturing: the possibilities inherent in those two little girls playing with each other's hair. This is leadership that is leading *away* from something undesirable—prejudice and conflict—but not *toward* what would be most desirable—joyful coexistence.

Consider a diversity training session conducted for Denver municipal employees. Participants had to watch a training video in which a white guy manages to say hateful things about Latinos, Poles, Jews, and "midgets"—all in less than two minutes![2] Meanwhile, the voice of the narrator confides that "we've all told more than a few" hateful jokes. Says who? Just because *some* people are racist, and crude to boot, is that a reason to assume that we *all* are and to expect each of us—in this case the rank-and-file employees who were put through the training—to "confess" to it?

My point is not that diversity training is unimportant, but that a fictional crude and possibly hateful white man should not be what it is about. Work is where many people have the most contact with "others." Many workplaces are less segregated than residential neighborhoods, houses of worship, and schools. And with the rise of global business, many more people are traveling and meeting other people who are definitely different. Yet business travelers often report being excited to meet these "others" and to experience a different culture.

What would a diversity training program look like that gave the lion's share of the participants the benefit of the doubt, presuming not that they are racists but that they are good people who don't hate others and are actually curious about them and—dare I say—to whom difference is *appealing*? What if the training presumed that most employees are quite interested in others and eager to meet them but would still appreciate guidance in how best to live and work most comfortably with others who are different ethnically, culturally, religiously, and in other ways? What would a diversity program look like that acknowledged the challenges and discomforts of engaging with "the other," but did not assume that these were rooted in hate, negative prejudice, or a sense of "us against them"?

We certainly see this pattern of assumptions about "us" *against* or *versus* "them" play out in public policy. As I will point out elsewhere in this chapter and throughout the book, many national and international organizations are very serious about tracking hate crimes and the potential for such crimes. The FBI, for example, publishes an annual Hate Crime Statistics Report. The European Union Monitoring Centre for Xenophobia and Racism has tracked the rise in anti-Semitic attacks and the rise of Islamophobic attacks following 9/11.[3]

Yet there is no comparable effort to track individuals and groups with positive attitudes about those who are different and the conditions most likely to generate and sustain such attitudes. As a result, we have come to understand a lot more about the angry segregationist than we do about the traveler who can't wait to immerse herself in a foreign way of life. We try to track former members of anti-American forces, such as Al Qaeda, to make sure they don't harm us; we are very interested in what conditions will keep them on this path or that. Do we track former American Friends Service Committee international exchange students to learn as much as possible about what sets some people on the path of lifelong interest in and passion for another culture? Of course we have much to fear from the former Al Qaeda members. But doesn't our increasingly pluralistic world have much to gain from some of those former AFS students? Northern Ireland's ambitious Shared Future initiative includes efforts to monitor its own impact on good relations between Protestants and Catholics "by monitoring the levels of incidents, including crime, motivated by hate."[4] They say they want to promote positive relations—and I'm sure they do—yet what they're going to keep track of is negative relations.

In each of these instances, we see leadership away from things we don't want—hatred, prejudice, discrimination, conflict—but no clear and evidence-based leadership toward what we do want—joyful, committed, and productive relations between different groups. The danger—certainly a real one—is regularly confronted, but the opportunity—just as real—is rarely seized.

In addition, our preoccupation with what we don't want is blinding us to the fact that what we do want is often present in our communities, waiting to be supported and amplified. As I will show, we have developed a collective aversion, through much of the research and writing on relations between groups, to seeing that there is a *positive* power of difference. Difference is not always a catalyst for hate, anger, and violence; it is often met, quite naturally, with respect, curiosity, and even enthusiasm. "Vive la difference."

## Where Is the Leadership?

This is a book about how ethnic, religious, social, racial, and national groups feel about each other and act toward each other—what I call *us-and-them relations* (and what social scientists typically call *intergroup relations*). The term itself is neutral, and the phenomenon is complex. I use the phrase *negative us-and-them relations* to refer to attitudes and behaviors such as hatred, prejudice, discrimination, and violence by members of one group toward members of a different group. I use the phrase *positive us-and-them relations* to refer to attitudes and behaviors such as proactive engagement, curiosity, and mutual exploration with respect to members of a different group and a desire to live and work with them. When there are positive us-and-them relations, "us and them" can become "us *plus* them."

Why don't we see clear and evidence-based leadership toward positive us-and-them relations? *Because, for the most part, this goal is not even recognized and legitimated as a possibility.* It may be expressed as a dream, perhaps—something that stirs us when we hear it from Martin Luther King Jr. ("I have a dream") or John Lennon ("Imagine all the people"), or we may hear it in a church, synagogue, or mosque, but we do not see this goal as achievable by reasonably ordinary leaders using repeatable and scientifically grounded methods. But why not? It's not that positive us-and-them relations are part of some unattainable spiritual realm. They are quite ordinary—something people engage in quite frequently and naturally—but those everyday occurrences have generally been ignored or even denied. Not only are they naturally part of our human repertoire but, as I will show, they can be nurtured. Negative us-and-them relations, on the other hand, are not as natural and inevitable as we are led to believe, but very much a by-product of how our leaders lead—defining constituencies and advancing the interests of those constituencies. This is not what leadership has to be. It is an unfortunate choice from among four basic alternatives.

Most leaders who find themselves having to deal with us-and-them relations take one of three approaches. Some deliberately choose to lead their own "us" against some other "them." The conflict may already exist, and the leader may be trying to ensure his or her own group's victory. In some cases, the leader exacerbates an existing conflict—or even conjures up a conflict where there hadn't been one—in order to solidify his or her own position of leadership. Of course this occurs on the political stage, but it also occurs in business and other organizations, when a leader hopes to get the group roused to action by fomenting competition with a rival.

Some leaders simply overlook us-and-them relations, either considering such matters irrelevant to their goals or else something they just can't do anything about. This seems more benign than actually creating or encouraging us-versus-them relations, but it doesn't always work out so benignly. There is a lot of research showing that the mere presence of strong leadership within a group can increase the likelihood of conflict with other groups.[5] Strong leadership doesn't necessarily cause conflict, but makes it more likely.

Some leaders recognize the need to deal with us-and-them relations, but they take too narrow a view of what can be done. That is what we are seeing in my nephew's middle school, in the Denver diversity training session, in the monitoring of Northern Ireland's Shared Future, and in many more examples to come. Here we find leaders trying to lead away from something negative—prejudice, discrimination, and so on—but not trying to lead toward something positive, at least not in any scientifically grounded and well-tested way.

And then there is a fourth way: leadership that tries to make sure not only that "us and them" does not degenerate into "us versus them" (or stay there if that's where it already is), but also that "us *and* them" becomes "us *plus* them." That approach, seldom acknowledged and even less often taken, is what this book is about.

How big a mistake is it to focus on the reduction of negative us-and-them relations and not on the promotion of positive us-and-them relations in any sustained, serious, scientific way? Imagine if we knew all about how businesses can cut costs but little about how they can generate income—simply because almost no one had bothered to study that. Then imagine a business leader, well versed in such one-sided research, trying to turn a failing business around only by reducing its costs—certainly very important—while doing nothing to generate new business. It would never work. But that is what the middle school's Pledge to Combat Prejudice amounts to—a commitment not to do the bad stuff, but no equivalent commitment to the good things that might be felt and done.

Of course, few business leaders would pursue such an absurd strategy. Most would know that generating something new and positive is something they must do and something that *can* be done by reasonably ordinary leaders. It's a challenge, but it's not magic. Our social, political, and educational leaders, on the other hand, do not typically see the creation of positive, joyful, productive us-and-them relations as something they must do and can do. For example, even a cursory review of recent acts, laws, orders, and initiatives illustrates. clearly that, while policy makers around the globe understand the critical need to build coexistence in diverse and often divided societies, they present their efforts as plans to reduce negative attitudes and hate. The very names of their organizations and events—from the European Union Monitoring Centre on Racism and Xenophobia to a UN seminar series called "Unlearning Intolerance"—focus attention on negative attitudes. The Organization for Security and Co-Operation in Europe has a High Commissioner on National Minorities whose mandate is "to identify and seek early resolution of ethnic tensions."[6] That's an important mandate—where there are national minorities, there can be ethnic tensions that might endanger peace and stability—but what about relations beyond tension? Why aren't they as worthy of a high commissioner's attention? All this reinforces the notion that we're somehow predisposed or wired or even predestined to act with hostility when we encounter people who are different—a notion that, as we will see in chapter 3, is unfounded.

As we build and improve our methods, policies, and interventions for reducing hatred, prejudice, discrimination, and conflict, why aren't we building and improving our methods, policies, and interventions for increasing our capacity and opportunity to be intrigued and even delighted by those who are different—to feel comfortable with them and seek their companionship? Why aren't we tapping the positive power of difference? Most leaders have been misled when it comes to leadership of "us and them." Their view of their options is unnecessarily narrow and ineffective. They are quite right about what needs to be avoided or eliminated—how could anyone miss it? But they don't know the full range of what is possible instead, which will be underscored in the next chapter. They know what to lead us *away from*, but not what to lead us *toward*.

## Hate Science—Necessary, but Not Sufficient

The scientific study of us-and-them relations took off in response to the Holocaust and to the violence attending the struggle for racial equality in the United States. The intergroup relations movement of the 1940s and 1950s enlisted social scientists and social reformers in a collaborative battle against hate. This movement involved a wide range of organizations—including the National Council of Christians and Jews, the Common Council for American Unity, the Service Bureau for Intercultural Education, the American Jewish Committee, the National Council of Churches of Christ, the National Catholic Welfare Conference, the Anti-Defamation League, and the American Jewish Congress—working to eliminate prejudice and discrimination against racial, ethnic, and religious minorities. These organizations sought to employ scientific research to analyze and counteract hate, prejudice, and discrimination. They funded action research projects, with social scientists working alongside practitioners. Agencies interested in the quality of human relations formed partnerships with university researchers.

At its core, the overarching research question motivating the science of us-and-them relations has been: how could such horrible things happen? This science has committed itself to generating not only new insights about such dysfunction, but also new practical knowledge. The "technology" to be derived from this science is a set of methods, policies, and interventions to make sure such things *stop happening* and, at its most ambitious, to make sure such things never happen again.

## Is There an Academic Hate Industry?

Because the intergroup relations movement focused on hatred and prejudice, it came to be supported by a wide variety of groups that could agree on the need to fight these scourges. One result, unfortunately, is that something like a codified hate industry has become entrenched in our universities, where it serves up a most unbalanced intellectual diet. There are hate conferences at prestigious universities. There are undergraduate and graduate courses on the psychology, sociology, anthropology, history, political science, and biology of hate—courses with titles such as "Hate in Cross-Cultural Perspective," "Hate Studies in Business," "Communicative and Social Cognitive Foundations of Hate," "Hate Crimes," and "Why We Hate." There are thousands of very-well-funded research projects on negative prejudice and hate. There are books aplenty on hate: *Why We Hate*, *Prisoners of Hate*, *Mass Hate*, *Who Hates Whom*, *Legacy of Hate: A Short History of Ethnic, Religious, and Racial Prejudice in America*, *Hate Crimes Revisited: America's War on Those Who Are Different*, and *Hate Hurts* are just a few of the titles.[7] There have been proposals for hate studies departments. There is even a refereed scholarly journal devoted to hate, the *Journal of Hate Studies*.

A scholar interested in these matters could have attended, just in recent years, a plethora of interdisciplinary conferences such as Landscapes of Violence: Conflict and Trauma Through Time, International Conference on Hate Crimes, Hate Speech Incitement and Genocide, International Conference on Hate Crimes: Preventing Hate, Violence and Conflict, and the No Hate Conference. The scope of such conferences ranges from one campus or community to regional to national to international. A particular fever pitch is reached on the hate conference circuit when the United Nations holds its semiregular World Conference against Racism, Racial Discrimination, Xenophobia and Related Intolerance, often referred to as the World Conference Against Racism.

This confluence of scholars, administrators, and publishing outlets, by persistently addressing the worst of the many possible relations between "us and them," makes it seem as if positive attitudes and behaviors toward others who are different are outliers, either unknowable or not worth knowing. For example, social scientists study cross-group friendships and contact between members of different groups as a way to reduce negative relations between groups, but do not study friendship as a path to something really positive such as deep interest in, admiration for, or affection toward a different group.[8] And yet friendship often serves as a gateway to a truly positive experience of a different group. It can do much more than simply counteract prejudice, which often was not even there to start with. Philip Rose, a Broadway producer and a white man who did much to bring African American playwrights and actors to Broadway—most notably by producing Lorraine Hansberry's masterpiece, *A Raisin in the Sun*—attributed his love of African American culture to his early experience as a bill collector in African American neighborhoods of segregated Washington, D.C. He made friends there who introduced him to some of the glories of their culture, such as jazz and gospel music, a gift for which he felt lifelong gratitude.[9] Similarly, the Greek-American musician Johnny Otis grew up in a racially mixed neighborhood and developed a lifelong love of African American culture. He taught about African American music and helped the careers of several great singers, such as Etta James and Jackie Wilson. As he put it, "I reacted to the way of life, the special vitality, the atmosphere of the black community . . . this difficult to describe quality . . . popularly known as 'soul.'"[10] How does hate—or the reduction of hate—help us to understand these life stories and so many others like them?

There is even a line of research investigating the effects of hate over time; for example, collective memory and intergenerational trauma. These are important and interesting things to understand but, again, when you look at the field of us-and-them relations as a whole, there's something wrong with its willingness to track hate back through generations while overlooking positive attitudes and actions that happen *today*, never mind seeking their distant roots or long-term effects.

When positive attitudes do appear in the research literature, the researchers themselves seem to adopt a cynical attitude toward them. One team of psychologists argued that whites hold both positive and negative attitudes toward African Americans, but the positive attitudes they went on to study were "sympathetic beliefs and feelings about the minority group as underdog."[11] Feeling sorrow and pity is a *very* limited and circumscribed form of liking an "other." Some scholars have even doubted that positive attitudes about the "other" can exist at all! Another team of psychologists developed a survey tool to measure racial attitudes that included a subscale to measure "ease of interracial contacts" with items such as "I would have no worries about going to a party with an attractive black date."[12] But this was included as a *lie scale*—that is, as a trap to see how much respondents would lie about their attitudes—rather than as a tool with which to measure actual positive attitudes. Confronted, however, with patterns in their own data, the researchers were forced to conclude that their subscale really *was* measuring positive attitudes that some white respondents had about African American people.

A pair of social psychologists have done interesting work on "dual racism."[13] Their "negative racism," is just what you would expect—generalized hostility toward African Americans. But their "positive racism" is not a generalized admiration for African Americans, as you might expect, but rather a "stereotypic admiration of Blacks." This includes attitudes such as, "A Black person is wasting an opportunity by not getting involved in athletics," "When music starts playing, I expect Black people to start moving to the beat," "Black people should take advantage of their natural abilities to sing and dance," and "Black people have a unique quality of sexuality that most White people don't have." Genuinely positive attitudes are not even considered! Is this really the best we can do to understand the full range of us-and-them relations?

Perhaps less distressing in one sense, but also more distressing for its resolute determination to see negativity in any interaction with an "other," was a research presentation I saw on the "discriminatory act" of "speaking slowly to an obviously foreign person."[14] I don't know about you, but if I were in a country where I could speak only a little of the language, I would be thrilled if someone were kind enough to speak slowly to me. It is, I suppose, possible that one might speak slowly to a foreigner while thinking how stupid he or she is, but it is absurd to *assume* the presence of such an attitude. In fact, nothing in the presentation showed that the behavior in question had a negative character. The researchers were studying "an obviously foreign woman who appeared to be lost." Honestly, why wouldn't you speak slowly while trying to give directions to a foreigner who looks lost? It makes sense to speak slowly when giving directions even to a native; he or she is more likely to remember them. The desire to see hate and discrimination everywhere blinds us to some of the other ways people quite naturally respond to the "other."

When it comes to understanding and tapping the power of positive attitudes toward the "other," we have seen nothing like the aforementioned intergroup relations movement, which, to its credit, embraced the tools of social science research. While practitioners on the front lines of us-and-them relations flail, realizing the world needs something better than "less hate" but not knowing how to reach it, social science is firmly entrenched in the study of hate. There are no coordinated movements bringing secular and religious organizations together with social science researchers in order to pursue that something better.

Even Gordon Allport, whom many see as having founded the scientific study of prejudice almost sixty years ago, noted that "it is the pathology of bigotry and not the wholesome state of tolerance that, as a rule, interests social scientists. It is not surprising, therefore, that we know less about tolerance than about prejudice."[15] Working in a different discipline, and from a very different perspective, political scientist Samuel Huntington recognized that, "Differences do not necessarily mean conflict, and conflict does not necessarily mean violence," even while he reasoned that "differences among civilizations are not only real; they are basic."[16] Huntington became famous, and in some circles infamous, for his analysis of potential cultural conflict in his article, "The Clash of Civilizations?"[17] Yet not one of the many who have found inspiration in these diverse thinkers takes up the challenge: to seek a scientific understanding of how and when difference leads to a positive response.

Social science graduate students quickly find that the academy legitimates and rewards the study of hate and is uneasy with the study of anything that seems, well, too positive, too preachy. I experienced this firsthand when I was applying to graduate school and had an interview with a professor well known for her extensive research on discrimination in the workplace. I asked what she had learned about organizations in which discrimination was rare or not a problem at all. She laughed—she seemed to find the question childish—and said, "As you get older, you will learn that discrimination happens." Needless to say, I hadn't found my research mentor, but I had been given a valuable glimpse of a widespread conservatism that keeps so many diversity professionals and the social scientists associated with them focused on hate and prejudice rather than on the positive relations one would think they want to understand and advance.

Of course, most teachers, school administrators, business managers and executives, consultants, politicians, civil servants, and so on are not social scientists. But social science research lies behind much of what they learn in school (not to mention how they are taught in school) and what sort of advice they are given when they have to make decisions or formulate policies. In effect, our social science of "us and them" is our foundation for developing technologies for advancing us-and-them relations. But while we've moved to evidence-based techniques and policies in so many arenas (health care, education, etc.) in the realm of us-and-them relations, we are still using techniques and policies based on general notions—in many cases, just shots in the dark. The results are multicultural fashion shows on college campuses, world-music flea markets, and the like. These are fine in themselves, but hardly enough to change and enhance the actual relations among different groups within countries, companies, neighborhoods, schools, congregations, and other bodies.

### The Media's Appetite for Atrocity

The same overwhelming focus on negative us-and-them relations is to be found in the media. In early 2001, for example, there began to be an influx of black Muslim Somali immigrants into Maine. They were about as "other" as they could be in the "whitest" and "least diverse" state in the nation.[18] In 2006, when a local idiot rolled a severed pig's head into a mosque during prayers—a deliberate abomination—the story was quickly picked up by the media inside and outside of Maine, even making the *New York Times*.[19] It made sense; what else would you expect from such a mismatch of cultures? *But it wasn't the whole story*. Many of the new immigrants were experiencing harsh winters for the first time in their lives, so some locals were donating winter coats while others were helping them understand and operate their furnaces. Members of a local adult learning center organized potluck dinners for American and Somali families—fostering cross-cultural friendships and bonds. Somalis and Americans tried each other's dishes, and Somalis taught Americans to tie headscarves and paint henna tattoos. These actions—and the feelings that motivated them—did not get the coverage that the hatred and stupidity did. Unlike the outbreaks of "us versus them," this outbreak of "us plus them" made the *St. Petersburg Times*, not the *New York Times*.[20]

Of course, this one-sided media focus has roots in human nature. Something that is wrong can be more attention-getting and more motivating than something that might be better. However, it is important to remember that this is a disposition, not a law. This is where leadership is so important, because with good leadership, we can focus on "the dream" as well as on "the fierce urgency of now."[21] In fact, a really inspiring leader, be it Martin Luther King Jr. or Steve Jobs, manages to give a dream the fierce urgency of now by articulating the vision and giving people a down-to-earth way to help bring it about.

There is a danger that having hate command an ever larger share of the collective consciousness is poisoning our collective imagination of how an "us and them" can be. Each time we learn about someone rolling a pig's head into a mosque, such things become a little less shocking and more what we expect. We wish more intensely for our leaders to stop that kind of thing from happening and give less and less thought to what our leaders might accomplish far beyond that. Reporters do need to tell us this awful news, social scientists need to understand it, and leaders need to do something about it. But none of them should stop there. We are letting the worst of the news become our underlying picture of us-and-them relations. We know the negative power of difference very well, but we are barely acquainted with the positive power of difference.

In other words, it is not by accident that the administrators in Marc's school, the politician proposing a hate-crime tracking center, and the diversity consultant bent on getting clients to see the vestiges of their own prejudices take the approaches they do. They are all steeped in a widespread cultural view that us-and-them relations are inherently us-*versus*-them relations. The problems are either already there or just waiting to explode. This is a cultural view that *feels* realistic—partly because the media keep telling us this is just the way things are—but is *not* realistic. As with a television reality show, we get preselected slivers and think we are seeing something real.

We will see in chapter 3 that, while the historical record suggests humans are capable of great fear, animosity, and aggression toward the "other," careful scientific examination does not support the view that this is the inevitable or even the most likely response. While it is true that some sort of fight-or-flight instinct resides in the amygdala (a part of our brain), it is not true that we come wired to run from strangers or else shoot arrows at them. The notion that we are nothing more than killer apes is more misinterpreted science than real science.

There are many possible reasons for the hatred and violence that have played such a powerful role in history, but here I am concerned with the role of leadership. Leaders tend to be guilty either of sins of commission (they provoke intergroup hostilities in order to advance their own or their group's interests) or of sins of omission (they don't move past the negative dimension of us-and-them relations to engage the positive dimension). The positive dimension, which I will discuss in detail in chapter 2, particularly calls for leadership precisely because, in some instances, it is an aspiration rather than a present reality.

## A *What-If* Science of Us and Them

What we have seen so far is that there is a leadership gap in us-and-them relations at many levels, from schools to nations. Leaders have been misled about what kinds of us-and-them relations are possible. They associate truly joyful and productive us-plus-them relations with religious or artistic messages, not with their own down-to-earth responsibilities.

We have seen that this leadership gap has roots in the social sciences, which—for historical and honorable reasons—focused early but too exclusively on hatred and prejudice. For me, then, there is another kind of leadership failure at work—the failure of science to pursue the full spectrum of possible us-and-them relations, both those that already exist and those that could exist. Such a one-sided approach is not only self-defeating, it is inherently unscientific. If you focus only on certain combinations of the variables and ignore the other possible ones, you will never thoroughly understand the phenomenon you claim to be studying—in this case, how an "us" and a "them" can relate to each other.

But in addition, to have us-and-them leadership that focuses on what we want, not just on what we don't want, we will need—and at first this may sound very unscientific—a *science* of "us and them" that focuses on what we want in the future, not just on what we don't want repeated from the past. Although neither science nor technology are inherently bound to serve social or moral ends, they certainly can (and often do) without being any less valid. Medical science, agricultural science, and materials science, for example, are frequently focused on what we wish we could have, be it long life or clothes that don't wrinkle. As long as truth is not compromised, this kind of what-if science is good science. Norman Borlaug, often called the father of the green revolution, was a microbiologist who devoted decades of work to wheat. Not wheat as he found it, but possible crossbred strains that would yield more grain than existing kinds of wheat and would resist diseases that killed existing kinds of wheat. He envisioned a kind of wheat that could help feed the hungry of Mexico, then India, then Pakistan—a wheat that could help save millions from hunger. In short, Borlaug was a scientist who studied things that did not exist and, because he did so with rigorous science, they now do.

Science prides itself on being value-free, but even scientists can forget what that really means. In attempting to understand a phenomenon, scientists cannot apply their values to determine the facts or their logical connections. But values can certainly influence what phenomena scientists seek to understand. As the economist James Tobin noted, "The most important decisions a scholar makes are what problems to work on."[22] Oncology is a science and the oncologist must study cancer cells as they are. But oncology exists because we want to preserve human life and eliminate cancer. Today, engineers are racing to figure out how to make cars go farther with less fossil fuel. This is clearly not just a matter of intellectual curiosity; they are practicing a goal-driven, what-if science. If the physical and life sciences can do that, why not the social sciences?

While the social sciences alone cannot frame the what-if questions that really matter, infusing them with humanity and aspiration, rigorous social science can be used to answer those questions. That's what the intergroup relations movement did, asking a what-if question of the utmost importance: can we have a world in which there are no race laws, no lynchings, no gas chambers? Social scientists seem to have lost some of their nerve since then. Having applied themselves to the problem of hate—for reasons that transcend science—they have hesitated to apply themselves in the same way to the positive dimension of difference. And just as engineers often seek not just an incremental improvement but a breakthrough, such as an engine with zero emissions, so too should some social scientists be seeking a breakthrough in how different groups see and act toward each other.

Sometimes what we want is already there but is being ignored by science. The medical sciences, for example, were once focused almost exclusively—and understandably—on illness and injury. But they have increasingly tried to balance the study of illness and injury with the study of well-being. After all, that's what we all want, and it has always been there; most people aren't sick or injured most of the time, and some people seem to have particularly good health. The fields of criminology and law enforcement have also been learning to focus on how and why people are law-abiding; after all, that's what we want, and it is much more common than crime. In short, sickness and crime are taking their appropriate places amid a wider spectrum of possible conditions or behaviors that do exist and are desirable and therefore need to be scientifically understood. The field of positive psychology has also taken this approach, studying the well-adjusted human functioning that is both normal and desirable, rather than focusing entirely on mental illness.

The science of us-and-them relations, however, is still almost wholly focused on one end of the spectrum of possibilities—hatred, prejudice, and discrimination—with little or no serious attention paid to the rest of the spectrum, to the positive us-and-them relations that *do* exist and that are certainly the goal. After all, there is almost always an "us" and a "them" at hand. Yet, most of the time, we are not at odds with some other group. In Africa, for example, there are an estimated 2,035 linguistic groups and more than 3,000 ethnic groups.[23] It is not uncommon to find more than 20 ethnic groups in one country. And yet, at any given moment, most Africans are not hating or fighting. Why not? We really don't know. It's mostly the hate we study.

Most readers of this book are likely to be curious about another's accent rather than disgusted or repulsed, intrigued by another's religious tradition rather than angered, interested in life in other countries rather than horrified. Yet science has next to nothing to say about these impulses toward "others," impulses that are both present and promising.

Thus, the problem is not at its core an overly fastidious "pure" science, it is a science that is already biased toward one portion of the spectrum of us-and-them relations and therefore disturbingly constricted. Progress in combating hate and prejudice is certainly progress. But, as we will see in chapter 2, it is not progress toward the best of which we are capable. A paper called "The Rocky Road to Positive Intergroup Relations" sounds promising until you realize that *positive intergroup relations* means, for the authors, low prejudice.[24] The authors conclude by saying they feel "encouraged that many low-prejudice people have the motivation to respond without prejudice in intergroup interactions." I don't mean to criticize any one paper or research project as insufficient on its own terms, but are positive intergroup relations really just a matter of people keeping a lid on their negative prejudices? Where is the ambition to study the attitudes that would make someone *want* to be with members of another group, *want* to know more about them, *want* to help them, *want* to live and work and go to school with them? We know these things happen. Yet our science has almost nothing to say about them.

More importantly, this gap in the science is reflected in what we actually see going on in governments, businesses, and schools. Here, too, the ambitions are too limited. A 2008 conference at the University of South Florida had the hopeful title "Welcoming Diversity and Conflict Resolution," but what it actually offered was the "know-how to combat everyday bigotry, hate crimes and prejudice."[25] Important skills, but do they add up to welcoming diversity? If we are ever going to realize the promise of joyful and productive diverse and multicultural societies, we are going to have to go well past this focus on the negative dimension of us-and-them relations and set our sights on the positive dimension of us-and-them relations that we now barely recognize. We will need a rigorous science of that positive dimension, a science that is introduced in the next chapter but is still just getting off the ground.

The same can also be said of leaders in most situations where there is an "us" and a "them." Many leaders do try to bring different groups together, but they have neither the full vision of "us plus them" as a goal, nor the scientific and practical grounding for their efforts that they should have. As we will see in chapters 3 and 4, their efforts are grounded in inaccurate, lopsided, or misrepresented science; in self-contradictory or self-limiting leadership strategies; or in wishful thinking. Just as Norman Borlaug pursued a what-if science of agriculture and helped put the world on a different path, we need a what-if science of us-and-them relations, a science that seeks to know what is possible and how to make it possible. With a fuller scientific knowledge of the full range of what is and what could be, we could develop technologies—methods, policies, and interventions—that are less cynical and more hopeful. Well-trained leaders at all levels could lead us not only farther from what we don't want, but closer to what we do want.

## Road Map

This book seeks to begin the journey not simply away from the prejudice, hatred, and conflict we do not want in us-and-them relations, but toward the joyful and productive coexistence we do want. Chapters 2 through 4 concentrate on the current gap in us-and-them leadership, chapters 5 through 7 on how leaders can do better.

This chapter has explained that leaders typically focus on trying to reduce or eliminate the negative kinds of us-and-them relations that need to be reduced or eliminated, but not on building and maintaining the best kinds of us-and-them relations of which we are capable. There is a scientific gap underlying this leadership gap: we need a less cynical, more hopeful what-if science of us-and-them relations.

Chapter 2 summarizes what I and others have learned so far about the positive us-and-them relations of which people are capable. An assumed range of possibilities that only runs from negative (prejudice and hatred) to neutral (tolerance) needs to be replaced by a two-dimensional model in which reducing the negative is one essential task of us-and-them leadership while building the truly positive is another.

Chapter 3 explains why we haven't focused our attention on the encouraging possibilities discussed in chapter 2. I explain the varieties of inaccurate, lopsided, and misrepresented science that keep leaders at all levels focused on reducing hate and prejudice to the exclusion of creating us-and-them relations that go well beyond mere tolerance.

Chapter 4 continues the discussion begun in chapter 3 with an analysis of common us-and-them leadership strategies (e.g., attempting to replace difference with a common identity) that doom us to disappointing results because they ignore too much of the full spectrum of us-and-them relations.

After chapter 4, the book takes up the leadership challenge first mentioned in this chapter. It presents what I and others have learned about how leaders at all levels can take a hands-on approach to encouraging and enhancing the positive dimension of us-and-them relations. Chapter 5 looks at what I call the *empathy error*. Leadership that makes use of empathic joy—feeling joy at someone's happiness or good fortune—will be much more successful in building positive us-and-them relations. Yet us-and-them leadership focuses too excessively on empathic sorrow—feeling sorry for someone's unhappiness or bad fortune—undermining rather than enhancing positive us-and-them relations. Chapter 6 examines how leaders can use displays of collective pride to contribute—surprisingly, perhaps—to positive us-and-them relations.

Chapter 7 stresses the importance of boldness in us-and-them leadership. There is a time for giant (and even risky) steps rather than the incremental progress and negotiation approach in which so many of our leaders are trained and by which they are ultimately limited. More is possible than most leaders and followers realize. In particular, I discuss the potential of the technology revolution. While it is not at all guaranteed that technology such as social networking will make a positive contribution to us-and-them relations, it is certainly possible, and I suggest a number of ways in which leaders can unleash today's technology to build us-plus-them relations.

My goal in this book is to document the human capacity for feeling drawn, in various ways, to those seen as different and to describe what social science has learned about the conditions under which such responses arise and thrive. Put another way, it is about the *positive* power of difference and how to tap that power. This book will not try to tell you what you—or society as a whole—should do, but it will give you a fuller picture of what we can achieve in our inescapably pluralistic world.

# TWO

# ANOTHER "OTHER"

*A More Realistic Model of "Us and Them"*

INTERNET CHAT group discussions are, of course, not an accurate tool for gauging us-and-them relationships, but they can give us a glimpse of some of the individuals who make up the statistics. In one such forum—a chat group with the disturbing name, "Why Turkish people hate Arabs"—I was struck by one participant's position: "I don't hate them. I simply don't like them."[1] Perhaps inadvertently, this young man has made a very important distinction, not between levels of dislike, but—just as he says—between liking or not liking and hating or not hating. Researchers have, by and large, failed to make this distinction. This is exactly the scientific gap that is reflected in the leadership gap described in chapter 1. In several examples, we saw leaders making a distinction between levels of dislike—the desired level being zero dislike, or tolerance—rather than between liking or not liking and hating or not hating.

By the end of this chapter, I hope you will agree that neither this possibly tolerant Turk nor I are splitting hairs. The difference between not hating an "other" and having positive feelings toward that "other"—the difference between "the other" and "the other other"—is very consequential. By the end of this book, I hope you will see how that candid Turk's comment contains the seed of something much finer and much more befitting our collective ambition.

## There Is a Positive Attitude Toward the "Other"

Who is "the *other* other"? It is the "other" who is definitely different, definitely one of "them" and not one of "us," but who is greeted with curiosity rather than suspicion, enjoyment rather than antipathy, comfort rather than unease. We see this type of us-and-them attitude in those two girls playing with each other's hair (described in chapter 1)—curious, not repulsed. We see it in a high-powered American executive who retires to Mexico because he so enjoys the Mexican people and culture, in a white teacher who works nights at a reggae club because she loves to be around Jamaican culture, in a Boston software engineer who takes the trouble to talk with several Russian-born coworkers to find out what life was like there and how strange American life seems to them at times, and in a New Yorker who spends as much time as she can either in Arizona with the Diné (Navajo) people, whom she loves, or back home seeking support for their struggle over property rights on Black Mesa Mountain. We see it in a Filipina who describes her experience meeting and befriending some Jewish coworkers; she so obviously enjoyed celebrating Jewish holidays with them and was so open in her admiration for their way of life that one finally pointed out to her that it was possible to convert. "I can't do that," she replied. "I have accepted Jesus Christ as my savior." This devout Catholic certainly saw her Jewish friends as an "other," but took great pleasure in their "otherness."

We see this type of us-and-them attitude when the book club in an all-white Midwestern suburb reads a novel about the African American experience with interest and curiosity, not anger and animosity. We see it in the Anglo who attends the Quinceañera of a coworker's daughter, not only with curiosity but also with delight. And we see it in the Muslim or Christian who attends a bat mitzvah, not with animosity or anger but with interest and even enthusiasm for an experience that means so much to "others." We see it in the teenager who enjoys having a diverse group of friends. We see it in the senior who straps on a backpack to travel the world, hoping to avoid the tourist traps and really experience a different culture. We see it in those who join the Peace Corps and the many, many more who will apply for the coveted slots, eager not only to meet but to help the "other."

In all these cases, people are deliberately seeking out the "other." There is nothing unusual about them doing so. Would people in 431 million homes in 170 countries be watching the Discovery channel if they were not interested in people different from themselves? Would millions of young people each year choose to be foreign exchange students? Would millions of families choose to host them? Would *Roots* have glued 120 million—a number far greater than the African American population of the United States at the time—to their TV sets? Clearly, it is as natural a thing for people to feel this positive power of difference as it is to feel the negative power of difference.

Yet even though these are all real people, how they feel and act is ignored—and even denied—by the middle-school Pledge to Combat Prejudice and by the majority of us-and-them leaders, policymakers, and scholars who see that the world is increasingly putting us in contact with "others" but conclude too narrowly that our challenge is to keep the inevitable hate and prejudice from getting out of control. The very real and very promising experience of being drawn to and interested in "others" and their difference is typically considered to be a theme for something like a world crafts fair and very rarely considered a proper object of scientific study, school curricula, and social policy.

Yet this alternative us-plus-them attitude can be found even in places where us-against-them attitudes are strong, widespread, and historically, politically, and economically entrenched. For example, my colleagues and I have found evidence of positive regard for the "other" among Jews and Arab citizens living in Israel.[2] We reasoned that, if we could find evidence of genuine liking in an area in which the social norm was negative or at least conducive to the negative, we would have strong evidence that the positive impulse toward the "other" really exists—even in harsh climates. With the help of Jewish and Arab researchers, we set out to directly examine the relations between Israel's Jewish and Arab citizens. Not the media portrayal, not the dominant story, but how Arabs and Jews who both had Israeli citizenship *actually* felt toward each other. According to Israel's Central Bureau of Statistics, the country has a Jewish majority of almost 80 percent and an Arab minority of approximately 20 percent. As in any pluralistic society, the quality of the relations between these ethnic and religious groups directly influences the well-being and vibrancy of the country. We interviewed over 1,000 adult Jewish citizens and 721 adult Arab citizens—in Arabic, Hebrew, or Russian—either by phone or face-to-face. We asked a lot of questions and we worked hard to make sure they were the questions we really wanted to ask. Some of our colleagues thought we were crazy—or at best wasting our time—asking about truly positive regard for the "other." One colleague warned us that not nearly enough people would report any such thing to make our effort worthwhile. Another colleague was simply bemused. But we persisted. Perhaps we would find less positive regard than negative regard, but we still wanted to study it. What we found was nothing short of eye-opening, even though we thought we were going in with eyes wide open—that is, looking for evidence of liking as well as of animosity.[3]

First, we found quite a lot of what we had been told wasn't worth looking for. Some 30.1 percent of Jews and 25.3 percent of Arabs reported positive attitudes toward the other group. What, then, is the full story here? What sort of us-and-them relations are actually present in this society? What is possible? A hint can already been seen in organizations such as Hand in Hand, a network of schools in which equal numbers of Jewish and Arab Israeli schoolchildren learn each other's languages and histories simultaneously.[4]

Second, we found that measuring the presence of positive attitudes allowed us to be much better at predicting who supported efforts at promoting coexistence. That is, if you wanted to know which Israeli citizens were most likely to support policies such as addressing the employment and income gap between Jewish and Arab citizens, you would do better to look for high levels of positive attitudes toward Arabs than to look for low levels of prejudice toward them. Again, there seem to be possibilities that only become visible through the fog of prior assumptions when you take the trouble to look for them.

Third, we found that both Jewish and Arab citizens of Israel significantly underestimate the degree of liking their own group has for the other group. Put another way, people who feel they are unusual in their positive regard for the other group are actually not as unusual as they think.

Other researchers have made similarly "unexpected" findings; for example, among Protestants and Catholics in Northern Ireland.[5] In 2008, the Good Friday Agreement had been signed, the IRA had decommissioned its weapons, democratic self-government had been restored, and a range of economic and social tensions (such as differential employment, education, and housing) had been resolved. Nevertheless, religious polarization in Northern Ireland was (and is) still so strong that vital aspects of life such as neighborhoods, shops, political parties, sports, and first and last names could be clearly identified as either

Catholic or Protestant.[6] For example, 94 percent of Protestant children attend de facto Protestant schools (state-controlled schools or voluntary schools—state-funded schools in which a foundation or similar, usually a Christian denomination, has recognized administrative influence); 92 percent of Catholic children attend a Catholic school (state-controlled or voluntary).[7] The us-and-them lines were clearly drawn. Yet when survey respondents were asked to list the emotions they experienced in response to "the average or typical person who is part of the other community," what came out were the expected negative emotions, such as anger, irritation, and nervousness, but also positive emotions, such as happiness, affection, and curiosity. In fact, respondents listed as many positive emotions as negative emotions.

History also offers examples of one culture's fascination with another—certainly a positive us-and-them attitude. Europe, for example, has had historical periods—like the nineteenth century— characterized by great cultural fascination with the East. Though some see in the period's artifacts only clichéd Orientalism, and even propaganda to support Western imperialism, others see many examples showing "obvious respect for the subject matter."[8] As Middle East expert Peter Scholl-Latour has observed, many works from that period reflect "feelings of astonishment and fascination."[9] In America today there is great fascination with Japanese culture, and vice versa.[10]

For political, community, business, and religious leaders—possibly even for cultural leaders—findings like these have very practical implications. To heal and rebuild a conflicted community, company, or entire society, leaders must of course reduce the ill will between groups. But what we see here is that they also have the option—and therefore the responsibility—to tap into and nurture a positive power of difference that may well be there but has always seemed invisible or at least trivial compared to the problems at hand. Leaders have the responsibility to understand and increase what we want, not just to understand and decrease what we don't want.

We can also catch glimpses of the "other" other in historical, biographical, and other writings. *Twice a Stranger* examines kinship affections between Turks and Greeks rather than the commonly studied animosity between these two "others."[11] *Anglophilia* argues that pre-Civil War American culture was characterized by a widespread affection for and attachment to the British people.[12] In both books, we glimpse the "*other* other."

While the kinds of us-and-them attitudes I have been describing have occasionally received some scholarly and practical attention, they have never moved in from the sidelines to be taken seriously as social goals and scientific subjects. Gordon Allport, a seminal social psychologist whose focused scholarly attention on hate and prejudice spawned much of today's social psychology of the relations between "us and them," saw that there was not only a condition of *not hating* the "other," but also something more—"a blend of sharing and actively enjoying the practices, the mores, the worldviews not just of others as individuals, but others as Outgroup members." While an *outgroup* (the social science term for a "them" different from "us") is often seen as an enemy, Allport acknowledged that it was also possible for an outgroup to be "appreciated, tolerated, even liked for its diversity."[13] Unfortunately, he only toyed with this idea and never seriously engaged it, opting instead to devote his formidable analytical insight to the nature of negative prejudice and animosity toward those seen as "other." Allport published his landmark study, *The Nature of Prejudice*, in 1954 and was aware both of the recent horrors of the Holocaust and of the prejudice against African Americans in many countries, particularly the United States. So it is understandable that he focused his intellect and effort on hate and negative prejudice, but nonetheless unfortunate for those interested in the "blend of sharing and actively enjoying" he had noted. *The Nature of Prejudice* has been an enormously influential book, and it is sadly telling that Allport's observation that difference does not have to go hand in hand with hostility is one of the very, very few points in that book that has *not* spawned further research.

## The Unnamed Attitude

Some ten years ago, I was working on a paper about leadership when I found I had begun a sentence I could not finish: "Some of the most important leaders push their people beyond negative relations and tolerance to . . ." To what? I couldn't think of a word for the opposite of prejudice, discrimination, and hostility toward people who are different. Tolerance was the absence of those ills, but what was the word for positive feelings and attitudes toward people who are different? What was the word for being an Israeli Jew and wanting to have more Arab friends? What was the word for being a teenager and wanting a summer job at a nursing home so as to be around elderly people? I couldn't find one. The reference staff at Harvard's Widener Library, who can find just about anything, could not find one either. When I asked if there were such a word in some language other than English, they still came up short, as did the students I met at the Harvard Kennedy School, who collectively were fluent in 104 languages. We can all name a string of negative *-isms*—sexism, racism, anti-Semitism, ageism, and so on—yet would struggle to name their true opposites. Tolerance? Acceptance? Respect? They all seem to fall short. The data my colleagues and I had been collecting were showing us something more active and engaged than any of those words suggested.

Reluctant to write out "positive attitudes or behaviors toward the members of another group" every time we wanted to refer to this unnamed attitude in a paper, my colleagues and I finally began using the term *allophilia*, derived from the Greek words for "liking of the other." One feels allophilia when one considers a group of people as a "them" rather than a part of "us" and is drawn to the members of that group, interested in them, or positively predisposed toward them.

This isn't just semantics. The lack of vocabulary for positive attitudes toward people who are different does not reflect the nonexistence of such attitudes, but rather the lack of attention paid by researchers and practitioners to those attitudes. The focus has been on reducing the negative, not on promoting (or even recognizing) the positive. This puts teachers at a disadvantage. Without a vocabulary for the positive, how can they inspire their students to reach for something beyond mere tolerance? Even TeachingTolerance.org, perhaps the leading resource for those interested in hate and hate reduction in schools—an organization whose very name uses the word *tolerance*—acknowledges the lexical shortcoming on its website: "'Tolerance' is surely an imperfect term, yet the English language offers no single word that embraces the broad range of skills we need to live together peacefully."[14]

Benetton, the global luxury fashion retailer, seems to have run into the same lexical roadblock. In 2011, the company launched what it calls the UNHATE Foundation, which was "[c]reated to oppose and undermine hate culture" and that will "combat hatred," "engage in the development of campaigns aimed at exorcising the 'fear of the other,'" and "contribute to the creation of a new culture of *tolerance* [italics added]." There will be an "UNHATE Campaign" that will include a global "UNHATE Day" and an "UNHATE Dove . . . built by recycling used war bullets for a 4 meter long dove that will be then donated to a country that has recently faced conflicts."[15] Perhaps coining a new term was meant to grab our attention, but it is telling that the term they coined for all this worldwide love and affection (the campaign features digitally fabricated images of world leaders [of groups often in conflict?] kissing) is *unhate*.

## Is Allophilia as Small as It Seems?

By this point, we have seen that allophilia is a real thing, an ordinary experience. It doesn't loom as large as hate does on the stage of local, national, or world events. Rather, it seems to be experienced as a more private matter, pigeonholed as "sweet" or "virtuous" but seldom extending beyond the local Franco-American friendship society or a world music festival. But in fact, we don't know if that is true or not. And even if it is, that doesn't mean that allophilia cannot have a wider effect and play a more powerful role than it currently does. After all, practical concern for people so distant that one had never and would never meet them was once very rare, to say the least. Today, that same feeling routinely fuels enormous worldwide aid efforts, with people giving their money and their time (for example, by reading or watching the news) to help those same distant strangers when they are struck by a tsunami or a terrorist attack. Times change and the scope and power of us-and-them attitudes can also change.

If nothing else, scientific honesty demands that we pay attention to allophilia. And I believe that, for most of us, our wishes for a world in which hatred does not do so much damage also demand that we not only pay attention to allophilia but also find out what can be done with it. How we can do something with it is the concern of chapters 5 through 7. In this chapter, we will look at what has already been learned about allophilia. What forms does it take? What functions does it have?

## The Second Dimension of "Us and Them"

For the most part, social science models of relations between "us and them" continue to focus on hate. This is particularly damaging because of the influence social science models have on public policies, educational methods, and corporate human resources practices. The positive attitudes and actions that are largely missing from social science models and theories are not likely to be found in policies and practices.

About ten years ago, I began, with the invaluable help of colleagues—most notably, psychologist Seth A. Rosenthal—to directly study positive attitudes toward an "other." Rosenthal and I were convinced that such attitudes really exist, but we were not sure how—or if—they were related to negative attitudes. This is an important scientific question with important practical implications. Can the policies and methods we saw in chapter 1—designed to dial down hate—really work? That is, can they make us like each other more? Do we need to do them differently, or do we need to do something else altogether?

My colleagues and I began our work as agnostics with respect to the specific nature of liking. That is, we did not assume, as many others in the field have done, that positive attitudes are the mirror opposite of hate and that the presence of positive attitudes can be detected or inferred from low scores on surveys designed to detect and track hate. Nor did we assume that negative and positive attitudes about the "other" are independent of each other. Rather, we let our research data guide us. We call our work the study of allophilia. As far as I know, the allophilia construct is the first concept ever designed to describe situations in which another is seen as different— as "other"—and seen with a positive orientation. (Note, I did not write "*but* seen with a positive orientation," although for me, too, as I noted in an endnote in chapter 1, it slips easily off the tongue.) My colleagues and I take this research on allophilia, conducted in settings ranging from the Middle East to Middle America, as seriously as many other social scientists take their research on hatred and prejudice. We believe it is providing the basis for a new and more realistic way to understand, describe, and perhaps one day transform relations among social groups. This new model considers not only the hate dimension, but also the positive dimension—the allophilia dimension. We do not study allophilia *instead of* hate. Both are there, and both must be understood. We typically study both at the same time, believing that both the level of hate and the level of allophilia in a community are necessary indicators of what is happening *and what is possible* in any given us-and-them situation.

The rest of this chapter describes what we have learned thus far. Although research on allophilia is still in its earliest stages, it has produced findings that are important for leadership as well as for social science. What emerges is a model of social relations that recognizes and elucidates allophilia both on its own terms and in relation to its "evil sibling," hate. Here is a summary of the main findings, each of which will be discussed more fully below:

1. **Allophilia is one of two dimensions of us-and-them relations.** The best way to understand social relations is to observe both the positive and the negative attitudes a person can hold toward different groups.

2. **Allophilia and prejudice are increased or decreased by different things, not simply by more or less of the same things.** For example, the conditions and interventions that do the most to promote or reduce allophilia are not necessarily the conditions and interventions that do the most to promote or reduce prejudice.

3. **Increases or decreases in allophilia and prejudice affect things differently in the world.** For example, the presence of allophilia in a particular situation will lead to different feelings and actions than will the absence of hate in that situation.

4. **Allophilia is multifaceted.** Allophilia can take a number of different forms, which can appear in different combinations, produce different outcomes, and be promoted or inhibited somewhat independently.

5. **Allophilia is not the same thing as love for one's fellow human.** Altruism and universalism are different and, in fact, less useful than allophilia in specific us-and-them situations.

6. **Allophilia—and changes in allophilia—are scientifically measurable.** Scientific study generally requires measurement, but for a long time there were almost no tools with which to study positive us-and-them attitudes. For this reason, my colleagues and I have developed a tool with which to measure allophilia.

## Two-Dimensionality

When two concepts have opposite names, such as *liking* and *disliking* or *trust* and *distrust*, researchers often treat the phenomena themselves as opposites; that is, as opposite ends of a single dimension or continuum.[16] This, in turn, implies that a reduction in one will cause an equal increase in the other. Just as less wealth means more poverty and less heat means you're colder, less hate of an "other" is taken to mean more affection and less distrust among groups is taken to mean more trust. To see this in action, listen carefully to how reporters, pundits, and commentators move between trust (as in "U.S. trust of China") and distrust (as in "U.S. distrust of China")—sometimes in the same sentence. The two are simply presumed to be the presence or absence of the same thing, opposite ends of a single continuum.

Scholars often do the same thing. Nothing reflects this assumption in the research community better than the *feeling thermometer* that is often used to measure attitudes in contexts as diverse as personal relationships and politics. People are asked to mark a point somewhere along a line, indicating by its distance from one end or the other how warm or cold they feel toward a particular individual or group. The assumption underlying this approach is that the less you dislike that individual or group, the more you like him, her, or it.

But, in many areas of life, this assumption of one-dimensionality is not necessarily true. As early as 1965, a researcher had concluded: "The custom of finding an arithmetic average of attitude and opinion rating that includes both positive and negative ratings now seems unjustifiable; it may literally be a mixing of apples and cabbages."[17] In the 1980s, a psychologist began investigating the influence of positive emotions. By not assuming that positive and negative emotions were simple opposites, she found that they each have something of an independent nature that was being missed when researchers presumed that the two were part of a one-dimensional continuum and could therefore be measured with tools such as the feeling thermometer.

This work was later extended in the *broaden-and-build* theory of positive emotions.[18] For an individual, a higher level of positive emotion correlates with a wider range of thought and action, a gain that does not correlate as well with the individual's level of negative emotions. Again, we see that while the positive and negative emotions sound like they should be simple opposites, in fact the presence of one is not at all the same as the absence of the other. Other researchers have found that one's experience of positive emotions has important implications for physical health and well-being and even for one's longevity, over and above the experience of negative emotions.[19]

Still other investigators have found, for example, that trust and distrust are not opposite ends of a single continuum but rather are two distinct and independent phenomena. That is, to understand the trust relationship between particular people or groups, you need to observe and measure both trust and distrust; more of one is not necessarily less of the other. In fact, we know from our own everyday experience that we can sometimes both trust and distrust (or at least not trust) the same person—it depends on what that person is to be trusted with. Any time you drive, you are trusting hundreds of strangers with your life, yet you would probably not trust many of them with your house keys or your credit cards. On the global stage, we often make alliances of convenience—our enemy's enemy becomes our friend—in which we both trust our ally in certain ways and distrust it in others. Research on the independence of such supposed opposites as pleasure and displeasure have come to similar conclusions.[20]

In the 1960s and 1970s, there was a widespread effort to desegregate American schools. This effort naturally gave rise to many social science studies and, in retrospect, we can see the problems of a one-dimensional view of us-and-them relations. A thorough review of the scholarly literature on school desegregation and intergroup relations found many shortcomings in the measurements used to determine whether or not school desegregation was changing how people felt toward "others." The review concluded that researchers looking for positive change should be reluctant to use measures of negative relations, even though that is what is available to them, and warned that there is "an implicit assumption that positive and negative attitudes are merely opposite ends of a continuum . . . Yet, empirical work on racial attitudes challenges this assumption."[21] Other research on the racial attitudes of students in desegregated high schools found that whites' attitudes are best described as clustering into two independent factors—a general negative evaluation of African Americans and a general positive evaluations of African Americans.[22] A particular intervention, then, might affect the positive views while having little or no effect on the negative views. Measuring the negative views might largely or completely miss what the intervention has actually accomplished. And yet, as we saw in chapter 1 with Northern Ireland's Shared Future metrics, researchers are still using measurements of hate and prejudice to find out how much good an intervention may be doing.

One might suspect that people claim to have positive attitudes toward the "other" when they are being interviewed by researchers, but do not actually feel this way in real life. In fact, researchers have addressed this suspicion. For example, a study of white high school students found that a majority believed that African American students exhibited many positive traits.[23] Strikingly, the African American students in that study recognized the positive attitudes that white students held toward their group. Evidently, the white students weren't just making it up to look good to the researchers. The researchers also found that the African American students viewed the white students' positive attitudes as independent of their negative attitudes. If those African American students could tell that some of their white schoolmates held positive attitudes about them, it's a pretty good bet that those positive attitudes were real.

Perhaps the strongest support for the possible independence of concepts and experiences that at first blush might seem to be simple opposites comes from research on the theory of *functional separability*, which says that positive and negative attitudes do not actually lie at opposite ends of a linear spectrum and therefore both have to be studied and measured—information about one cannot be inferred from measurements of the other.[24] Put another way, one's level of happiness cannot be said to be the simple opposite of one's level of sadness. In addition, a change in a negative attitude does not necessarily coincide with an equivalent change in the "opposite" positive attitude. We can see this, too, in ordinary circumstances: one can, over time, become disappointed with one or another aspect of a friend while still feeling the same affection for him or her.[25] Though researchers often persist in assuming bipolarity, research evidence of independent dimensions is accumulating for more and more attitudes.[26]

To understand the concept of independent dimensions more intuitively, think of debt and income. Both affect your financial well-being. But they can go up and down independently. Getting a raise can help you lower your debt, but it does not lower your debt all by itself. If you are a gambling addict or a shopaholic or medically unlucky and uninsured, your income and debt can go up at the same time. And—this will be a key point for the rest of this chapter and this book—to improve your financial state, you may need to increase your income *and* reduce your debt, which are two different tasks accomplished in two different ways. (Getting a better-paying job is one thing; breaking your habit of getting takeout instead of cooking at home—or perhaps even brewing your own cup of coffee instead of frequenting a neighborhood Starbucks—is quite another.)

One reason that apparent "pairs" such as trust and mistrust can turn out to be more independent than we thought is that different processes may help generate and maintain them. To illustrate: If you are sitting at home and you want to be warmer, you could turn off your air conditioner. But that is only going to get you as warm as the ambient temperature. You would have to turn on the heat to get any warmer than that. Making the house less cool and making it more warm, although they might seem to be the same thing, are actually different effects brought about by the use of different appliances.

What does all this imply for us-and-them leadership? Allophilia research is showing that positive and negative attitudes toward members of other groups—allophilia and hate—constitute one of those related-but-more-independent-than-commonly-recognized pairs.[27] Us-and-them relations therefore call for a two-dimensional approach in which allophilia and prejudice are not assumed to be mirror opposites and are therefore understood to involve two quite different tasks for leadership. Nonviolent resistance is a somewhat extreme example of differentiating between the positive and negative dimensions of us-and-them relations. Given a state of negative us-and-them relations (such as racial segregation in the American South or British colonization in India), one group recognizes that it is the object of another group's prejudice or hatred, but chooses to respond as much as possible along the positive dimension by attempting to respect rather than diminish the individual members of that other group, to legitimate rather than denigrate them; in effect, to love rather than hate.

Here is another way to think of the leadership challenge that results from recognition of the two-dimensionality of allophilia and hate: Planting seeds in a weed-choked garden will probably not be successful. But simply pulling weeds will not make any new plants grow. One needs to plant *and* weed—and one needs to do the two of them in a coordinated fashion. Similarly, an intervention to fight prejudice cannot automatically be expected to increase allophilia.

### *Uniquely Caused*

Allophilia and prejudice, being partly independent dimensions, need to be increased or decreased by different factors, not just by more or less of the same factor. Think again of income and expenses. An increase in your credit card interest rate increases your monthly expenses but does not affect your income. An austerity budget decreases your monthly expenses but does not affect your income. By the same token, an increase in your salary does not in itself reduce your credit card interest rate or your monthly expenses. Nevertheless, expenses and income can be interconnected at times. You have the option to use an increase in income to pay down your credit card debt or to buy a more efficient water heater, which will decrease your monthly expenses. To improve your financial well-being, you would seek ways both to increase your income and to decrease your expenses.

A practical outcome of allophilia and prejudice having independent causes is that, as leaders search for ways to promote allophilia, they cannot simply look for the causes of hate and try to reduce or eliminate them. Allophilia will have its own patterns of causes that must be brought to bear. In the second half of this book, we will see some examples, such as empathic joy, displays of group pride, and some new uses for networking technology.

Classic research on what social scientists call *operant conditioning*—the manipulation of consequences to modify behavior— offers insight into the independence of the causes of prejudice and allophilia. Psychologist Kurt Lewin, widely considered a pioneering researcher of social, organizational, and applied psychology, examined the conditions under which one feels attraction to another person versus repulsion toward that person.[28] The perceived benefit or enjoyment of being in a relationship with that person and the perceived harm or discomfort of being in a relationship with that person were both important factors, but not as simple inverses of each other. A wealth of subsequent research has also supported the idea that these basic processes (benefit/attraction, harm/repulsion) are distinct and independent, and it is no great leap to apply this to attraction and repulsion in us-and-them contexts. We will see in the second half of this book what conditions are particularly important for allophilia to thrive.

## Distinct Outcomes

Another result of prejudice and allophilia being partly independent attitudes is that we can expect them to have their strongest effects on different kinds of behavior. It seems intuitively obvious, for example, that certain dangerous and deadly actions are more likely in a person who feels more hatred and prejudice toward a particular group than in someone who feels less hatred and prejudice toward that group, and indeed, research supports that intuition. So we certainly know what negative prejudice can do. But what can allophilia do? What kinds of behavior are more or less likely in a person who feels more or less allophilia toward a particular group?

Research on this question suggests that allophilia makes it more likely that an African American in California will stand up for Mexican farm workers, that an American retiree will volunteer to tutor Iraqi refugees in English, or that a straight person will advocate for gay rights. Research in Northern Ireland found that Protestants who felt more negative emotions (such as anger, irritation, and nervousness) toward Catholics were more likely to avoid them, keep their distance from them, have nothing to do with them, argue with them, confront them, or oppose them. However, these negative actions did not show a strong reverse correlation with positive feelings (or lack thereof); that is, knowing which Protestants had the *least positive* feeling toward Catholics did not tell you which ones would try to avoid Catholics. Avoiding Catholics turned out to be a function of *having* the negative feeling, not of *lacking* the positive feeling. Positive feelings on the other hand (such as happiness, affection, and curiosity) were significantly stronger predictors of such positive actions toward "others" as making friends and supporting coexistence.[29]

We are all so used to thinking of *liking* and *not disliking* as the same thing. They really are not, and that's a powerful tool for leaders who want to heal us-and-them conflicts and, more generally, to improve us-and-them relations wherever there is an "us" and a "them." Reducing hate—that is, achieving tolerance—will serve to curtail negative acts, and that alone can be a big step forward. But an individual's low level of hate toward a particular group is not very strongly associated with his or her active support for members of that group—a necessity for a genuinely cohesive community, whether neighborhood, business, or nation. It turns out that such positive behavior is more strongly associated with how much the person *likes* the other group than by how much he or she *does not dislike* that group.[30] (As the chat group participant at the beginning of the chapter said, "I don't hate them. I simply don't like them.")

My colleagues and I found much the same thing in a study in which we paid a group of white participants to complete a questionnaire that included a measurement of how much allophilia they felt toward African Americans and then offered them a chance to earn additional money that could be used in different ways. One option was to donate that money to a scholarship fund for African American students. We found that those who felt more allophilia toward African Americans were significantly more likely to make charitable donations to a scholarship fund for African American students than those who felt less allophilia toward African Americans.[31] And the presence or absence of allophilia was a stronger predictor of those who made the donation than the presence or absence of many different hate and prejudice measures.

We replicated this finding in a study in which we measured white participants' allophilia toward Latinos and also their feelings of hate and prejudice toward Latinos.[32] (In fact, given the smorgasbord of hate measures available, we measured hate and prejudice many, many different ways.) Again, we found that the more allophilia a white participant felt toward Latinos, the greater his or her willingness to contribute to an organization that supported Latino college students. But we also found that allophilia was a better predictor of such generosity than the hate and prejudice measures. That is, if you wanted to predict whether a participant would help Latinos, it was more useful to know how much allophilia he or she felt for Latinos than to know how much prejudice he or she felt against Latinos. It was the presence of allophilia, not the lack of prejudice, that was more strongly connected to the willingness to donate.

Census research finds that multiracial Americans have become the fastest-growing demographic group in the United States. That is, more and more Americans check more than one box for race on surveys run by the U.S. Census Bureau, an option that was first offered in 2000. Demographers attributed this in part to more social acceptance and to high-profile multiracial public figures such as Tiger Woods and Barack Obama. The emergence of this group prompted my colleagues and me to wonder what influences people's support of the members of this group? A study we conducted on the attitudes of U.S. citizens of different ethnicities found that the impulse to step up and support people who identify as multiracial was in fact more strongly predicted by how much allophilia there was than by how little prejudice.[33]

To see how these findings relate to real us-and-them leadership, let us consider cross-ethnic mentoring. Minorities can benefit greatly in their careers from having mentors.[34] For this reason, mentoring high-potential minorities is a perennial concern for companies. While minority protégés may gain certain advantages from mentors of the same minority group, minority mentors are too often in short supply. And in any case, some research has found that cross-race and cross-ethnic mentors are also particularly valuable for young, talented employees from minority groups. Members of a majority group can therefore be extremely effective mentors for minority group members—if they are motivated to do so. But as we have just seen, people who feel allophilia toward a particular group are more likely than people who simply don't feel hate for that group to take such action. In schools, too, promoting allophilia might, in the long run, seed a society with a small but disproportionately motivated group of people more willing than most to help the "other."

The fact that allophilia and prejudice have their strongest effects on different outcomes is not just a matter of the attitudes that members of a majority group hold toward the members of a minority group. Allophilia has been found to predict the proactive support of members of one minority group for another minority group.[35] And allophilia can be felt by members of a minority group for members of a majority group.

It has been said that for evil to prevail, it is only necessary for good women and men to do nothing. Recognizing that the presence of allophilia is a stronger predictor of proactive support of an "other" than is lack of hatred raises important questions about who is a "good" man or woman—someone who feels no hate or someone who does feel allophilia?

## Multifaceted

An important aspect of allophilia—for leaders as well as for researchers—is that it is not one simple quality that you have in such-and-such an amount. Positive attitudes and emotions, like negative ones, can come in different shades and flavors. Love for one's children, for example, can take such forms as selfless love, indulgent love, tough love, and material love. Over several years and studies of allophilia both in the United States and abroad, my colleagues and I have found that allophilia can take five distinct forms:[36]

- **Affection**—Having positive feelings toward members of the other group

- **Comfort**—Feeling comfortable and at ease with members of the other group

- **Kinship**—Feeling a close connection with members of the other group

- **Engagement**—Seeking interactions with members of the other group

- **Enthusiasm**—Feeling impressed and inspired by members of the other group

The different forms of allophilia need not all be present; rather, they can be present in various combinations and to varying degrees. For example, an Armenian businessman or government official can be genuinely eager to engage with Turks without necessarily feeling particularly comfortable with them. A white American reggae fan can be enthusiastic about Jamaicans without feeling any particular kinship with them; for that matter, an African American reggae fan can be enthusiastic about Jamaicans without feeling any particular kinship with them. Of course, the five components can all come together, too.

This means that leaders may be able to develop the particular kind of positive us-and-them relations they feel are needed or that they feel will be most achievable in the near term. For example, the degree to which one feels comfort with the "other" is more closely related to subsequent social ease in interaction with the "other"—finding it easy to talk, not feeling awkward or self-conscious in interactions. This might be crucial for political negotiation but less important for fund-raising. Engagement with the other is more closely related to learning about the other—wanting to expand one's knowledge about another culture. This might be crucial for work in international aid agencies but less important in well-integrated communities in which positive contact is already common.

The actions of some high-profile public figures can help us understand the five forms of allophilia.[37] For example, Britain's Princess Diana publicly displayed great *affection* for an "other"—HIV-infected children in developing countries. In the late 1980s, most people were afraid to get too close to anyone with HIV, yet the whole world saw photos of Princess Diana hugging HIV-infected children in Africa. For Western audiences, these children were most certainly the "other"; they were stigmatized by this still-mysterious disease and further separated from both the princess and most ordinary citizens by poverty, ethnicity, and/or geography. Diana's hugs communicated affection; something far more positive and powerful than tolerance or lack of prejudice.

President Bill Clinton is famous for displaying great *comfort* with African Americans. As governor of Arkansas, he invited local African American leaders to his home for impromptu gatherings and later, as president, he reached out to this community in an unprecedented way. People interviewed for the book *Bill Clinton and Black America* remarked on his move to Harlem, his love of soul food, his attendance at African American churches, and his scores of close African American friends, colleagues, and appointees, not to mention the fact that he knew all three verses of "Lift Every Voice and Sing."[38] Michael Frisby, senior vice president of the public relations firm Porter Novelli, said, "The thing I will never forget is that Clinton was *so* comfortable talking to me. There was no uneasiness at all" [italicized in original].[39] Hugh Price, president of the National Urban League, observed, "There was a comfort level in his dealings with African Americans, in his interfacing with African Americans, going to the churches, connecting, preaching, and baring his soul with us."[40] Attorney Johnnie Cochran commented, "Bill Clinton is probably the most comfortable Caucasian around black people that most of us have ever seen. He feels totally comfortable around black people."[41] And novelist Toni Morrison famously called Clinton the first black president of the United States.[42]

Martin Luther King Jr. was perhaps the most powerful example of moving not just beyond hate, but all the way to love of an "other." His leadership offers a treasure trove of inspiration for social science research on the how, when, and why of allophilia. One striking aspect of King's practice of leadership was his expression of *kinship* with others. Himself a Baptist minister, he displayed deep religious and moral appreciation for Judaism and the Jewish people. He did not see his identity as a Baptist compromised by kinship with this "other." His belief that Christianity and Judaism shared a common source of ethical inspiration, indeed kinship, was a rather radical notion for a Christian minister at that time. King went even further. He used Moses and the Hebrew prophets as models for the civil rights struggle as much as he used Jesus. He made a habit of connecting the suffering of the children of Israel to the plight of African Americans under Jim Crow laws. King would refer to Abraham Joshua Heschel, a prominent rabbi and author who walked beside him in the protest march at Selma, as "my rabbi."

Nelson Mandela exemplifies *engagement* with the "other." He was steadfast in his commitment to engage with a specific group very different from his own—the white Afrikaners who collectively, and in some cases individually, had imprisoned him and oppressed his people. At the 1995 Rugby World Cup finals, Mandela, by then the president of South Africa, cheered for the national team, the Springboks, which had always been regarded as a powerful symbol of white South Africa. He even sported the team captain's jersey. Mandela did these things deliberately so that two "others" with a very bad history would be able to willingly engage each other rather than just try not to hate each other.

World-renowned cellist and UN Peace Ambassador Yo-Yo Ma has become a prominent face for the feeling of *enthusiasm* toward an "other." His passion for bridging different cultures and musical traditions sets him apart from most other classical musicians. He has collaborated with musicians, artists, filmmakers, and choreographers from the Kalahari bush to Brazil, and he always seems to be having a ball. His enthusiasm for the other—and his wish to instill such enthusiasm in others—reaches its peak in the Silk Road Project, which highlights the music and other aspects of various cultures to be found along the ancient trade routes connecting Asia and Europe, many of those cultures little known in the West at the time.

Of course, neither I nor you, the reader, nor the most exacting biographer can claim to know what is (or was) in these particular people's heads. And even if they were motivated by allophilia, there may have been other motivations as well—people are complex. But their actions do offer leaders at all levels and in many situations a set of vivid images of what allophilia can look like in its various manifestations. And the fact that allophilia can take many different forms gives leaders some latitude as they face their uniquely perplexing us-and-them situations. There are many ways to be an allophiliac us-and-them leader. If you don't seem to resemble Mandela or King at all, you might resemble Diana or Ma. If your situation does not allow for advancing enthusiasm, you may be able to advance engagement. In this way, we see that advancing allophilia is something that ordinary people aspiring to lead can do in their own time and place.

### Different from Universalism

Allophilia is sometimes confused with *universalism*—the belief and feeling that all people are one. When people think about better relations between different groups, it is easy for them to assume that the only goal is a loving brotherhood of humankind. Allophilia is not incompatible with universalism; universalism can facilitate allophilia, and allophilia can facilitate universalism. Allophilia, however, is a positive attitude toward a *particular group*. Is this too limited a goal? It may not seem quite aspirational enough. In fact, in some settings, it may not even seem politically correct.

Why, then, am I pushing both leaders and social scientists to seize the possibilities of positive attitudes toward particular groups rather than to focus on universalism? A very practical reason. One could conceive that a person might help members of another group purely from a moral imperative. It is not clear, for example, that gentiles who risked their lives to protect Jews from the Nazis necessarily had positive feelings about Jews beyond seeing them as fellow human beings with a right not to be persecuted. Nevertheless, my colleagues and I have found in our research that one's behavior toward a particular group is much more closely correlated to one's feelings toward that particular group than to one's universal or altruistic feelings about humankind.[43] That's not to say that a love of all humankind does not exist and is not a worthy goal, but only to say that it doesn't turn out (so far) to be what motivates the kind of us-and-them behavior we are typically looking for, especially in situations in which us-and-them divides are a live issue. For example, had Mandela emphasized his overall love of humankind rather than taking specific steps to engage the Afrikaners of South Africa, would he have been as transformative in such a polarized us-and-them situation?

In other words, if you are wondering whether I am likely to bestir myself to help some Somali immigrants, you'll do better to check—or to cultivate—my positive feelings toward Somali immigrants than my overall love of humankind. Or let's say you are a corporate human resources director responsible for increasing the presence of Latinos in your company's upper management. You are trying to drum up enough mentors for your young and promising Latino managers and wondering if I (a non-Latino) can be recruited to the cause. You'll do better to check—or to cultivate—my positive feelings toward Latinos than my overall love of humankind.

This fact is really just a reflection of a more general truth. Decades of trying to understand when attitudes can predict behaviors has yielded one very solid finding in the social sciences: we can predict behaviors more accurately by measuring specific attitudes. Thus, if we are concerned with how a particular "us" treats a particular "them," then understanding how that "us" feels about that particular "them"—not how that "us" feels about humanity as a whole—is the best predictor of behavior.

What about religious leaders? Isn't it their job to preach a love of all humankind, all of whom are children of G-d? There is, of course, no reason for religious leaders to abandon that teaching, but there are many situations in which they also need to preach some group-specific allophilia in order to address specific tensions within a congregation or neighborhood—the particular children of G-d who need to get along at a particular place and time. (This topic is taken up again in chapter 7.)

### Measurable

If allophilia is to be studied scientifically and used effectively by leaders facing real us-and-them situations, then both social scientists and leaders must be able to measure it. Being able to measure a phenomenon allows us to track it and to conduct research on it. We can even run experiments and then remeasure the phenomenon, allowing us to answer critical questions about where it comes from, what effects it has, and—perhaps most important—when and how it changes.

Measurements are an indication of what we think is important, but sometimes they miss the mark and we realize that something different needs to be measured. Right now, for example, we have many aggregate measures of national wealth, but we are sometimes surprised by what studies tell us. People in the richest nations do not report being the happiest and, in some cases, are well down the list. Bhutan made itself an exception—and the butt of many jokes—when it began to measure "gross national happiness." Although King Jigme Singye Wangchuck first used the term in an offhand remark, he had in mind a serious goal—a Bhutanese society that was materially prosperous, yes, but also culturally and spiritually rich. The Centre for Bhutan Studies went on to develop a survey instrument that would measure overall well-being in that particular society. The goal of Bhutan's measurement, and of the growing movement around the world, is to help the government stay on track with the policies it pursues to improve GNH. Are they making a meaningful difference? In such cases, measurement is not simply an academic exercise; it sets the stage for effective leadership.

Politicians in some countries, including the United Kingdom, France, Canada, and in some municipalities in the United States are now looking into tracking something like Bhutan's gross national happiness in their own census research. When the U.K.'s Measuring National Well-being Programme was launched in November 2010, Prime Minister David Cameron said the purpose was to "start measuring our progress as a country, not just by how our economy is growing, but by how our lives are improving; not just by our standard of living, but by our quality of life."[44]

The ability to measure allophilia is also important because researchers are more likely to undertake—and funders are more likely to fund—studies of phenomena for which there are developed and validated measurement tools. For example, despite many concerns about consumer confidence measurements—questions about what exactly they measure and whether or not they are valid—consumer confidence continues to be widely reported and discussed in policy circles and in the media because there are straightforward, accessible, well-established ways to measure it. When it comes to tools for measuring social science phenomena, it is truer than it should be that "if you build it, they will use it."

When colleagues and I first began our research—long before we had articulated what we had come to see as the missing link in the study of "us and them"—we were designing a research study that should have gotten two groups to really appreciate and like each other. Failing repeatedly to observe the effects we expected, we carefully examined each part of the experiment: Were the experimental manipulations correct; that is, had we created the interdependent conditions we thought we had? Were the people we recruited blind to what was going on or had they somehow figured out what we were looking for and decided to play games with us? Finally, as we read through the items we were measuring in our questionnaire, we realized that something absurd was going on. The questions on our survey that were supposed to assess attitudes toward others all had to do with various shades of hate. But our participants all had low levels of hate to start with, so the level of hate wasn't going to change much *no matter what we experimenters did*. More importantly, we were trying to create something positive between our two groups, so hate wasn't even what we were trying to change. It really wasn't what we wanted to know about. But it was the only thing we had the tools to measure. In fact, when my colleagues and I began our allophilia research—in part, in response to that "aha" moment—we found more than *two hundred* different published measures of hate and negative prejudice toward another group but not a single tool specifically designed to measure a construct of positive attitudes toward another group.

The result was that a researcher interested in the positive attitudes Latinos might have about African Americans might find herself using a tool designed to measure negative attitudes and then inferring the presence or absence of positive attitudes from low or high scores, respectively, on measurements of negative attitudes. My colleagues and I had fallen into this very trap: we were trying to measure the relative presence of positive attitudes using measures of negative attitudes. We had not consciously decided that they were the same thing. We simply knew that we were interested in us-and-them relations and that we wanted to use a well-validated instrument and that led us naturally to social science's abundance of tried-and-true measures of negative prejudice and hate. But as we came to learn, this won't do at all; the presence or absence of negative attitudes does not say enough about the absence or presence of positive attitudes.

At that point, we realized we would have to develop our own tool with which to measure the positive attitude toward an "other" that we were trying to investigate. Since then, my colleagues and I have put much of our effort into understanding how to measure allophilia in a direct, valid, and reliable way. Experimental psychologist Seth Rosenthal, social psychologist R. Matthew Montoya, and I developed the Allophilia Scale, a tool to measure one's allophilia for a particular group of which one is not a member.[45] The scale measures the five factors of allophilia—affection, comfort, kinship, engagement, and enthusiasm—discussed earlier. To score high in allophilia for, say, African Americans, one would agree strongly with a series of statements such as "I respect African Americans," "I am at ease around African Americans," "I am truly interested in understanding the points of view of African Americans," "I am motivated to get to know African Americans better," "To enrich my life, I would try to make more friends who are African Americans," and "I am interested in hearing about the experiences of African Americans." As you might imagine, these are not the kinds of questions that hate researchers often use in their scales. But allophilia researchers find them very exciting. Finally, then, with the scale in place, we are looking at the full range of us-and-them attitudes, not just half the spectrum. At the same time, instead of looking only at the sources of the kind of world we don't want, we are also looking at the sources of the kind of world we do want. To put it another way, my colleagues and I believe that the Allophilia Scale can be a tool of leadership.

For example, the Allophilia Scale can be adapted to measure organizational climate, giving businesses a much better way to track the openness, curiosity, and camaraderie that are needed if diversity is to serve as a boost to innovation, as is often hoped (an aspiration discussed more fully in chapter 4). More generally, human resource people can keep an eye on the most productive us-and-them attitudes, not just the most divisive ones, and tailor their initiatives to boost the company's strengths, not just gnaw away at its assumed weaknesses. By the same token, the leaders of my nephew Marc's school, whom we met indirectly at the beginning of chapter 1, could devise more productive ways to make the most of their school's diversity rather than just manning the guns against an assumed threat of intolerance.

The Allophilia Scale is versatile. We have used it to study attitudes toward people of various nationalities, ethnicities, religions, and sexual orientations; we have even used it in schools engaged in rivalries. In many situations in which there is a clear sense of "us and them," the Allophilia Scale has allowed us to identify the degree to which individuals have a general liking for members of the other group. Other researchers are using it to measure attitudes in many different settings; for example, to tap the presence of positive attitudes toward immigrants in Italy.[46]

Early on, we made a strategic choice to measure allophilia as an explicit attitude; that is, as an attitude that a person is conscious of having and that a researcher can therefore determine simply by asking the person, rather than as an implicit or unconscious attitude that at best can be deduced from the implicit associations a person makes. (Implicit attitudes toward "others" will be discussed in chapter 3.) One advantage of our decision is that the scale is usable pretty much anywhere by anyone on any budget. Like a chemical engineer trying to understand what makes a heart-valve implant wear down so that someone else can later develop one that won't, we are using the scale, alongside more traditional hate and prejudice measures, to conduct science in a purely scientific way, but we very much intend that science to be used to make people's lives better.

Do people tell the truth about their levels of allophilia? We find that allophilia is actually easier to measure than hatred or prejudice because people rarely have any reason either to fake or hide allophilia. While there is often social pressure to deny being hateful or prejudiced, there frankly just isn't much social pressure to report feeling particularly positive toward members of other groups. And indeed, whenever we administer the Allophilia Scale, we find a normal distribution—a few people at the low end, a few at the high end, most somewhere in the middle—which is a good indication (though not a proof) that people are answering the questions truthfully. Further, the Allophilia Scale has been shown to distinguish between genuine liking for another group and two types of deceptive response that can sometimes undermine an explicit attitude measure: a desire to please the researcher by presenting oneself well (known as *self-presentation bias*) and a desire to conform to social norms (known as *social desirability bias*).[47]

Finally, we have administered the scale in a few situations in which one might expect great social pressure to claim allophilia (testing very religious and spiritual individuals) and in other situations in which there would be little or no social pressure to claim allophilia (testing Jewish and Arab citizens of Israel, whose groups generally have no qualms about expressing animosity for each other). We reasoned that, in these contexts, allophilia might be particularly difficult to measure—in the first case because of strong norms to present oneself as allophiliac and in the second case, described in chapter 1, because there would be such strong social pressure against feeling and reporting positive attitudes toward the other. Yet even in these situations, the Allophilia Scale provided a normal distribution, although the means—the statistical averages—were in different places, as would be expected.

There is particular value in a measurement tool that allows us to measure new things that matter in the world. As discussed in this chapter, the measurement of allophilia allows us to more accurately predict positive proactive behavior toward an "other." That will allow us to balance out the research and practice on hate crimes with a new body of scholarship—and associated practice—on instances of people enjoying and wanting to help those of a different group, from the cross-ethnic mentor to the Mainer showing a Somali immigrant what winter heating is all about.

I hope that other tools will be developed by other researchers to measure the spectrum of positive attitudes toward an "other" of which humans are capable and that these tools will be used by governments, NGOs, school systems, corporations, community groups, and others engaged in us-and-them leadership. The important result of our work to date is that allophilia is a real phenomenon that can and should be measured so that we can bring all the power of social science to bear on understanding and applying it.

## A More Realistic and Promising Model: Progress Toward the Goal

Research into the two-dimensional model of how people can feel about members of groups other than their own—and particularly into the long-unrecognized positive dimension, allophilia—can give us a more complete scientific model of human behavior. A more complete scientific (Newtonian) model of the physical world made it possible to build a civilization that the previous (Aristotelian) model could never have allowed, both because the new model could more accurately describe what existed and because it had greater power to model what *could be*. So, too, a more complete scientific model of us-and-them relations (the two-dimensional model) not only gives us a better understanding of the us-and-them relations that exist today, but has greater power to model what *could* be; that is, people's willing, active, and joyful engagement with members of groups other than their own.

Mental health therapists often find that their patients are stuck in cycles of counterproductive behavior such as bad relationships because they focus on the bad situation they are in rather than on the better situation they would rather be in. Societies can make the same mistake, and I would argue that we are. I would also suggest that research communities can make this mistake and that the social sciences are doing so by burrowing further and further into hate studies. The two-dimensional model offers the way out of this trap.

In particular, the two-dimensional model may better reflect the attitudes and values of a rising generation. More and more, we are hearing arguments that young people are freeing themselves from the previous generation's emphasis on prejudice and "the struggle." This, the argument goes, is the generation of world music and the World Wide Web. A model incorporating allophilia may be more likely to capture this generation's attitudes; hate and prejudice will not be absent, but the picture will be complex, with much more interest, curiosity, and enthusiasm with respect to "others."

The two-dimensional model is more realistic in yet another sense. It is a model of intergroup relations that can accommodate the most idealistic visions of diversity and multiculturalism but that demands more honesty than proponents of these schools of thought often demand of themselves. It requires us to stop hedging our bets by straddling the fence, claiming that "we are all the same" but also that "diversity is our strength." (The inadequacy of these positions will be taken up in chapter 4.) It is our responses to the real differences between groups that need to be understood and addressed—but again, the full range of those responses, not just the negative responses that cause all the problems. The two-dimensional model also forces us to acknowledge that the constant orientation to hate is not a way forward. This model demands precision—it insists that we define and measure allophilia as well as hate. In return, it makes room for that full range of responses to the "other" of which we are capable.

# THREE

# A LOPSIDED SCIENCE

**L**EADERS HAVE a hard time coming to grips with difficult us-and-them situations, in part because they often assume that it is natural for different groups to be at odds with each other. Although this seems to be pretty obvious and amply borne out by history, it is actually not a scientifically well-grounded fact, but often more of an assumption. As I will show in this chapter, there has been more than a little of seeing what you expected to see and seeing what you were looking for in the scientific study of us-and-them relations. This selective perception is one factor underlying the gap in us-and-them leadership. It amounts to a pattern of choices that led to the sidelining of truly positive us-and-them relations.

This chapter will look back on some of that past research. Why bother looking back if I am going to question what I find? Why not just look forward? We need to take a hard look at the accumulated scholarship on attitudes toward difference to appreciate how consistently it has avoided the subject of *positive* attitudes toward difference. The sheer magnitude of the one-sidedness will give you a powerful sense of how much we have missed and how important it is to finally claim this largely uncharted territory.

## Is It "Just Human"?

A young Muslim woman living in the United States decided she would rather attend even an unaccredited Muslim university than several prestigious and accredited but non-Muslim schools. "We want to learn from people who look like us, talk like us, think like us, eat like us," she explained. "It's only natural—it's just human."[1] Is she right? After all, she's only a first-year student, not an expert.

Eva Young, on the other hand, was presented as a "diversity expert" to listeners of a National Public Radio (NPR) segment, "Value of Diversity Training Tough to Measure." At the time, she was president of a diversity consultancy, Eva Young and Associates. Asked to explain why it is hard to find objective evidence that many diversity training programs accomplish anything, Young replied: "You know, we're talking about changing people's biases, inviting them to explore their assumptions, learning about differences. We understand the brain doesn't like differences that much. So we're asking people to rewire the brain."[2] Is she, an NPR-identified expert, right?

Scientifically, there's no real answer to her claim. What does it mean to assert that the brain doesn't like differences? We couldn't function without the brain's ability to discern differences, ranging from the difference between a moving object and its background to the difference between the singular and plural forms of a noun. And what exactly does she mean by "rewiring the brain"? There is, as we will see, surprisingly little solid evidence that the brain is "wired" to engage in the kind of hostility toward difference that her diversity training is supposed to counteract. Yet the show's host let this answer pass as expert opinion, without challenge.

Imagine an expert in math education claiming that no one could show solid results for a particular style of teaching math because "the brain doesn't like math that much, so we're asking students to rewire their brains." Would the host of an NPR show have let such an absurd comment pass without challenge? But the host interviewing Ms. Young was displaying the same gap in understanding us-and-them relations that we have been seeing all along. As a culture, we have become increasingly comfortable—far too comfortable, this chapter will show—with the notion that the human is somehow wired to be hateful, or at best very distrustful, toward the "other."

## Myths of the Hateful Human

If we turn from diversity consultants to the psychologists, social scientists, and anthropologists who make it their life's work to understand human dynamics in deep ways, what do we find? Too often, we simply find more sophisticated versions of the same nonsense. What follows is a discussion of some of the more influential forms of the myth that people are naturally hostile to any group they see as the "other." Some of the terms, such as *automatic categorization* and *minimal groups*, may not be familiar to readers who are not involved with social science research, but the behaviors to which they refer are familiar, and you will be able to see how, brick by brick, social science has somewhat unreflectively built a wall beyond which it cannot see the positive power of difference.

### Misunderstanding of Automatic Categorization

Not only has social science focused too much on hate and prejudice, but some legitimate scientific results on us-and-them relations have been misinterpreted in such a way as to perpetuate the myth that people are naturally hostile to "others" and to make it even less likely that researchers will turn to the subject of positive feelings for different groups.

For example, researchers have found very solid evidence that people are inclined to use categories; in particular, to use social categories to understand their social world. Categorical thinking—whether perceiving a chair as a chair fundamentally similar to other chairs or perceiving a creative act as fundamentally similar to other creative acts—is certainly real. But in the scholarly atmosphere I have been describing, this valid empirical finding has morphed into the unsupported notion that our brains are wired not only to categorize people but also to feel hostility based on these categories. This notion is not necessarily stated outright; sometimes it is inherent in the presentation of other findings. For example, in every social psychology textbook that I have seen, discussions of the propensity to categorize are found in chapters on discrimination and hate. But how strong is the evidence for a link between categorizing people as "other" and feeling hostile toward the "other"? One team of social psychologists found that there was "almost no empirical evidence" to support this hypothesis.[3]

In fact, there has also been evidence all along of *positive* categorization—situations in which we categorize a group as "other" and have accompanying positive feelings toward them. While some of this evidence has been collected in the allophilia research my colleagues and I have been conducting, other evidence predates our research.

Leaders take note: if category differences are not necessarily a cause of animosity, then they do not have to be minimized in order to minimize intergroup conflict.[4] In other words, we do not have to stop thinking of ourselves as "us" and some other group as "them" in order to avoid feeling hostility toward "them." Yet, as we will see in chapter 4, this is exactly what many attempts to improve intergroup relations—whether by diversity consultants, school committees, or UN agencies—are trying to accomplish.

### Misunderstanding of Implicit Association Tests

Categorization is the association of words and ideas. One of the great spotlight moments in us-and-them research has come with the popularization of the implicit association test (IAT) in the social sciences and the media. The popular interpretation and treatment of this technique gives us a valuable view of what is missing from us-and-them research and us-and-them leadership. We will even see that some of what is missing is hidden in plain sight.

Implicit associations—that is, unconscious associations people make—have been studied for a long time with a number of techniques. A computer-based association test, first developed by psychologist Anthony Greenwald and his colleagues and later applied to social relations, refined, and popularized by Greenwald and his colleague psychologist Mahzarin Banaji, turned the general study of implicit associations toward the more specific study of implicit associations made for social groups.[5] Greenwald, Banaji, and their fellow researcher psychologist Brian Nosek, went on to create IATs that could be easily administered—and could even be taken online— unleashing a flurry of research on implicit bias and a storm of public attention. The IAT is an experimental task that requires the rapid categorization of various stimuli presented on a computer screen. Quicker responses are interpreted as having been easier, and the stimuli are therefore interpreted as being more strongly associated in the participant's memory. An IAT may test whether you make more positive or negative associations with the young or the elderly, with white faces or with black faces, with thin people or fat people, and so on. The majority of people who take an IAT "discover" that they have some previously unsuspected relative bias; that is, a bias toward one of two specified groups.

The popularity of the IAT as a research tool led to a website where anyone with access to the Internet can take a variety of implicit association tests.[6] As I write, the website reports that some eight thousand people each week take an IAT. The IAT has even reached the apex of media buzz: it was the subject of its own episode of the *Oprah Winfrey Show*.[7]

Among some social scientists, there are concerns about the IAT. Some point out that seemingly small changes in the environment in which the IAT is administered can lead to dramatic changes in the scores. An individual's score can vary if he or she takes the test a number of times, leading many—including the IAT's lead researcher—to conclude that the test is more suitable for research involving many individuals than for diagnosing the attitudes of any one individual.[8] Some researchers contend that what the IAT measures is not an individual's actual level of prejudice or bias at all, but simply the fact that we know that some groups are more disadvantaged than others.[9] Finally, some wonder whether—or in what circumstances—IAT results (or implicit associations in general) tell us about how an individual will actually behave. After all, if I have a bias that not only fails to make itself known to me but also fails to motivate anything I do, then what difference does it make? Studies of the correlation between measured implicit bias and actual biased behavior so far have produced mixed results.[10]

I am persuaded by the mountain of evidence that the IAT does measure something different from one's explicit attitudes, but I think we need to accumulate more data before we know exactly what the test is measuring and the conditions under which implicit and explicit measures most strongly correspond to actual behavior. The story of the IAT is still being written. For many in the general media, however, the IAT is already telling a story too good to pass up: we're all racists, whether we think so or not. Those who think they are not are, in fact, closet racists, with racist sentiments seething just below the surface. Hate is what there is, hate is our natural response to the "other," hate is everywhere—a bit like bedbugs.

As if that weren't bad enough, several misconceptions about the IAT push the study of positive attitudes toward others—and the application of such attitudes—even further into the academic, social, and media shadows. For example, the IAT does not actually measure your absolute attitude to another group—positive or negative, hate or affection. It measures your *relative* preference for one group compared with another, not your actual level of regard for either. This relative-measurement approach unwittingly reinforces an us-versus-them perspective because it does not allow for the study of one's attitudes toward a group, only one's preference for one group (often "us") *over* another group (often "them"). It is founded on and reinforces, then, a notion of a necessary trade-off: more affection for "us" means less for "them." Yet, as we will see later in this chapter, such trade-offs are not inevitable; feeling good about one's own group does not necessarily require or cause hostility for other groups.

A further misconception is that the IAT is finding racism in everybody. It is telling that, as far as I know and as far as I can find by combing through the journals again and again, there has not been any systematic discussion—popular or scholarly—of people whose IAT results tip in *favor* of African Americans, the elderly, the disabled, and the other usual groups who are seen as the "losers" in the IAT contest. One study found that some 75 percent of white IAT respondents implicitly favor whites over African Americans.[11] But what about the 25 percent who are showing either no bias at all or a bias *toward* African Americans? Such people, even if they are "only" one in four, could have a very beneficial impact on particular communities or organizations. But as long as they are ignored in the research and in the media frenzy that often surrounds the IAT, we will learn nothing from the IAT about a type of attitude that ought to be of the greatest interest to us.

In November 2001, soon after the terrorist attacks of September 11, Project Implicit, anticipating a backlash against Arab Muslims, launched an Arab Muslim IAT task on its website.[12] Perhaps unsurprisingly, they found that 50 percent of the U.S. participants, when asked to express a preference for one name over another, preferred names that were foreign but *not* Arab Muslim to those that were Arab Muslim. But is that really, as researchers in one paper refer to it, "anti-Arab prejudice?"[13] If I prefer the name *Dominique* to the name

*Ibrahim*, it doesn't prove that I have any negative feeling about the name *Ibrahim* at all, only that I like the name *Dominique* better. In any case, 25 percent of the participants *did prefer* Arab Muslim names to other foreign names. Presumably, the remaining 25 percent had no preference for either. Yet I have found no interest—scholarly or practical—in this result. Can Islamophobia be considered endemic if a quarter of the population has not caught it and another quarter seems to have its *opposite*—a preference for something associated with Arab Muslims? If the 50 percent is showing us a genuine "anti-Arab prejudice" as some researchers claim it does—which, as we see, is a very questionable claim—might not the 25 percent be showing us a genuine Islamo-*philia*?[14] Isn't this worth looking into, especially by those trying to exhibit leadership in the relations among Muslim and non-Muslim communities, both in the Middle East and in Western countries?

Research has shown that implicit attitudes can be very malleable.[15] For example, simple exposure to highly valued older people, such as Mother Teresa, reduced implicit bias against the elderly on an IAT.[16] Similarly, exposure to word pairs linking *elderly* with *good* concepts and *young* with *bad* concepts had the same effect.[17] Some see this malleability as a serious weakness in the IAT: how reliable can it be if the results are so unstable? But there may be something worthwhile in this instability if it indicates *changeability*. The IAT's instability suggests that it measures environmental associations and reflects the effect of exposure on one's attitude rather than reflecting any inherently "true" attitude. If so, the results suggest that we're not naturally hostile to the "other," but instead very, very susceptible to clues in our environment indicating how to think about "others." The challenge for researchers, then, is to look at those who buck the trend. A social science focused on hate sees this malleability of experimental results as either a weakness in the experiment or, at best, a puzzle. A social science equally focused on positive us-and-them relations and on what-if possibilities would see it as an opportunity for us-and-them leadership. And the challenge for leaders is to act on this human malleability in two dimensions—trying to change us-and-them relations along the allophilia dimension rather than just along the hate dimension.

### Overassumption of Biological/Genetic Determinism

The myth of the hateful human reaches beyond particular cognitive functions—such as categorization and association—to our very genes. The view that we are genetically wired for hostility to "others" gained strength as it became clear that humans are not, as had once been thought, the only savagely violent primates, the only ones that kill their own kind. It became endlessly fascinating to look at the hostility shown by chimpanzees, orangutans, baboons, and gorillas to their own kind for a deeper understanding of hate and aggression among humans. But the comparison is liable to a number of errors that contribute to our hate-centered myopia with respect to us-and-them relations.

The first such error is that we tend to pay too much attention to violence among primates and too little to the caring and cooperative behaviors they also exhibit. For example, research shows that capuchin monkeys (*Cebus apella*), a social and cooperative South American species, show a sense of fairness, including a willingness to share food.[18] We seem willing to believe that violence among chimps indicates our own inherent violence, but we don't also believe that caring among chimps indicates our own inherent tendency to care for others.

The second typical error in comparisons of human and primate behavior is that, when we look to primates to show that our own worst behavior toward others is innate, we underestimate—or ignore—the extent to which primates, including ourselves, are influenced by environment as well as by genetics. One primatologist/neurobiologist pointed out that the less aggressive and more cooperative species tend to live in lush rain forests where food is plentiful and life is easy.[19] And, in any environment, genetics can be overcome by learning—even for animals. Primate species that seem to have genetically violent traits built into their natures have nevertheless been observed to live in peace. A researcher in a region of Ethiopia containing two species of baboons with markedly different social systems trapped a female of each species and released her into a troop of the other species. Each female, when confronted by a threatening male, reacted in a way that was normal for her own species but was quite a faux pas in her new situation. Yet within an hour—one hour!—each was able to put aside her genetic heritage and adopt the social rules of her new group.[20]

A third way we give too much credit to biological/genetic determinism is by focusing on our captivating resemblances to the primates while underestimating how *different* we are from them, particularly in our ability to shape our own physical and social environments. The lessons we can learn from primate behavior are limited because how we wish to live can be very different from how nature would have us live. Nobody says that because we are genetically designed for walking, we should not fly. We try to learn what we want to know and we try to go where we deem worthy of going.

We may someday be capable of scientifically proving or disproving the assertion that we have some genetic programming that predisposes us in certain contexts to hate. To date, it certainly has not been proven. Even if there were any such thing as a gene for hatred, that would not be the whole story. Genetics, as we have learned in the nearly sixty years since the discovery of DNA, is far from deterministic. Genetic potential can be expressed or unexpressed, triggered or suppressed, depending on many, many other circumstances, both chemical and social. While our *capacity* to hate may have a genetic component, the notion of being *programmed* to hate others is clearly far too simplistic, reductionist, and falsifiable by our own experience. The absence of explicit reference to allophilia—by whatever name one gives it—in social policy and social science studies is a result of our past research choices and methodologies, not of any prewired incapacity to feel it.

## Assumption That Positive Feelings Are "Tainted"

The assumption, acknowledged or unspoken, that humans are inherently or genetically anti-"them," that there is little or no positive power of difference, can lead researchers, policymakers, and leaders to misrepresent—or just miss altogether—evidence to the contrary. For example, when social scientists encounter positive feelings about the "other," they often explain these feelings away as something else. Some argue that low-status groups have positive attitudes toward higher-status groups, but that these feelings are a product of envy.[21] No doubt those who are low on the totem pole can envy those who are higher up, but why would we assume, without evidence, that envy is the *only* possible feeling in such circumstances? And how do we explain away the regard of those higher up for those below them? Accounts of colonial India often show that individual Indians were capable not only of resenting, envying, and even hating the British but also of deeply admiring them. And many individual British people in India were deeply drawn to its culture and people.

Some scholars have even doubted that positive attitudes about the "other" can exist at all, as we saw in chapter 1 when a team of psychologists, while designing a test, planned to interpret as lies any reports by white participants of their positive regard for African Americans.[22]

Others argue that, while people do sometimes have positive feelings about the members of other groups, such feelings are undermined by simultaneous negative feelings.[23] For example, a non-Asian may admire Asians for being hardworking but, according to these theories, will also see them, as a group, as sly and conniving. According to this theory, one can feel what the researchers call *unmixed posi-tive regard* (what an everyday person might call *liking*) only toward one's own group or toward groups that serve as social reference groups (the high-status groups in society that others wish to emu-late), both of which can be seen as extensions of oneself.[24] Regard for the truly "other," in this view, is inevitably tainted.[25] Evidence for this kind of mixed and ambivalent liking has been found in studies of some peoples' attitudes toward a number of social groups, including the elderly, Asians, and Jews.[26]

When I first read these "tainted regard" papers, I was confused. Does this mean that I can't genuinely like other groups without deep ambivalence? I had always felt that people could. But rereading the papers, I noticed that the researchers had asked survey participants what they thought "people in general" feel about particular groups. As their instructions explained: "We are not interested in your personal beliefs but in how you think they [the group in question] are viewed by others."[27] So the real finding was that widely held positive stereo-types (such as "Asians are smarter") are matched with widely held negative stereotypes. That doesn't at all mean that an individual can't have positive feelings about another group that are not "tainted," but the studies have often been interpreted that way!

My colleagues and I decided to replicate the research, but with a difference: we asked respondents what *they themselves* felt about members of other groups, not what society in general feels. Con-cerned that people might just want to present themselves favorably by claiming to hold positive attitudes, we conducted our test among Jewish and Arab citizens of Israel, people for whom a sense of "us and them" is an aspect of everyday life and for whom there would be little or no social pressure to feel unmixed positive regard for the other group. And we certainly got plenty of negative responses. All told, the majority of respondents did report mixed (positive and negative) atti-tudes or else purely negative attitudes. Nevertheless, some 24 percent of our respondents reported unmixed positive regard for the other group. Not a majority, but not a phantom, either. The prevailing theory had predicted we would see unmixed positive regard only for one's own group or for those groups that were the clear "paragon" of a community. Why then, were we seeing it among Arab Israelis for Jewish Israelis and vice versa?

We concluded that unmixed positive regard for the "other" is—or at least can be—a real part of us-and-them relations. It is a natural part of the human repertoire, present to some extent even when it is not being nurtured. Even if most members of an "us" have only negative feelings about members of "them," or only mixed feelings, there can be a minority with unmixed positive feelings. They are a minority well worth identifying and understanding, particularly for leaders in us-and-them situations. This minority can be powerful if leaders choose to make the most of it. As a colleague—an experienced facilitator in high-conflict zones—proposed, a leader with a careful eye can usually spot followers who have the most interest in and aptitude for intergroup collaboration and make good use of them.[28]

### Misreading History

Another version of the myth of the inherently hateful human asserts that history proves that hatred of the "other" is a dominant feature of human social interaction. Look at all the wars, the persecutions, and so on. But this point was well refuted by two political scientists who observed, "Though both journalists and the academic literature on ethnic conflict give the opposite impression, peaceful and even cooperative relations between ethnic groups are far more common than is large-scale violence . . . Yet theories of ethnic conflict seek to explain tension and mistrusts and spirals of violence, rather than the peaceful and cooperative relations that are by far the more typical outcome . . . If our current theories are true, we would expect much more violence; the theories over-predict violence."[29] In other words, we can look at all the wars and persecutions, but we are obliged to look as well at the less gripping but far more common—and infinitely more desirable—*absence* of war and persecution.

But even if hatred is not prevalent, doesn't history at least prove that it is an inevitable part of human nature or human society? History proves no such thing. At different times, history could easily have proven that human sacrifice, the rule of kings, and death by pneumonia are inevitable or that the natural average human life span is thirty-eight years (as it was in the United States in 1850). What has been is not necessarily what must be or all that can be. Most disciplines and practices know this; the world of us-and-them scholarship and leadership still needs to get the message.

## *Misunderstanding of Minimal Group Research*

Far and away the most influential work done on us-and-them relations has been the *minimal group* studies, so called because they seem to show—and very vividly—that people assigned to groups on even minimal grounds will still have negative feelings (prejudice, discrimination, and even hostility) for arbitrarily assigned outgroups. In other words, people slip into this pattern at the drop of a hat, showing how natural and even inevitable it really is. In fact, the minimal group research, although very ingenious and compelling, has been frequently and seriously misunderstood. It does not tell us what it at first might seem to tell us.

Minimal group researchers begin by creating an "us" and "them" out of thin air, either by dividing a group of study participants into subgroups or teams according to some very arbitrary criterion or else by creating one group and simply telling them that there is another group that is different in some way. In one experiment, for example, children were randomly given red or blue T-shirts to wear. Once the participants have been grouped, the researchers set up a scheme to allocate something of value—such as food, money, or prizes—either to the members of one's own group or to members of the other group. With startling consistency, what researchers see is that the participants—typically complete strangers to each other—take their arbitrary groupings seriously and display relative bias toward those in their own group.

Social psychologist Henri Tajfel and his colleagues conducted the earliest and still the seminal research of this kind in 1971.[30] This research then led Tajfel and John Turner, Tajfel's student at the time, to develop social identity theory, by far the leading account of intergroup hate and conflict taught in universities around the world.[31] This theory says that each of us strives to enhance his or her self-esteem. Because we each have both a personal identity and various group identities (I, for example, am myself, but I am also an American, an academic, and so on), we can boost our self-esteem through our own achievements or though the achievements of a group with which we identify. (I can be proud of my own achievements, proud of the achievements of my academic discipline, proud of my country's achievements, and so on.) But there is a third option for enhancing self-esteem: we can try to bring another group down. This, according to the theory, is what we see happening in minimal group experiments and, more importantly, what we can see happening all around us.

Minimal group research is still a frequently used research technique, and social identity theory is very widely taught in modern social psychology. Together, they help create a culturally pervasive picture of groups ready to become hostile over the smallest and most arbitrary of differences. An "us and them" is always, according to this view, kindling for the flames of hate.

Yet the theory is wrong.

For one thing, we are led to believe that all one has to do is put different-colored T-shirts on a group of strangers and—voilà!—one has created friends, enemies, loyalty, and conflict. A minimal cause seems to have produced a very large effect; this must really be telling us something fundamental. I disagree. The people who participate in these experiments do not drop down from Mars. They have all been socialized in a world in which identification with one's group and loyalty to it are considered normal and proper behavior. That is, they have been socialized to the norm of group interest—to favor one's group and to denigrate an outgroup. We all learn, for example, that you play a sport to help *your* team win and beat the *other* team. Research on the norm of group interest finds that taking into account the interests of one's own group before taking into account the interests of other groups is a pattern of behavior that is actively taught and fostered in many societies.[32] It is something many societies uphold as a rule—an unwritten rule, but a rule nonetheless. Tajfel himself actually acknowledged that participants took their socialization—what he called a *generic norm* of intergroup behavior—with them into the supposedly minimal conditions of his experiments, but that part of his argument has been largely overlooked.

Not only is the evidence from minimal group research strongly supportive of the norm of group interest—that is, how we treat an "us"—it is *not* strongly supportive of conclusions about how we treat a "them." Minimal group studies show more evidence of ingroup preference than of any particular attitude toward an outgroup. In fact, some researchers have reviewed previous minimal group experiments in the literature and have also repeated the experiments, finding that the participants' bias was more a matter of attachment to their own group than of hostility to the other group. That is, there was empirical evidence for the desire to enhance one's own group; there was no empirical evidence for the desire to denigrate the "other." Minimal group researchers have seen and continue to see in their studies what they want to see—a vision of innate, irrepressible "us against them" attitudes.

In addition, it is hard to say that the grouping in these experiments is truly done in any minimal way; that is, that the group starts out having no particular meaning for its members. In the social setting of the experiment, almost the *only* information the participants are given by the experimenters (who are the authority figures in that particular setting) is which group they are in and which group they are not in. The ingroup-favoring norm in many societies dictates that group members should act to benefit their group.[33] Thus, while the basis for the grouping in these experiments is indeed minimal, the centrality of the grouping to the situation is *maximal*. What minimal group experiments are picking up is likely not a predisposition for us-and-them conflict but rather the extent to which we follow social norms when there is really nothing else to go on. My colleague R. Matthew Montoya devised a reliable way to directly measure the degree to which individuals do or do not buy into the norm of group interest. In several studies, he and I were then able to study how adherence to that norm in general could explain the degree to which one did or did not favor one's ingroup and denigrate an outgroup in practice—in some cases, months and months later.[34] We found that one's adherence to the general social norm of group interest is a far stronger predictor of the degree of competition or cooperation one will later exhibit toward specific outgroups than any drive to identify with any particular social group.[35]

It is important to note further that in minimal group studies—as in IAT studies—there is often significant variation in how the participants act. In one set of experiments, participants had a chance to allocate money to other participants who were identified only by a code number and group membership. In fact, nearly a third of the participants tended to allocate the money quite fairly, with little or no consideration for group membership. That is another aspect of minimal group research that tends to be ignored. For some reason, the large group of people who do not show any bias is deemed uninteresting. This seems to reflect the same mind-set that I encountered with the professor mentioned in chapter 1, who had spent a career studying discrimination in corporations yet seemed uninterested—in fact, downright dismissive—of a potential student's interest in exploring and understanding the many instances in which there was *no* discrimination.

In one minimal group study, participants allocated not only rewards but also punishments. When it came to handing out punishments, discrimination between "us" and "them" faded markedly or disappeared altogether. Participants tended to be even *less* willing to dole out painful punishments to members of an "other" group than they were eager to dole out rewards to members of their own group![36] Certainly this finding, which has been replicated many times, does not fit with the myth of the hateful human or the disturbing lessons students are continuously encouraged to take away from the minimal group research.

All told, minimal group research findings do not seem to indicate that we are prone to hatred.

### Assumptions About an "Us and Them" Trade-off

It has been widely accepted (and sometimes blindly assumed) by social scientists that the more attached one feels to one's own group, the less positively one will feel toward members of other groups. Indeed, a systematic review of decades of research found that "most contemporary research on intergroup [us-and-them] relations, prejudice, and discrimination appears to accept, at least implicitly, the idea that ingroup favoritism and outgroup negativity are reciprocally related."[37] While researchers have debated whether hostility toward "them" is a consequence of strong psychological identification with "us," as Freud argued early on, or whether, as others have noted, strong identification with "us" is a consequence of conflicts in the world with a "them," both sides seem to agree that there must be a trade-off.[38] There is no room in these theories for a strong attachment to one's own group that coexists with—or may even stimulate—a strong attachment to another group.

But if we dig deeper, we find no evidence that such a trade-off is inevitable. Researchers have shown that feeling strongly positive toward one's own group does not necessarily lead to antagonism toward other groups. In fact, the tendency for a trade-off, if it does occur, seems to show up most clearly when the research is experimental; that is, conducted among minimal groups created by the experimenters. But studies of the group affiliations of real people in the real world are less likely to show a clear relationship between identification with one's own group and bias toward another group.[39] For example, a study of the many ethnic groups in South Africa, some of which have a long history of hostility, found that a strong identification with one's own group did not correlate strongly with intolerance for others.[40] For neither the black majority nor the white minority did strong ingroup identity lead to much intolerance toward an "other." These findings suggest that conflict is not the necessary result of group attachments—that "us and them" does not have to be "us versus them," even if it has been in the past.

R. Matthew Montoya and I have examined conditions in which even the opposite might be observed; that is, strong attachment to one's own group might predict *more positive* evaluations of other groups. We found that a positive attitude toward another group can actually be stronger for people with stronger positive identification with their own group when there are cooperative relations between the groups; this finding held both in a laboratory study in which we created minimal groups and in a field study of students at different universities.[41] Similarly, a team of political scientists found that stronger social identification with what they called *black racial identity* was positively correlated with *more* positive feelings toward "others."[42]

An anthropologist studied field notes from studies of 186 traditional societies, looking for the sources for strong affiliation with one's own ethnic group and of hatred for outsiders. She found no evidence that the two attitudes were connected and concluded that positive feelings about the ingroup and negative feelings about an outgroup are not the negatively correlated yin and yang people imagine; in fact, hostility toward outsiders seemed best predicted by *hostility and violence within a society* rather than by strong affection and attachment within that society.[43]

The work of political scientists, social psychologists, and an anthropologist has converged on findings that should be seen as nothing short of liberating for us-and-them leadership. Although it is sometimes possible to cynically trade external hostility for internal cohesion, we see that a leader need not even consider paying such a price for internal cohesion because such trade-offs simply are not necessary in order to achieve it. The ingroup/outgroup trade-off is therefore not good leadership. The advantage cannot last, and the trade-off will eventually do more harm than good. For one thing, it requires creating or maintaining an enemy—always a liability.

Looking in the other direction, we see that the misguided notion of a necessary trade-off also implies that, if positive relations with the "other" are the goal, they might come at too high a price—the loss of group cohesion. Again, no such trade-off is necessary, and no such price must be paid for positive us-and-them relations. In fact, strong group identification can actually stimulate allophilia for others when the norms of the group support it. If there weren't such a cultural focus on hate and prejudice, we would already know a lot more about this phenomenon and how it might be put to use at many levels, from defusing school rivalries to strengthening international coalitions.

### Assumption of Hate Can Mask Many Real Causes of Conflict

The scientifically unfounded conviction that hate is a natural reaction to an "other" can blind both leaders and scholars to some of the actual causes of hate and prejudice, such as necessary competition for resources or simply the *perception* of the necessity of such competition. This, in turn, can shut the door on trying—or even seeking—a whole class of potential solutions, most notably keeping an eye out for when resources are limited and preempting conflict by setting up joint groups to make fair allocations. More important still, good leaders can be vigilant about not allowing false *perceptions* of scarcity and illusions of "necessary" competition to take hold.

Increasingly, historians are finding suggestive evidence that ethnic and cultural differences can easily be invoked in a conflict of which they were not the cause. A number of studies, for example, have suggested that what seem to be ethnic conflicts in Africa are actually conflicts involving ethnic groups but not primarily for ethnic reasons. One political scientist found two ethnic groups, the Chewa and the Tumbuka, both living on both sides of the border between Zambia and Malawi. In Zambia, the two groups were friendly, but in Malawi they were very much at odds.[44] This suggests that there is an inferential error in the argument that cultural differences are at the root of the world's conflicts.[45] Worldwide, there are far more juxtapositions of different groups—ethnic, racial, religious, and so on—than there are actual conflicts.

It seems that it is not differences per se between groups that rouse hostility, but differences (1) that have become politically or socially salient and (2) to which negative meanings have been attached. This can be missed by researchers who measure *perceptions* of differences—not actual differences—and find a relationship between those perceived differences and such problems as poor economic growth, political instability, and civil war. The reason this is the tail chasing the dog is that people tend to perceive cultural differences when they have become politically or socially salient for negative reasons! As we will see in cases throughout this book, the media—which often determine what is or is not salient in modern societies—are prone to focus on such cases. Of course, the most politically or socially salient differences might well be the ones that are associated with conflict. A more rigorous testing would instead look at the degree of *actual* difference between groups and try to establish a relationship between actual differences and problems such as poor economic growth, political instability, and civil war. The main point here for us-and-them leadership is that leaders have to be less concerned about the differences and more concerned about the social and political meanings attached to them.

In Rwanda, for example, European colonizers gave preference to the Tutsis—who were a minority but were believed to be taller on average (more like the Europeans)—over the Hutus, who were a majority but were believed to be shorter on average. Tutsis were given privileged access to education and jobs; there are reports of a minimum height requirement being instituted for access to college! In order to tell who was Tutsi, colonial officials required everyone to carry an identity card complete with a tribal label. A *card*—not differences that could be discerned by one's own senses—had to identify "us" and "them." Colonial discrimination—not an instinctive or "natural" hostility toward the "other"—largely sowed the seeds for the hatred between these two groups that finally erupted so murderously in the Rwandan genocide of 1994.

## The Wrong Norms

As we have seen, careful examination of some of the most famous scientific "demonstrations" of man's supposedly innate and genetically programmed inhumanity to man shows that we may be much more shackled or misguided by our social environment than by our genetic makeup. Hamas television runs a popular children's program, *Tomorrow's Pioneers*, which featured among the cast a Mickey Mouse–like main character named Farfur. Though presented in a children's educational format similar to that of such shows as *Sesame Street*, the character spouted anti-Israeli, anti-Jewish, and anti-American hatred.

Eventually, Farfur was beaten to death on the show by an actor playing an Israeli.[46] A child narrator further explained what had happened to Farfur, so it could not be missed. If the preschoolers who watch this show grow up full of hatred, we won't need an expert to conclude that their environment will have had more to do with it than anything in their genetic code.

Even in the United States, our academic, social, and media environment is pushing us, not to feel hatred and commit violence, but to believe that hatred or the lack of hatred define the full range of our capacities. Much as Madison Avenue would like to convince us all that we have an inherent body odor problem that needs to be solved (with conveniently available antiperspirants), the "hate industry" in all its forms seems determined to convince us that we all have an inherent hate problem that needs to be solved (with various methods of antiprejudice, antiracism, and so on). But, also like Madison Avenue, it will lead us to believe that our problem can never quite be solved, just kept at bay, so that we keep buying more product.

The media, in particular, are well aware that hate grabs people's attention (which, in turn, influences the attention paid to hate by policymakers and even to some extent by scholars). But what we see and hear in the media shapes what we think is normal. The media thus become a funhouse mirror, exaggerating one of our worst features until we don't remember what we really do or can look like.

An outrageous—yet fairly typical—example turned up in an issue of *Newsweek*. The cover asked, "Is Your Baby Racist?" Inside, there was an article titled "See Baby Discriminate" and the teaser, "Kids as young as 6 months judge others based on skin color. What's a parent to do?"[47] The article itself offered no evidence whatsoever that babies are (or for that matter are not) racist. In fact, of the nine research studies described in the article, only one was a study of babies! In that study a psychologist found that babies will stare significantly longer at photographs of faces of a different race than their own than they will at photographs of faces of the same race. Indicating? Indicating that they find the face out of the ordinary. What's the problem here? I confess I spend extra time looking at particularly beautiful people; does that show I have a prejudice *against* them? Most of the other "evidence" in this article had to do with middle school and high school–aged children—children well on their way to mastering society's lessons—and had little to do with racism in any ordinary sense of the word.

I find it implausible that the article's authors—two award-winning "deep" journalists—could actually have thought that the material in this article justifies any claim that babies are (or for that matter can be) racist. But someone—whether the authors or the publishers—assumed, quite correctly, that such a claim would get attention for opening up a new frontier of hatred. All involved did their bit to narrow our view of the potential range of us-and-them relations and what goals leaders can set for themselves and those they lead.

How harmful or harmless is this? Vague and unstated cultural assumptions have enormous power, not only over what people think and do, but also over what they *cannot* think or do. Cultural assumptions, such as the inherent tension in us-and-them relations, shape social norms, the unwritten rules about what is allowable or forbidden, appropriate or offensive, normal or weird. We are drifting too close to a state of affairs in which those who do not feel hate toward others and those who actually enjoy other groups for their difference are seen—and see themselves—as deviant. We begin to create a confusing mess in which hate is increasingly cast as normative—what one should do or what most people are doing—in order to get people to pay attention to it and fight it.

*That's a very dangerous gamble.* Study after study finds that most people tend toward what they believe to be normative—that is, to the attitudes, values, and behaviors of those around them—even when they consider the norm to be irrational or even morally wrong.

Social psychologist Solomon Asch, for example, in a classic study, gave his experimental participants a "vision test," requiring them to make judgments such as which of two lines was longer.[48] Among the participants, Asch planted some *fake* participants who gave responses that were clearly wrong. Surrounded by people insisting on something obviously incorrect, some 32 percent of the actual participants would conform strongly, despite what they could see right before their eyes. Some 43 percent more would conform to some degree, leaving only 25 percent who could not be convinced to deny the obvious truth. If people end up thinking that it's more normal, natural, and human to dislike the other than to enjoy or admire the other, they may no longer think it makes sense or is worth the effort to fight what they take to be human nature. Better, perhaps, for different groups to just keep to themselves and not provoke each other's "natural" dislike—and that would only be the most benign outcome of such a transformation.

## Institutional Problems with the Science of "Us and Them"

Some of the errors leading to our focus on hate and prejudice and our failure to take allophilia seriously—or even to notice it at all—are institutional rather than conceptual or methodological. Social science, like any science, is conducted by real people pursuing real careers in real institutional and organizational settings. Pride, status, career, taking the path of least resistance, and historical happenstance all play a role in what knowledge is pursued or not and what problems are addressed or ignored.

### *Social Science Blinded by Its Search for Legitimacy*

As noted in chapter 1, the social scientific study of intergroup relations (us-and-them studies) emerged as a significant academic discipline very much as a response to the horrors of the Holocaust and then to the horrors of American racial segregation. To some extent, then, this branch of the social sciences arose with a moral agenda. It was necessary for humankind to understand its own capacity for such evils in order to prevent them from recurring. The study of hate thus gained what marketers call *first-mover advantage*. Being first to a market (in this case, the marketplace of ideas) with a new kind of product (in this case, concepts, theories, and measurements of us-and-them relations) lets you define that market and can confer a strong advantage in staying ahead of competitors. Hate was the proximal problem, and therefore hate was the subject.

At the same time, the social sciences have always had something of an inferiority complex with respect to the so-called hard sciences (such as physics and chemistry) and have often sought to gain legitimacy by mimicking them, whether or not that mimicry is appropriate or justified. The more quantitative the approach, the more sophisticated the physical or statistical equipment, the more legitimate the research is assumed to be. And indeed, there is much to be gained from using sophisticated statistical and analytical techniques (many of them now managed by increasingly complex software) and sophisticated technology such as MRI scanners. In particular, social science became increasingly sophisticated at measuring hate and prejudice. This has had the unintended effect of keeping social scientists' eyes glued to those types of attitude and behavior.

And of course, in academia, relevance plus legitimacy plus success can be a good formula for research funding. Funding breeds more success and its own kind of legitimacy. In short, the study of hate got off to a good start and became entrenched in the academy. The study of people's positive attitudes toward those who are different never had that kind of initial impetus and never gained that kind of foothold. If you were interested in intergroup relations ("us and them" relations), the bad stuff was where the action was—and still is.

Another aspect of scientific legitimacy also kept the study of positive us-and-them attitudes in the shadows. Scientists pride themselves on objectivity—on discovering what really *is*—regardless of anyone's opinion of what *should be*. Studying the existence of hatred is seen as within the domain of legitimate science, as long as one remains objective and not normative or, as some put it, "value-laden." But as we have seen, affection, comfort, kinship, engagement, and enthusiasm with respect to different groups also exist, so it would seem that the objective study of such attitudes is also legitimate science. Unfortunately, such responses to the "other" tend to be seen as the proper subject matter of religion or ethics, and that's enough to make them seem improper subject matter for science. These phenomena seem too concerned with undefinable and unmeasurable "goodness." In 1935, a psychologist described a comparable "flight from tenderness" in his own field; in repudiating theology, he suggested, psychology had overreacted and deliberately blinded itself to the tender aspects of human relationships so often emphasized by religions.[49] This attitude is gradually being overcome in fields such as evolutionary biology, where there is a vigorous inquiry into the evolutionary origins and neurological—even biochemical—bases of morality. But the bias against "goodness" is still very much the norm in the social sciences, and the field of us-and-them relations is not merely biased in this respect, but completely lopsided. Social science graduate students quickly find that the academy legitimates and rewards the study of hate and is uneasy with the study of anything that seems too preachy. It is seen as quite ordinary to study hate of the "other," the negative power of difference, but rather strange to study enjoyment of the "other" in its otherness, the positive power of difference.

A true science of "us and them" would of course be as interested in the positive—the "us *plus* them"—as the negative—the "us *versus* them." Scientists examine how concrete can be reinforced; it's an interesting problem, but the motivation is clearly to keep people safe in tall buildings and on long bridges. Why would it be unscientific to examine—scientifically—how to reinforce social relations in diverse communities, companies, and societies so that people can be happier, more productive, and, in many cases, a whole lot safer? It is time to examine the more positive cases of "us and them." We need to put those who feel affection, comfort, kinship, engagement, and enthusiasm with respect to an "other" under the microscope, examining in detail the individual, situational, and social characteristics that nurture or hinder such natural feelings. Yet we have seen throughout this chapter how evidence of such feelings is often ignored or cynically redefined.

As naturally as discoveries in the physical and life sciences lead to new technologies, discoveries in the social sciences should lead to new policies and practices by which to achieve a particular society's aspirations. Social science expertise on the power of hate was used in landmark legal decisions. And just as the physical and life sciences are sometimes asked to contribute to the development of a desired technology—but can only do so by adhering to the standards of science—so the social sciences can be asked to contribute to the development of a desired policy or intervention—but can only do so by adhering to the standards of science. Finally, just as a society's values must help determine which physical and biological technologies are worth pursuing or prohibiting, those values must determine which developments of social science should be put to use or prohibited.

### Measurement That Is Institutionally Enshrined

Social scientists tend to study what they can measure, whether or not that is what is theoretically or practically most important. As I mentioned in chapter 2, there are now hundreds of validated measures, scales, and tests of hate and prejudice. When social scientists become interested in researching us-and-them relations, they are therefore likely to use those tools and thus to measure what those tools measure.

Even when researchers want to find out something about positive relations, they use scales and measures of hate or negative prejudice and interpret low or falling scores as evidence of positive or increasingly positive attitudes. But as we saw in chapter 2, hate measures cannot reliably inform you about something other than hate because goodwill toward a group is not simply the absence of hate.

In addition to the proliferation of tools for measuring hate, the research literature offers a constant proliferation of new ways to think about hate. For example, we have *ambivalent racism*, *aversive racism, symbolic racism, modern racism, racial resentment*, and *implicit racism*, to name just a few.[50] We have theories and models of hate and social context, hate and fear, conscious and unconscious processes and hate, threat and hate, anxiety and hate, hate and rejection, and intergenerational hate. Granted, there really are many varieties and gradations of negative us-and-them relations, ranging from mild disaffection to murderous violence. The problem is that the field of us-and-them relations as a whole is so lopsided. These nuanced parsings of hate—each of which, by its mere existence, tends to spawn more research—have no equivalent yet in the literature on positive relations between "us and them."

### Lack of Scientific Humility

The study of hate and prejudice, having taken the lead over the study of positive us-plus-them attitudes, maintains that lead not only because researchers tend to ask certain questions and overlook others but also because many researchers have become more and more willing to make bold pronouncements with a lack of conditionality that is surprising, given the far-from-complete state of our knowledge of how groups feel and act with respect to each other.

What accounts for this loss of humility in the social sciences? I don't know for sure. Possibly a desire to generate buzz and sell books. Possibly—and this would be more excusable—a desire to avoid sounding too wishy-washy and too equivocal to participate in public policy discussions. Social scientists have a lot to contribute to public policy, but we should not forget that science is an iterative process. Do we really think we have finally achieved perfect understanding—with perfect accuracy, reliability, and objectivity—with our MRIs and fMRIs? Judging from how MRI and fMRI findings are often discussed in the popular press, even by researchers, one might think so. Today, they seem like state-of-the-art science, but we are far from knowing for sure what they are telling us. For example, certain brain-imaging studies of a part of the brain called the amygdala, which plays a central role in fear and aggression, appeared to support the discouraging view that humans are hardwired to fear the "other." When subjects were shown the face of someone of a different race, the amygdala became aroused and ready for action, even when the face was shown so rapidly that the subject did not consciously see it. But more recent studies point to a different conclusion. When people who had spent time with other people of various races were tested, the amygdala did not become aroused in response to the face of someone of a different race. It seems that fear of the "other" is not so hardwired after all. And there are sure to be many, many more surprises. Having seen in this chapter how persistently science has avoided the study of positive rather than negative attitudes toward difference, it is far too soon to say that science has proven what we can or cannot be or that it has told us all we can learn about how to live together.

# FOUR

# MISGUIDED STRATEGIES

W HEN WE look at how situations involving different groups are actually handled by communities and nations, corporations and congregations, we see many vestiges of the us-*versus*-them assumptions and misinterpretations discussed in chapter 3 and too little, if any, recognition of the presence or possibilities of allophilia— of "us *plus* them." In this chapter, I will show what is missing from a number of the strategies and approaches most commonly used to solve us-versus-them conflict and more generally to bring "us and them" together more productively.

## Diversity Diversions and Multicultural Mistakes

You may have already been wondering: what about the diversity and multicultural movements—aren't they pushing the agenda beyond the limited choice of hate and the reduction of hate? Unfortunately, these movements are not much help. In fact, I would argue that, on the whole, they *strengthen* rather than loosen the grip of hate. Of course, I don't mean they preach or incite hate. But neither do they offer any serious alternative to hate as a determinant of us-and-them relations, so that we are left with the one-dimensional model of hate and the reduction of hate. Furthermore, they too often eschew rather than embrace the power of rigorous social science.

### A Mixed but One-Dimensional Message

The major shortcoming of the diversity movement is its mixed message. Spend time with diversity experts, immerse yourself in the diversity literature, and you are likely to hear two conflicting messages with no explicit attention to the contradiction. The first message is: diversity is our strength—each different group brings something valuable to the table. The second message is: deep down, we are really all the same. Depending on the day—and sometimes on the feelings of the diversity trainer—one message or the other will be emphasized. Often, both messages are emphasized in the same training session. With anti-hate training beginning so early (in elementary and even preschool) and offering such a confused message about what difference is, how important it is (if it all), and how it should be treated (if at all), we shouldn't be surprised when the recipients of such training emerge confused. Imagine this as a public health campaign: "Vegetables are important for your health. Go ahead and eat them because they're really no different than any other food group." Sociologist Marlene Mackie has observed possible perceptual roots to an *egalitarian dogma*—the quickness with which people say that because everyone is equal, everyone is the same, and as a result ignore differences between groups.[1]

The real problem here is that the diversity movement is deeply ambivalent about the fact that different social groups really can be quite different from each other. It is frankly amazing how far some leaders will go in denying difference in the name of diversity. Taking the we're-all-the-same position to an extreme, the Rwandan government—as part of a reeducation campaign in the aftermath of the 1994 genocide—actually outlawed ethnicity. Whereas Rwandans had been required to carry ID cards identifying them as Hutu or Tutsi, all are now to be termed *Rwandan*. Different ethnic groups cannot be named in newspapers or textbooks. A nebulously defined crime of *divisionism* has been added to the penal code and discussing ethnicity can land one in jail.[2]

Sensible people will acknowledge that some difference is real, but do not always realize how real it is. Of course, many traits—such as tenderness toward children or amusement at pratfalls—are common within many groups. All the same, national, ethnic, and religious groups often socialize their members in quite different ways, with quite different results. In my classes, when the national diversity of the student body permits, I often show students slides of foods, each of which someone in the class finds mouthwatering and someone else finds stomach-turning—not owing to the idiosyncrasies of personal taste but because these students had been brought up that way in their own cultures. One such food is water bugs, which resemble giant cockroaches but are used in Thailand to add aroma to sauces. Is your stomach churning simply from the thought of biting into a crunchy water bug? If socialization is powerful enough to lead people of different groups to have such different *physiological* responses—not even to a particular food or even a picture of it, but merely to a written description of it—how can we think that people of different ethnic, religious, and national groups will not differ meaningfully in more important ways?

The other claim of the diversity movement—that diversity is our strength—is not as patently false as the claim that we're all the same, but it is certainly misleading. For example, it is frequently argued that ethnic diversity increases a business's capacity for innovation and creativity. The prestigious Drucker Foundation's magazine, *Leader to Leader,* ran a cover story entitled "How to

Put Our Differences to Work." The author's counsel to business leaders is a common one—to make "diversity a conscious priority for explorations, collaborations, and teams to generate new ideas for innovation."[3] But so far, there is little solid empirical research linking diversity to innovation, which has led some disappointed leaders to conclude that it's simply not true that diversity is our strength.

A more scientifically grounded diversity movement could have taken a more realistic approach. Diversity is a not a priori a civic or business strength. On the contrary, it has clearly been a contributing weakness and problem for many an organization and many a society. But it *can* be a strength, because there is a natural and nurturable positive power of difference. We have, for example, good empirical research showing that innovation is more likely in the context of positive emotions.[4] Diversity, therefore, might well increase a business's capacity for innovation *if the different groups have positive feelings about each other*. In other words, the necessary condition is not simply a lack of hostility toward diversity but rather the presence of positive feelings about diversity—allophilia. A one-dimensional model of us-and-them relations can't make this distinction, but a two-dimensional model can.

And that, I believe, is the diversity movement's Achilles' heel. Whether or not we say it or think it explicitly, we are operating largely on a one-dimensional model, with a palette of human possibilities ranging from hate, prejudice, and discrimination to, at best, the complete elimination of hate, prejudice, and discrimination. In other words, difference can either be a problem or, at best, not a problem, which leaves people torn between trying to defend it and deny it. What's missing is the second dimension of us-and-them relations— allophilia. With a two-dimensional model, one has the option of truly enjoying, admiring, and feeling drawn to difference, without needing to justify it in utilitarian terms. Think again of the example in chapter 1—those two little girls playing with each other's hair; diversity wasn't their strength, it was their delight.

## Trying to Talk People Out of Prejudice

Diversity training and diversity initiatives often include an effort to talk or train people out of their existing stereotypes with "the truth"—educating people about past discrimination, about the assumed if too often elusive benefits of diversity, about the positive qualities of members of another group. But research has found that how we act toward others seems more a result of our feelings about them than of our rational or informed thoughts about them. In fact, controlling for how much one emotionally likes another group— rather than what ideas one has about that group—can account almost completely for one's level (if any) of biased behavior toward that group.[5] This suggests that, even if we could get rid of every stereotype about, say, people with disabilities—clearly demonstrating that the stereotypes are not accurate—some people would still feel uncomfortable around the disabled and might still be biased in how they evaluate and how they act toward members of that group.

The situation is different with a two-dimensional model of us-and-them relations. With the aforementioned research in mind, my colleagues and I designed the allophilia construct to be largely an emotional construct.[6] That is, the Allophilia Scale includes some measures of cognitive orientations—what one *thinks* about another group—but focuses most on emotional responses—how one *feels* about the other group. Thus, when we measure allophilia with the Allophilia Scale, we are measuring something more closely correlated with how one will *act* toward members of that group. Interventions that go beyond reducing prejudice to promoting allophilia—a set of positive feelings and orientations rather than a set of positive stereotypes—can then be monitored with a measurement tool that really lets you know whether you are moving toward the kind of us-and-them relations that the diversity movement would aim for if it dared.

## *Losing the Fight for Lack of the Proper Goal*

The current diversity movement, by not coming to terms with its fundamental contradiction, is gradually undermining its own cause. Given that this movement has been around in some organized form since the late 1960s, it hasn't made much of a dent in the amount of tension and conflict between groups in the world. This, in turn, has increased people's cynicism about whether it is even possible to do anything about tension and conflict between groups in the world. Perhaps the current amount of us-versus-them conflict is simply the way it is and always will be—getting better here and worse there but never really going away. This is the very attitude we saw repeatedly in chapter 3. To avoid this surrender, we need to stop insisting we're all the same and have a little more faith in people's interest, ability—and actual desire—to engage difference.

This is where you might think the multicultural movement would have stepped into the breach. Multiculturalists express no doubt that differences can matter. Often, they even espouse a vision of positive relations between different groups. One would think this movement would have made its own discovery of allophilia, yet it has done little or no more than the diversity movement to set forth a serious alternative to hate of the "other" and the reduction of that hate.

I think what we most need is to focus not on multiculturalism but rather on *interculturalism*. We do not need scholars to prove the existence or power of group difference; we can all see with our own eyes that cultural, ethnic, linguistic, national, and other types of groups can and often do differ in meaningful ways. We do desperately need scholars to help illuminate the conditions under which these interactions can be most productive. This would help communities and leaders to focus on strategies that help different groups intersect and, in particular, strategies that promote positive productive engagement of the "other" when the differences come to the fore. Religious communities, for example, could complement their efforts to develop their own individual communities with efforts to learn about other religious communities. This is the opposite of the common multiculturalism strategy of encouraging—sometimes even pushing—groups to express their uniqueness (that is, what makes them different) for its own sake. Cultures are certainly worth preserving. But I believe this will—and *should*—happen much in a more natural bottom-up way if the various cultures in a multicultural community, organization, or society enthusiastically enjoy each other's differences and if leaders keep an eye out for opportunities to promote and encourage connections in the context of positive emotions. An interesting example is the particular form that interculturalism took in Smyrna, Alexandria, and Beirut in the nineteenth century:

The cities of the Levant were never a melting pot of peoples; rather a grid of self governing communities, enforced by separate schools, places of worship, hospitals, burial grounds, clubs, charities, newspapers, and libraries . . . And because the divisions between the communities were so absolute, there was a remarkable spirit of tolerance within a Levantine city. No one felt that their children were in danger of being submerged by another culture, and so there was a propensity for sharing and acknowledging the various festivals and rituals of different faiths. This arose not out of any interest in a multi-faith fusion, but as neighbors with a taste for being amused by different dishes, street processions, dances and tunes.[7]

### *Weak Scientific Foundations*

Strategies employed by the diversity and multicultural movements are often weak in their very foundation—the science on which they sit. Their scholarship is surprisingly and overwhelmingly—almost obsessively—about hate and how to reduce it.[8] For example, there have been many studies of how personal contact between members of different groups affects attitudes toward those different groups. (I will say more about these studies later in this chapter.) Yet the results are measured with hate scales—that is, the researchers measure the degree to which contact between groups reduces hate, but not how much it increases allophilia. This lopsided approach is adopted in study after study not only of contact, but also of the other commonly studied potential pathways to more positive intergroup relations, such as cross-group friendship, shared goals and identities, and intergroup forgiveness and reconciliation. If our goal is to understand and tap the positive power of difference, why not use a scientific tool, such as the Allophilia Scale described in chapter 2, specifically developed to measure the presence of positive attitudes and relations? We need to look for evidence of what we really aspire to when we try to increase contact between groups.

Too commonly, advocates and proponents of multiculturalism—even those trying to lead from inside the academy—simply refuse to use the tools of social science to examine, test, and ultimately validate or invalidate their assertions and models. In turn, their real-life interventions are, as several scholars have noted, too long on articles of faith and too short on rigorous social science. Various scholarly reviewers bemoan the weaknesses of research on how and how well diversity training actually works.[9] These weaknesses include failure to use valuable sources of information such as third-party reports from colleagues and supervisors, minutes from meetings, and employee evaluations; overreliance on self-reported data; failure to conduct research in settings and with populations that resemble the actual targets (for example, using social science graduate students to test a training program used by insurance company executives); failure to randomly assign participants to groups that receive training and control groups that do not in order to be clear what is a cause and what is an effect; failure to distinguish what role is played by individual elements of the training such as role-playing exercises, lectures, and videos; use of assessment questionnaires that make it embarrassingly clear what the "correct" answer is supposed to be (for example, "Do you discourage biased statements in your workplace?"); and failure to distinguish participant feedback from actual evidence of the training's impact. Yet many, if not most, U.S. employers continue to offer (or require) diversity training and many of the same tools and techniques are used by nonprofits working for the betterment of society.

Lack of bona fide program-impact assessment means not only that effort might be wasted on something ineffective, but also that lessons are not learned that would render interventions more effective over time. It's as if physicians simply tried different medicines without the benefit of rigorous controlled studies and without even communicating the results of their own efforts to each other. As a result, decades of investment in the diversity movement have not yielded great dividends.

For example, diversity training has often made inappropriate use of interventions invoking blame, shame, and separation of different groups of employees.[10] What this means, in practice, is making white males—and increasingly all participants—aware of the degree to which their attitudes and behaviors toward other groups can be insulting or oppressive. But research has already shown that shame produces a tendency to *withdraw, hide,* or *escape.*[11] These are hardly the building blocks of a healthy, productive, and innovative organizational culture—and some diversity consultants are starting to agree. One criticized "the shame-and-blame where you call people in and make them feel bad," while another explained, "Nobody wants to get into a corporate classroom and be beaten up and made to feel guilty."[12] When researchers began to look more reflectively and rigorously at the shame-and-blame approach, they discovered that it often creates a backlash, leaving minority group members feeling stigmatized and blamed, farther on the outside than ever.[13] (And that's not to mention the effect on those who are required to submit to it but are not actually "guilty as charged"; likely a *very* sizable group.) Although this approach is less common now, it is still too common and it has already turned many people away from the goal that motivated the diversity movement in the first place.

Ironically, even some of the criticism of diversity training reflects the same inadequate scholarship that undermines the training itself. One sociologist claimed, "To understand where diversity training goes wrong requires some understanding of the causes of prejudice . . . Simply put, humans have a tendency to like those who are similar to them and to dislike people who are not. Although not proven, sociobiologists believe that such tendencies have a biological basis."[14] But if it hasn't been proven (and he's quite right about that, as we saw in chapter 3), why is he presenting it as something fundamental to our understanding of human behavior?

### Diversity Is a Fact, Not a Goal

Diversity is a fact, but I think we would do well to sidestep it as a concept and proceed in both research and in our practice to a more basic—and, I believe, more useful—inquiry: what is the full range of possibilities when an "us" and a "them" are together? In particular, what are the more positive and productive possibilities, and what conditions make them possible? Put in terms of the two-dimensional model presented in chapter 2, the question becomes: how can we increase the allophilia that members of one group feel toward another group?

It can be unproductive and actually harmful when politicians and religious leaders come out for or against diversity or, worse still, when social science researchers seek to understand whether diversity is "good" or "bad." This approach encourages people to treat the relations of a perceived "us" and a perceived "them" as a fixed state, either good or bad, rather than as something that can—and every day does—take many possible forms under various conditions. This stance robs leaders of the chance to choose from the full range of us-and-them possibilities. Until we invest in a comprehensive scientific understanding of all of the ways an "us" and a "them" can relate to each other, rather than focusing on one portion of the possibilities, we can't say that our diversity experiment has failed. Rather, it hasn't begun.

## Alternatives That Offer Too Little

One of the key points of this book is that the positive power of difference is both natural and nurturable, so that promoting positive attitudes toward others is something that civic, business, religious, educational, and political leaders *can* do and therefore *should* do.[15] In many cases, it is what leaders would like to do, but they don't realize that positive us-plus-them relations are a definable and achievable goal, over and beyond the reduction or elimination of negative us-and-them relations. Lacking a complete two-dimensional model of what is real and what is possible, leadership itself can become an obstacle.

The most obvious case is when leaders deliberately lead by dividing; that is, they solidify their standing in their groups by stirring up hostility or rivalry with other groups. I have called this the *ingroup/outgroup leadership trade-off*.[16] Leaders do this because history shows over and over that it can work. We can find it everywhere, from sports to business to international relations. How much team spirit has been stoked by getting Yankees fans to hate the Red Sox and vice versa? I learned only too well when I moved from Boston to New York and didn't think to retire my Sox cap at the New York state border.

Nevertheless, many leaders do recognize and try to practice alternatives to the ingroup/outgroup leadership trade-off. But the most common alternatives are alternatives only on the surface. At bottom, they rest on the same assumptions on which the trade-off rests—that different groups can either hate each other or, at best, not hate each other.

## Tolerance

The goal of *tolerance* is simply the goal of not hating something or someone or some group and does not inherently go beyond that, although people are often *thinking* of something nobler when they use the word. The goal of *acceptance* can imply a little more in the way of positive feeling, but it is still a passive state, far from willing and active interest, admiration, or engagement. As we will see below, tolerance and acceptance are states from which it is easy to slip back into intolerance. Without any countervailing positive force, there is nothing more than the absence of hate to prevent a rebirth of hate. Unfortunately, the absence of hate is not up to that task. *Tolerance* is therefore a trap, a state so lukewarm that it serves to reinforce the power of hate as the dominant concept of relations between "us" and "them." When one is floating on a raft in the middle of the ocean, one may be dry, but the ocean is still a dominant presence.

## Dismissing Positive Difference—a Bipartisan Mistake

Sometimes leaders who seek to unite different groups try to *transcend* the differences. They emphasize similarity and play down or just ignore difference, trusting that, with the proper effort and attitude, the similarities will somehow prevail over the differences and the problem will cease to exist. In American politics, this is true of both liberals and conservatives, although they have distinct ways of going about it. Liberal leaders too often try to evade difference by broadcasting the mixed and ultimately ineffective message of the diversity movement: our diversity is our strength, but we are all the same. Conservatives, on the other hand, often try to evade difference by saying, in effect, "We must all become the same," either through assimilation or through an emphasis on shared identities or shared goals. Both the liberal and the conservative approaches are ultimately doomed to fail because they so seriously underestimate not only how much our differences matter but also how positive a factor those differences can be.

## Overreliance on Shared Goals and Identities

Most approaches to improving relations between an "us" and a "them" focus on broad social categories. This makes sense. These are the basic building blocks. Various approaches differ, though, in what they do with these building blocks in order to improve relations.

Some approaches focus on increasing the extent to which people are seen as individuals rather than as members of groups. These models are what social scientists call *decategorization* models because the idea is to look past the categories.[17] *Recategorization* models, on the other hand, focus on changing the perceived categories themselves, so that "we" and "they" are combined into a single "us."[18] Such recategorization may be achieved by creating what social scientists call *superordinate identities* (for example, "We are all Americans") or *superordinate goals* (for example, a group of business leaders and environmental activists might be able to agree that "we are all working to preserve the environment"). More recently, we have seen the development of *dual categorization* models, which focus on encouraging groups to have both shared and distinct identities because it turns out that trying to replace distinct group identities with one shared identity can have undesirable effects (described below).[19]

Emphasizing—or even creating—shared goals and shared identities is a commonly studied and commonly attempted method for improving intergroup relations. National leaders in Singapore and Mauritius, for example, have been successful in uniting very multicultural societies largely through the common goal of economic development. In Mauritius, there was an additional underlying and unifying fear of the consequences if the country were to remain dependent on the volatile price of sugar cane. It is easier and more common to emphasize shared identities or shared goals that already exist than to create them, but leaders do sometimes attempt to replace different group identities with a brand new common identity. One example was Mustafa Kemal Atatürk's attempt to create a single Turkish identity out of the various ethnic groups living in the territory that was left after the collapse of the Ottoman Empire following World War I. On a more ordinary scale, schools plagued with gang warfare sometimes try to create and promote a strong school identity to be shared by all students.

Shared goals and shared identities can be independent routes to recategorization. In practice, they are often intertwined. As people begin working toward a common goal, they feel more common identity and, as people feel more common identity, it is natural for common goals to arise.

Defeat of an enemy in war may be the most frequently discussed example, perhaps because it seems the most plausible. As a colleague once quipped, "Peace on Earth will come about when there is an invasion from Mars." A common enemy—or even the mere perception of a common enemy—can indeed promote and support a shared identity, at least as long as the threat is convincing. Many New Yorkers, living in one of the most diverse cities in the world, reported a marked increase in what could only be called camaraderie after the 9/11 attacks. People noticed neighbors helping neighbors more than they ever had before and were surprised by eye contact and greetings on the street instead of the averted gazes characteristic of many big cities. Around the country and even around the world, people were prepared to say, "We are all New Yorkers," echoing John F. Kennedy's famous declaration in 1963 of the Free World's solidarity with East Berliners cut off by the Berlin Wall. Terrorists had probably never seemed so threatening to the whole world as they did after wreaking such destruction on the largest city in the world's most powerful country. U.S. embassies around the world were showered with flowers, even in countries politically hostile to the United States. As many researchers have noted, the relations between groups in conflict become more congenial when the groups are confronted with a common enemy.[20] Many New Yorkers lament that the camaraderie has passed. And the international manifestation did not outlast the strain of differences over the invasion of Iraq. Indeed, the post-9/11 recategorization into a broad encompassing "we" went the way of many shared goals and identities; there was an initial positive effect that eventually dissipated for reasons I will discuss below.

But shared threat still seems to be—to leaders' minds—the best tool they have for trying to bring groups together. Almost eight years after those attacks, Barack Obama's 2009 speech to the Muslim world, delivered in Cairo, would rely heavily on the same "technology," using a sense of shared threat in an attempt to forge a common identity and goals. He even seemed to define human brotherhood as the joint facing of mutual threats:

> For we have learned from recent experience that when a financial system weakens in one country, prosperity is hurt everywhere. When a new flu infects one human being, all are at risk. When one nation pursues a nuclear weapon, the risk of nuclear attack rises for all nations. When violent extremists operate in one stretch of mountains, people are endangered across an ocean. When innocents in Bosnia and Darfur are slaughtered, that is a stain on our collective conscience. That is what it means to share this world in the twenty-first century. That is the responsibility we have to one another as human beings.[21]

Shared goals and shared identities—whether evoked through speeches or actively promoted through various forms of cultural assimilation—can have powerful unifying effects. They are critical in a pluralistic country, yet they have serious limitations, which is why, throughout history, they have been only moderately successful and never sufficient in transforming us-and-them relations.

**First, shared goals and shared identities can ignore what matters most.** During 2009–2010, a newly sworn-in President Obama followed up on a campaign pledge to overhaul the U.S. health-care system, and congressional Democrats began that work with zeal. The stakes were high, ranging from coverage for many who were uninsured to the growing costs of the existing system, let alone a more inclusive system. President Obama offers a particularly compelling opportunity to examine the practice and malpractice of us-and-them leadership. He has explicitly stated the need for leadership in several areas of us-and-them polarization, and he is widely portrayed in the media as aspiring to bridge difference—or perhaps more accurately, to transcend it. In the battle over health-care reform in the United States, for example, liberal and conservative Democrats were seen to have very different philosophies, very different constituencies, and very different interests. In particular, they had very different ideas about how to control costs. What they did have in common was the politically popular goal of expanding coverage, so the president and the congressional leadership focused on that goal. Was that a successful instance of leadership that brings different groups together? Not really, because the looming cost avalanche was largely ignored. The effort wasn't even politically successful because the unresolved cost issues seriously undermined wide support for the whole reform package and will lead to reduced investment in other social services for the neediest in the coming decades. I don't claim to know how President Obama could have overcome the differences between liberal and conservative Democrats, but it is clear that pushing them aside to pursue only a genuinely shared goal did not work.

What we see in this example is that *shared* goals are not necessarily the *most important* goals, any more than what's most essential to a pair of neighboring countries will necessarily be found along their border. Leveraging shared goals can be worthwhile when it helps groups move toward the most important goals. Leaders have a responsibility not to forget—or let others forget—which are really the most important goals. A different version of the same problem can be observed in President Obama's relations with Republicans during the same health-care battle. Obama assured the public that he wanted to get past the us-versus-them stand-off between the two parties, but when it came down to it, he invited key Republicans to watch the Super Bowl with him (a declaration of shared identity—"We're all Americans and Americans love the Super Bowl and a good beer") but did not include them in key meetings to overhaul the nation's health-care system (which certainly came across as a declaration of insurmountable difference—"We'll never agree on shared goals and how to reach them and it's too much trouble trying to deal with you on this"). It is hard, if even possible, to maintain a healthy coexistence on the basis of shared identity without working together toward important shared goals. The two work best when reinforcing each other; one will not suffice as a substitute for the other.

The interfaith movement offers another example of how much more difficult a shared identity can be in real life than it is on paper. It is common for interfaith proponents to emphasize that Christianity, Judaism, and Islam are all Abrahamic faiths and that this common identity should provide a strong foundation for working together. But interfaith leaders tend to stop at this somewhat technical fact of history, afraid to move on to the real differences between these three living religions and cultures, because the differences are implicitly equated with conflict. A model of interfaith action based on a two-dimensional model of us-and-them relations would be able to separate the task of addressing and reducing the very real us-*versus*-them conflicts and the task of addressing and increasing the equally real possibilities of us-*plus*-them affection, comfort, kinship, engagement, and enthusiasm. Such a model would recognize that similarities are real and important and are the foundation for positive relations. It would recognize that differences, too, are real and important and can also be the foundation for positive relations. Once properly understood, more far-reaching but also workable interfaith solutions could be undertaken, assessed, and refined.

**Second, shared goals and identities as a method of achieving coexistence often presuppose a threat and may even aggravate it.** Replacing "us" and "them" with "we" is most often attempted in order to combat a common threat—real or perceived. Reread the excerpt, earlier in this chapter, from President Obama's speech to the Muslim world. References are made to financial collapse, pandemic flu, terrorism, and genocide. The vision of interdependence is a lopsided one, a vision of interdependence in the face of *threat* (in chapter 7, I will discuss such *negative interdependence* in contrast to *positive interdependence,* which is conducive to allophilia).

The nations in the European Union—at least until their recent and very serious financial difficulties—had for decades been experiencing historically unprecedented levels of integration and cooperation. A common European identity has been embraced, while distinctive national identities remain. One motivation for adopting this shared identity may well have been a fear of the intra-European rivalries that had spun out of control so violently during the two world wars. But another significant motivation was to compete more effectively with "others"—namely the United States, China, and India. It's not inconceivable that the EU's success in creating a shared European identity, if it doesn't fall prey to the current financial crisis, will provoke or exacerbate economic tensions with one of these competitors.

Third, to the extent that shared goals or identities are successful, they homogenize diversity and may sacrifice its benefits. The benefits of diversity are real but too easily romanticized. There is some, though not voluminous, research suggesting a relationship between greater diversity and greater creativity and versatility of thought and action in small groups.[22] But diversity advocates have been too quick to see this as proof that diversity is "good" anywhere it occurs; if things don't look that way, it's because the benefits of diversity have gone unappreciated or have been undermined. But, as I said earlier in this chapter, it is not helpful—it is indeed far too simplistic—to simply declare that diversity is better than homogeneity. Diversity is a condition from which many different outcomes are possible, depending on the specific context and the approach one takes to it. It is often a long, hard slog to overcome the differences that divide groups, and the effort often overshadows the gains. Early efforts will be awkward and can easily stall out or break down. But—and this is a crucial *but*— if, over time, a community, school, company, or entire society can learn how to put in place the conditions in which the positives of difference can emerge—to leverage the upsides of diversity while minimizing the costs—there is a pay-off. What we need now is a much better scientific understanding of us-and-them relations, undertaken with more of an engineering orientation; that is, a determination to understand the conditions under which various desirable and positive benefits of diversity can be brought about, increased, and preserved.

An extensive 2001 study of forty American communities, conducted by political scientist Robert Putnam, found that higher levels of racial and ethnic diversity corresponded with lower levels of many forms of *social capital*—a term used both in social science and economics to refer to a variety of social relations that make a community "work."[23] For example, Putnam's study looked at public behaviors such as participation in community projects, contributions to charity, and voting in elections; private behaviors such as spending time with friends versus watching TV alone; and attitudes such as how much a person trusted people of a different group and of his or her own group. Putnam's results seemed to indicate that diversity was a serious liability, not actually creating problems but undermining the behaviors and attitudes that would make a community a safe, healthy, and happy place to live. Putnam himself took no stand against diversity but others have used his findings to do so.[24]

But instead of trying to figure out whether such research findings prove that diversity is either good or bad, suppose we took a different scientific approach. Were there any communities—or even neighborhoods within communities—in Putnam's study that bucked the trend? A rigorous study of high-diversity communities with high social capital (along with a study of the high-diversity communities with low social capital and why the two seem to be connected) could be of great practical use to leaders in those communities. As I said in chapter 3 with respect to IAT results, if we want a pluralistic world that really works, let's look carefully wherever we see a glimpse of it. Instead of focusing *entirely* on the large majority of IAT takers who seem to show prejudice or the large majority of diverse communities with lower-than-average social capital, let's also look very carefully at the meaningful minority of IAT takers who seem to show a positive attitude toward the "other" or the minority of diverse communities with higher-than-average social capital.

From there, we will need leaders willing to support social policies founded on a two-dimensional science of us-and-them relations. Leaders too often show a shortsightedness—frankly, a lack of leadership—when they go for the short-term momentum of a shared identity and abandon the more ambitious goal of a community or society that is adept at making the most of its own diversity.

**Fourth, identities and interests that are downplayed in the name of shared goals and identities often come back.** Genuine differences in interests and identity can be kicked down the road, but rarely can they be willed away. Ethnic identities, for example, are resilient, persisting in the face of prejudice, conflict, discrimination, and aggression.[25] Group differences that *seem* to have been overcome by a shared identity are more likely still there, but under the radar. It is shockingly easy for a self-interested or shortsighted leader to revive them, as we saw in Yugoslavia and then Rwanda. Assimilation can lead members of both a majority and a minority to abandon their sense of the minority as an "other," but that sense of otherness can easily be revived. Before the rise of Nazism, many German Jews were integrated into German society to a degree that too many of today's immigrants and guest workers in countries around the globe don't come close to approaching. Yet the Nazis found it easy to convince many "real" Germans not only that those Jews were an "other," but also that they were a threat to the rest of the country. As we saw in chapter 3, differences between groups are not always taken to be very meaningful; other factors can come along to make them more politically and socially salient—sometimes with deadly results.

**Fifth, encouragement of a shared identity can become enforcement.** If the replacement of group identities with a broader identity turns out to require the suppression of irreconcilable differences, it could require more forceful coercion than any democratic society could tolerate. We see this happening now in China, as the government seeks to defend its tight control over the Internet as part of its attempt to block anything that it considers a threat to national unity.

### A Mixed Approach Misses the Point

Some leaders recognize that shared-identity and shared-goal approaches—in effect, strategies of promoting similarity and demoting difference—have downsides as well as benefits. Instead, these leaders advance the mixed message I noted above in my discussion of the diversity movement: "We are all similar. We are all different." Such a message may be technically defensible (groups, or for that matter any individuals, can be similar while having important differences), but it communicates little. More importantly, it really misses the entire point. What's holding us back from a more successfully pluralistic world is not any failure to understand that different groups are indeed both different and similar and that both dimensions matter. What's holding us back is that we still know so little about the *positive* aspects of the difference dimension. We all can likely agree that similarity helps, and we all agree that difference can be a problem. But we hold to the mistaken notion that difference is almost always a problem—either an active problem or one in abeyance. We haven't gotten past the overly simplistic and frankly wrong idea that a person's response to another group's difference is pretty much always some shade of dislike, either active or latent, and that the solution to problems of pluralism must be some version of hate reduction, either by reducing the negative attitude itself or by reducing or replacing the difference that we think provokes it. Instead of perpetuating these mistakes, we need to understand that both similarity and difference can be the cause of positive relations and that to ignore difference as a source of positive relations is to blind ourselves to the best of our choices.

## Implications of Shared Goals and Identities for Citizenship

The limitations of shared identities and goals discussed above are especially relevant to the increasingly vexing question of citizenship in pluralistic societies. Citizenship can be understood as a dedication or obligation to the common good; at least, to certain forms of the common good, such as public safety, education, and economic growth. Governments of many countries with diverse populations realize that their citizens' sense of citizenship is becoming an acute problem, but few know what to do about it other than to keep trying the usual methods of encouraging a shared identity. But strategies of similarity are not enough to keep groups together over the long haul.

We must think as well about difference and the still largely unexplored conditions under which the positive power of difference is a force for attraction rather than a cause of discord.[26]

Finally, we have to remember that even a two-dimensional model of us-and-them relations is not all-inclusive. Some groups are not only different but intolerable. I am not at all advocating that a society should find ways to encourage affection, comfort, kinship, engagement, and enthusiasm for the members of terrorist factions and racial supremacy groups. There is no reason that inquiry into the practical and theoretical appreciation of difference need be or should be equated with the normative mandate to appreciate any and all difference.

### Leaving Leadership to Followers

Strategies for improving us-and-them relations can be as big as a national policy or as small as planning an event at a primary school. And while we all have a chance to do our part in our own relations with people of different groups, it is especially important that leaders do their part. Leaders really do have a different and essential role to play. Yet they often leave us-and-them situations for their followers to sort out ("That's *their* job, not mine"), underestimating how much their own attitudes and behaviors—at least their perceived attitudes and behaviors—influence those of their followers.

For example, a common practice of diversity efforts is to try to increase contact between members of two groups. The theory seems to be that if, for example, Israeli Jews and Arabs from neighboring countries just have more chance for contact, more opportunities to get to know each other at the individual level, they would lose their animosity for each other's groups. It seems like common sense (and has moved many a wealthy donor to open up his or her pocketbook to fund a program). But is our common sense correct?

Contact theory is the most commonly studied us-and-them theory, and there is a wealth of social science research on how much and under what circumstances contact does help people lose their negative prejudices. Yet what does that research tell us? Of all the factors affecting the success of intergroup contact that researchers have studied, the most important is whether or not there was support from an institutional authority.[27] Formally recognized leaders' support of intergroup contact predicts an effort's success better than any other factor. In practical terms, this means that if a diversity council or some members of a church are running a program to bring groups into contact, it is much more likely to be effective if the human resources director, minister, or school principal (or, better still, the CEO, the bishop, or the mayor) is enough of a presence—and really walking the talk—to make participants feel that this leader really approves of what they are doing. This is a challenge to leaders who, too often, leave the work of improving us-and-them relations to those followers who feel a calling for it. Ignoring a solid body of research showing how and when leadership matters, many civic and business leaders have failed to give the necessary boost to the efforts they themselves have supported. (This topic is taken up in more detail in chapter 7.)

## Training the Old Kind of Leader, Hoping for a New Kind

To change how something is done, you often need to change how it is taught. Us-and-them leadership is certainly an example. U.S. President Woodrow Wilson noted, "Interest does not tie nations together; it sometimes separates them. But sympathy and understanding do unite them."[28] Yet this is not at all what is taught in the business schools, law schools, and schools of public policy from which so many of our public- and private-sector leaders emerge. In these institutions, the dominant approach is economics, which favors a negotiation perspective. Negotiation as a dominant framework is taught both theoretically (how to understand the world) and normatively (how to accomplish goals in the world). These schools indoctrinate aspiring leaders in a style of negotiation that pursues what is called *enlightened self-interest*—exploring interests that my group and your group have in common and pursuing options that offer better outcomes for both groups.

This doesn't sound so bad, especially in comparison with, say, a leader's absolute focus on his or her self-interest—the kind of leadership Machiavelli notoriously described in *The Prince*. Nevertheless, enlightened self-interest is insufficient on several grounds. First, it is inaccurate. Rooted in a one-dimensional model of us-and-them relations, it aims at the supposedly necessary balancing of unavoidable human selfishness and hostility with respect to "us" and "them." One does consider the interests of "them" in this approach, but *only* in the service of advancing "us."

But making the best of competing interests is not the only alternative. This approach lacks the allophilia dimension and forgoes everything that actively working the allophilia dimension might make possible. It allows for an "us *and* them," but not an "us *plus* them." While science accumulates research results showing that positive regard for others is as natural a human capacity as hatred or prejudice—and, more generally, that prosocial orientations are as natural to humans as our selfish ones (as we saw in chapter 3)—it remains for society to decide that it wants to nurture this capacity. That, in turn, calls for leadership. If our leaders are guided by self-interest—even in the kinder, gentler form of "enlightened" self-interest—how transformative will they be?

Second, enlightened self-interest does not take us far enough. Leaders trained in this approach typically say (and may well believe) that their goal is "the common good." But the common good cannot reliably be achieved when other groups are considered only to the extent to which accommodating them advances one's own group's interests. We need to break free from the myth that pluralistic communities (whether large or small) can thrive as a collection of groups, each advancing its own interests. To truly pursue the common *good* rather than common *interests*—even to believe that there is such a thing as the common good—would require far greater interest in and engagement with the "other." At the international level, for example, this would require Americans to become much more interested in and engaged with, say, the Chinese than we are today, going well beyond courting relationships to advance our own interests. One promising example is the rise in the study of Chinese in American middle and high schools, in some cases thanks to teachers sent from China.[29] Language is one key to a much deeper level of engagement with an "other"; a scarcity of Arabic-speaking Americans has been a serious obstacle to successful engagement with the Arab world. Mutual engagement would also require an effort—undertaken in part by the U.S. government—to encourage Chinese and Arabs, for example, to be much more interested in and engaged with American people and culture (a subject taken up in chapter 7).

Finally, common interests can shift even while the common good remains the same. I taught a class in which I referred to the European Union as an amazing "experiment." A student from an Eastern European member country rather angrily insisted that the EU is not at all an experiment, but rather a fact. How, she demanded, could I fail to understand that Europe has become a single entity, like the United States? But, interestingly, a student from a Western European member country came to my defense. This was more than ten years ago and now, with the strain of the European financial crisis and talk in some countries of secession (or expulsion) from the EU, calling the EU an experiment seems far less controversial. But at the time, when there was much "EU-phoria," how could two members of the same "group" have seen it so differently? Precisely because the EU is an "us" largely based on enlightened self-interest; that is, a combination of the interests of its several members. Western Europe looks to the

East for markets, resources, and lower-cost labor; Eastern Europe looks to the West for markets, investment, and advanced technology. Both coalitions look to each other to create and grow a regional block to ensure a more solid footing in the global order as other countries—most notably China and India—rise in economic and political power. German chancellor Angela Merkel put it to her own citizens in terms of enlightened self-interest: "We do not need to love our currency. We need to evaluate how much it helps us, and the euro does so in every aspect. We should remind ourselves of one thing: We face an increasingly intensive competition with vast countries like China, India, or Brazil. In order to compete, Germany needs allies. The euro creates such allies. A strong and efficient euro-zone is the best protection for our welfare state and our jobs. It is also thanks to the euro that the number of Germans in employment is higher today than before the crisis."[30]

But as interests diverge—for example, as it becomes more and more expensive for Germany to bankroll the EU—it becomes easier for those who think of the union as a tally of self-interests only to think about ending it. In the end, the degree to which the EU can weather the tensions that threaten to dissolve it will depend not on the enlightened self-interest that brought it together, but rather on whether each country's goodwill toward the others is felt to be a "fact." As one Greek citizen put it, "I like this whole European family. We have exchanged ideas and cultures all these years being together. I don't want to leave them. It's my family now, but I don't like their currency."[31] For her, the trade-off of trouble for "family" makes sense, even if it wouldn't stand up to a sober assessment of enlightened self-interest. It is such feelings of kinship with the "others" that could, for example, move Germany to continue its participation in the EU even when its own interests are not being immediately served or perhaps are even being damaged a bit. In other words, the allophilia dimension will be needed.

The genuine pursuit of the common good should not have to rely on the occasional appearance of a charismatic leader such as Martin Luther King Jr. or Nelson Mandela. A comprehensive scientific investigation of the positive dimension of us-and-them relations, both *what is* and *what could be,* would eventually make its way—as science often does—into the practical realm of policies, practices, and programs that could help instill and promote allophilia in particular circumstances. In other words, there would be tools that leaders at all levels, with or without any special charisma, could reliably use to make us-and-them relations more positive and productive.

But the distance that separates this possibility from the current view of leadership and how it is taught can be seen powerfully in something that *failed* to take place. In 2006, Robert M. Sapolsky, the Stanford primatologist/neuroscientist whose work was discussed in chapter 3, published a fascinating article called "A Natural History of Peace" in *Foreign Affairs,* a highly influential journal published by the Council on Foreign Relations and read by many world political and business leaders.[32] Sapolsky has done some of the most interesting work supporting the view that, "Contrary to what was believed just a few decades ago, humans are not 'killer apes' destined for violent conflict, but can make their own history."[33] The article discussed this work, presenting a rigorous, scientifically grounded challenge to the prevailing view of us-and-them relations, particularly at the international level. He assumed (as presumably did the editors who chose to run the piece) that this more realistic understanding of human nature would stir up those who think about leadership. Sapolsky reports, however, that he did not receive a single response.[34] In the age of blogs, not receiving one response to an article in *Foreign Affairs*—particularly one that takes issue with the prevailing wisdom—is incredible. Clearly, his message fell on deaf ears. By this point, I hope readers can see why.

## Stunting Childhood Curiosity

What our future leaders learn—or don't learn—in graduate school is important, but we all learn lifelong lessons about how to feel and think about the "other" much earlier in life. And once again, we can find examples of a well-meaning approach that is actually making it harder than necessary for us to achieve a successfully pluralistic world in which different groups live and work together, not only because they have to but because they want to.

For example, few of us would deliberately teach children to hate others who are different, but we might very well teach them to suppress their natural curiosity about others who are different. Yet curiosity about what makes others different may be a natural entry into positive attitudes toward different groups.

One day, as I was walking in a park with a friend who gets around in a motorized scooter due to a physical disability, a little boy came over and said, "Cool car! Can I hop a ride?" His mother grabbed his hand, gave it a rough squeeze, and snapped, "Jason, it's not a car. Don't bother her." In doing so, she sent a clear signal that his curiosity was not appropriate. To this little boy—and to just about anyone—my friend, with her scooter and her legs curved from arthrogryposis multiplex congenita (a condition in which one's lower limbs do not develop properly in the womb), was undeniably different. But what to make of this difference? To the boy's mother, it was probably something to be pitied and definitely something not to be explored. Had her son approached a golfer in a golf cart or some people riding an electric cart in the airport—people who were neither "pitiable" nor very "different"—she probably would have found his boundary-crossing more permissible. But to the boy, my friend's difference was not only interesting but actually inviting. Whatever it was about her, she got to ride around in this "cool car." Yet the next time he sees someone so intriguingly different, he may keep to himself. Almost certainly he will have learned to do so by the time he is an adult. A chance to encourage the growth of allophilia, born of initial curiosity about difference, was certainly lost.

Earlier in life, when I worked at a child-care center, there was a single Jewish child, Rachel, in a class of some thirty preschoolers. The center provided lunch, but Rachel's mother packed her a kosher meal. Children, I came to discover, love to reverse roles—to instruct adults. As I was serving lunch on my first day of work, one child after another eagerly informed me that I shouldn't give one to Rachel—she couldn't eat it. When I asked them why (Rachel happened to be playing elsewhere), they really had no idea—it was just something different and interesting about their classmate. Their teachers had never offered them an explanation, though it might have been a good opportunity to open up the subject of people's different religions. It seemed that here, too, difference was to be "respected" by leaving it alone rather than explored and enjoyed, for example, by asking if one might "hop a ride" and experience a scooter. A wonderful moment to tap curiosity, rather than define what was off-limits, had been missed.

Growing up as an insulin-dependent diabetic, I would often have to carry lancets and syringes to school in order to take and test blood samples and to inject insulin. A school lunchroom aide charged with making sure I made it through lunch without any incident encouraged me to do this in a bathroom stall, suggesting I would be more comfortable "in private." But as any diabetic knows, a bathroom stall is a difficult place to inject insulin with syringes, to swap out insulin pump cartridges, and so on. And to do all that while staying sanitary and avoiding infection is nearly impossible. The bathroom counter with the sinks wasn't any better, because it was usually wet. Finally, it occurred to me to simply just do it at a lunch table; those were kept pretty clean, and there was plenty of room to maneuver. To boot, this way, I could check the menu to decide how much medicine I needed and I wouldn't have to come in late and join a conversation in the middle. The lunch lady looked at me a bit askance. People asked me a lot of questions: Does it hurt? Do you *have* to do it? But I became quite comfortable satisfying their natural curiosity about someone whose daily routine was so different from their own. And by not hiding in the bathroom, I was not reinforcing the idea that this difference was something that I needed to hide and everyone else needed to leave alone.

In contrast, I recently heard an African American woman on the radio complaining about all the "dumb" questions her daughter's white classmates asked about her hair when she started at a new school. This woman's daughter, she acknowledged, was one of the first African American girls her classmates had met. Of course, I don't know the exact circumstances, but I wonder if, again, an opportunity was missed to open borders rather than enforce them. My observation is that girls are often interested in each other's hair. My nieces, especially when young, loved to touch women's hair and the two girls I mentioned in chapter 1 were certainly crazy about each other's hair. If you're a white girl meeting a black girl for the first time, that black girl's hair is something different and may well be very interesting. And if you're a black girl meeting a white girl for the first time, that white girl's hair is something different that may well be very interesting. At least it could be, if you feel you are allowed to be curious.

## The Two Wolves

From presidential palaces to playgrounds, we see approaches to handling us-and-them relations that can be characterized as a kind of triage, responding to the most immediate threats posed by difference as well as can be done with our limited social science resources. In a one-dimensional model, similarity is seen as a cause for positive relations and difference as a cause for conflict and hate. One tries to reduce hate of the "other" as a triage nurse would try to stop the bleeding. But we can do better than triage (and for that matter, even triage is often intended as a first step leading to more specialized care). As shown in chapter 2, we already know more—and could know a lot more than that—about the full range of possible us-and-them relations. Were we to pay more serious scientific attention to this missing dimension of us-and-them relations, it could lead to new "technologies"; that is, we could be more adept and experienced at cultivating the kinds of intergroup relations we would most like to have. So far, almost all the attention has gone to hate and prejudice. I don't argue that hate and prejudice don't deserve all the attention they receive. But that doesn't mean that additional attention should not be paid to the real alternatives—not just the absence of hate, but active feelings of affection, comfort, kinship, engagement, enthusiasm, curiosity, and admiration with respect to those who are different.

There is a Cherokee tale of an old man who instructs his grandson that there are two wolves inside each of us. One wolf is evil—it is anger, envy, jealousy, sorrow, regret, greed, arrogance, self-pity, guilt, resentment, inferiority, lies, false pride, superiority, and ego. The other is goodness—it is peace, benevolence, and kindness. These wolves are in a constant battle with each other, he tells his grandson. The boy thinks this over, then asks, "Grandfather, which wolf wins?" The old man replies, "The one you feed."

The focus of the social sciences on hate and how to combat it, to the exclusion of allophilia and how to instill and support it, is too one-sided, like a science of medicine that has much to say about illness but nothing to say about good health or a political science that studies only tyrannies and failed states and ignores successful democracies. Any individual social scientist can of course legitimately study whatever interests him or her, and any donor can legitimately give money to whatever program she or he wishes to fund. But in the aggregate, there is something systemically unbalanced in the way we have sorely underinvested in understanding how to get groups to like each other more.

Socially, by paying so much more attention to our potential worst behaviors, which we wish to avoid, than to our potential best behaviors, which we wish to achieve, we are foreclosing on our best chance for peace in a world of increasingly (but not automatically happily) diverse societies. If people are going to keep moving and mixing, if our policies and economies are going to be more and more interconnected, we need to know how different groups of people can best live together, not only without conflict, but constructively and cooperatively. This will require more than an absence of hate for the "other"; it will call for curiosity, interest, and enthusiasm, too.

If we really wish for a world of productive coexistence, we have been feeding the wrong wolf. We have evidence of our capacity to respond to the "other" with feelings of affection, comfort, kinship, engagement, and enthusiasm. In the case of many other human aspirations—to live longer, to end famine, to rescue people from mental illness—we have set to work with our science to understand, in richer ways, what exists and what *could* exist. Why aren't we doing that with coexistence? Chapters 5 through 7, share some of what I have learned—from my own research, from the research literature, and from the world—about how and when the positive power of difference flourishes and what leaders can do to encourage and enhance it.

# FIVE

# TAKE EMPATHY IN A NEW DIRECTION

Our sympathy with sorrow, though not more real, has been more taken notice of than our sympathy with joy.

—Adam Smith, *Theory of Moral Sentiments*

**A**S FAR AS WE currently know, it is only human beings who can imagine what it is like to be in someone else's shoes. It is an ability with profound effects. It might have helped prehistoric hunters to be able to imagine what their prey would do. Complex human societies would be inconceivable without the ability to imagine what other people might do or wish or fear under particular circumstances. This is different from—and more sophisticated than—simply inferring how another might instinctively react. It is an ability so facile that we often don't even notice it in the course of our busy days.

And we go even further. We not only imagine what others are feeling, but also feel something ourselves in response. You see a homeless man shivering on a park bench and you "feel sorry" for him; that is, you *actually feel* some measure of discomfort and sorrow. You see the stricken look on a politician's wife as her husband admits to the world that he's been having an affair and you feel embarrassed for her—you may even physically cringe. By the same token, you walk by a small park, see a child swinging as high as she can and loving it, and you feel happy. You may even feel joy. You see newlyweds—even complete strangers—emerging from a church, and feel happy. You see someone arriving at an airport, suddenly surrounded by family and smothered in hugs and kisses, and feel happy for the whole joyous group. Many a camera company has based an advertising campaign on this ability of ours to feel an emotion in response to someone else's experience.

This combination of imagining what someone else is feeling and then feeling a related emotion oneself is how I and many (but not all) social scientists define *empathy*. When the feeling is negative, such as sorrow or embarrassment, in response to another person's experi- ence of something unpleasant, undesirable, or harmful, many social scientists call it *empathic sorrow*; a more ordinary word for it is *sympathy*. When the feeling is positive, such as happiness or pride in achievement, in response to another person's experience of some- thing pleasant, desirable, or beneficial, social scientists call it *empathic joy,* but it is telling that there is no ordinary word for that in English. Around the world, there were many expressions of empathic sorrow for Americans after the terrorist attacks on Septem- ber 11, 2001. For a number of reasons, there were many expressions around the world of empathic joy for Americans after the election of Barack Obama on November 4, 2008. One of the primary reasons was that the nation's election of its first African American president seemed to indicate that a mighty step forward had been taken.

We know sympathy can be a powerful force, mustering worldwide help for the victims of a tsunami, hurricane, or earthquake. But is empathic joy also a powerful force? Does *it* ever save lives or cause millions of dollars to flow? If not, then what—if anything—*does* it do? Infants are not always such fun, yet we care for them. Is it because we feel empathic sorrow for their weakness, their hunger, their vulnerability in the world, their dirty diapers? Perhaps. But, that's not the whole story. We also feel happy for them—empathic joy for their beguiling smiles and their capacity for seemingly infinite satisfaction with simple things. We seem hardwired to spread joy—infants smile before they can even recognize a human face—and we are wired to receive it. Anything that makes us respond to infants the way we do is certainly doing something in the world and might well prove to be a force in us-and-them relations.

Perhaps the effect of empathic joy is nowhere so immediate as in our response to human infants, but that is not the only form of it we can see. The population of Senegal is 95 percent Muslim, but you might be fooled—as one visitor was—at Christmas.[1] It's a national holiday there, and the government strings Christmas lights across main streets in the capital city, though few of the nation's small Christian minority even live there. In some villages where Christians and Muslims live together, they celebrate each other's holidays. As one citizen explained, "Officially, we Muslims don't celebrate Christmas. But the Catholics are our neighbors. So, we all celebrate all the religious holidays."[2] Of all Christian holidays, Christmas is one of the most obviously joyous, and it seems the Muslims of Senegal are able to share some portion of another group's joy.

These Muslims and Christians are well aware of conflicts going on elsewhere. But they are not merely avoiding conflict with each other; they are a valued part of each other's lives. "It's our tradition, this cohabitation," said one Christian. "When we're born and baptized, our Muslim neighbors are there. They help us all the way, even into the grave."[3] In this chapter, I argue that the very human ability to feel someone else's joy is much more important than merely an occasional human interest story. It can contribute to our ability to feel affection, comfort, kinship, engagement, and enthusiasm for members of groups very different from our own. Leaders can use it to tap the positive power of difference, changing an "us and them" into an "us plus them."

## Empathy, Empathic Joy, and Empathic Sorrow

Before I take this subject up in detail, let me attend to the unglamorous but important business of definitions. Among the various branches of the social sciences, the term *empathy* is used in differing and even contradictory ways.

For example, some researchers suggest that *empathy* should refer strictly to the emotional experience of being affected by someone else's condition, an experience often resulting from what social scientists call *perspective taking*—taking someone else's point of view. Other researchers argue the opposite: the word should refer strictly to the intellectual act of perspective taking, while other terms, such as *sympathy,* should be used for the resulting emotions.[4] Since we rarely respond to someone's engagement, promotion, or new baby with a sympathy card, presumably these researchers intend *sympathy* to mean, more narrowly, being emotionally affected by someone else's *unhappy* condition. Still other researchers use *empathy* to refer to an experience that is both emotional and cognitive—either because both the cognitive and emotional elements are taken to be intertwined, or because the emotion is taken to result from the cognitive state of perspective taking.[5] Some researchers even use *empathy* and *sympathy* interchangeably. Imagine if all physicists were free to adopt their own definitions of "neutron," "proton," and "electron." Perhaps it is no surprise that the social science of "us and them" is not as advanced as it needs to be.

I use *empathy* to refer to the combined experience—the perspective taking and the resulting emotion. If the resulting emotion is sadness, I will refer to it as *empathic sorrow*—what is ordinarily known as sympathy. If the resulting emotion is joy, I will refer to it as *empathic joy*. Empathic joy and empathic sorrow are therefore two possible forms of empathy itself.

## The Empathy Error

Some of the researchers who consider empathy as either entirely or partly an emotional experience do not specify that the emotion is either positive or negative. So, presumably, they are allowing for either. Yet almost without fail, what they actually study are negative emotions such as pity, sympathy, sadness, and sorrow on behalf of another, not positive emotions such as happiness or joy on behalf of another. Why not?

It is not just that there has been research on empathic sorrow but hardly any on empathic joy. It's that there has been *lots and lots* of research on empathic sorrow but hardly any on empathic joy. Despite the valuable work on empathic joy done by Edward Royzman and Paul Rozin, which I will discuss below, empathy research has been largely fixated on "a negative emotional state anchored in and tending toward the alleviation of another's *misfortune* [italics added]."[6] Some researchers outright ignore empathic joy, defining empathy as "our capacity to understand and feel the suffering of others even though we have never experienced that particular suffering ourselves."[7] Even the promisingly named *empathic-joy hypothesis*, a well-studied phenomenon in the psychological sciences, takes as its starting point another individual's suffering; it considers happiness or joy to be the emotions one might experience at the *end* of that suffering.[8] Sound familiar? A bit like the goal of antiracism being simply "no racism," a bit like replacing hate with "unhate."

We have also been led astray, in my analysis, by a tendency on the part of researchers to think of sympathy for an "other" as a form of liking that "other." It continually amazes me that people think of pity and sympathy as positive emotions. I consider sympathy only a qualified form of liking. Certainly it is preferable to hate. But is sympathy really positive, in the sense in which most people mean "positive?" Is being felt sorry for anything like being liked or admired? We don't think of someone else's self-pity as a positive emotion, even when that person has good reason for it, so why would pity for others be particularly positive? One very influential body of research serves as an example of this mistaken identification of sympathy as a positive emotion; it defines "pro-Black attitudes" as feelings that African Americans are disadvantaged and deserve sympathy.[9] Yet other research has shown that sympathetic recognition of prejudice toward African Americans is not the same as unconditional positive feelings or beliefs about them.[10] That is, one can acknowledge that African Americans are too often treated badly in America without feeling any particular goodwill toward them. This may help explain why, for instance, increased scores on a social science measure called the Pro-Black Scale are not necessarily linked to increased support for policies that would benefit African Americans, such as increasing the number of college scholarships for them.[11] What about just plain appreciating and liking African Americans and appreciating their history and culture? Is that not possible? Is it not even worth looking into? The successful American retiree mentioned in chapter 2 might feel sorry for far-less-well-off Mexicans he meets, but he would not be so delighted to have retired among them simply on that account. Sympathy can be a very powerful experience and can motivate worthwhile actions to remedy injustice, but it should not be confused with a foundation for a durable diverse community. It is merely, at best, a triage for the injustices that brought the sympathy about.

Why is the ability to rejoice in someone else's good fortune—surely one of the finer things about our species—of so little academic, educational, and political interest? We see it not only in the one-sided academic research on empathy, but also in the real-world policies and interventions that are meant to harness the power of empathy in order to improve relations among groups. This superabundance of attention to empathic sorrow relative to the scarce attention paid to empathic joy—this overall and gross imbalance in social science and social policy—is what I refer to as the *empathy error*.

## The Power of Empathic Joy: Why the Empathy Error Is an Error

Empathy has been at the center of the study of positive social relationships. Writing in 1897, the psychologist Theodore Ribot called sympathy "the foundation of all social existence."[12] As one modern researcher put it, "Traditionally, empathy has been viewed as the basis for all positive social relationships."[13] Programs ranging from corporate diversity training to school curricula use empathy to improve relations among different groups, but it's usually empathy for a group's misfortunes; that is, empathic sorrow.

Imagine a family that only gets together for funerals, never for weddings, birthdays, graduations, or baby showers. Fine for a movie comedy, but warped in real life. The fact that the study and application of empathy has been so lopsided toward the negative—empathic sorrow—means that our understanding of positive social relationships is distorted and our ability to promote them is deficient.

There is no question that sympathy can promote increased sensitivity to and less negative treatment of minority groups that are often subject to discrimination, such as immigrants and the disabled. It may well be true that it is "difficult to hate the people with whom you empathize."[14] Nevertheless, empathic sorrow does not lead one to like the "other" more. But empathic joy—almost completely overlooked in our social, educational, and organizational programs as well as in social science research—can help build allophilia. Compared with sympathy and pity, empathic joy is more strongly associated with behaviors such as reaching out to members of other groups and actively supporting them.[15] Here is something leaders can use, not simply to heal old wounds but to build new strengths in the groups they lead.

Some studies have suggested that it may be easier to empathize with victims who are familiar or who are similar to oneself than with victims who are unfamiliar or different. But the fact remains that we can and do empathize with those who are unfamiliar and different. Which of our human capacities, then, do we value and try to bring to their fullest expression? The philosopher David Hume may have gotten it right when he stated that he believed it was perfectly natural for people to empathize more with their kind than with strangers, but, as this bias may be incompatible with being moral, efforts must be made to organize society so as to minimize it.[16]

There is already a wealth of research showing that positive and negative emotions operate differently; as we saw in chapter 2, they are more two-dimensional than had been previously thought. This includes evidence gained from a broad range of methods—from neurological research to large-scale surveys. Collectively, this evidence indicates that positive and negative emotions are parts of distinct emotional systems and that it is the positive emotions that are more strongly associated with positive thoughts and actions.

Research has begun to show the unique role of positive emotions not only in interpersonal relations within a group, but also in relations between groups.[17] For example, positive emotions are particularly important for building connections between groups. One study found that positive emotions are stronger predictors than negative emotions are of the impulse toward positive attitudes and behaviors toward an "other."[18] But are positive attitudes important only in a few particularly favorable us-and-them contexts? If an "us" and a "them" are often in conflict, for example, do positive emotions ever come into play? As we saw in chapter 1, evidence from studies in places such as Israel and Northern Ireland suggests that positive emotions and associated attitudes are present even in the context of long-standing conflict between groups—situations in which we might expect only hate.[19]

What all this suggests for leadership is that arousing empathic sorrow—getting people to feel sorry for another group's suffering—is not interchangeable with arousing empathic joy. Arousing empathic joy can bring with it the benefits that are more associated with positive emotions than with negative emotions: positive thoughts, enhanced memory (including better recall of pleasant events), more exploratory and more flexible thinking, and the psychological states that prepare a person to build friendships and social networks.[20]

Arousing empathic joy is more likely to promote positive behavior, such as helping others, than arousing sympathy is likely to do. This may have been what was happening in a very suggestive study of people who were volunteering to help gay patients suffering from sexually transmitted diseases, AIDS, and hepatitis.[21] The researchers wondered what factors contributed to a volunteer's willingness to help, as measured by time spent with the client, practical help provided to the client, and length of service in the volunteer organization. Specifically, the research team examined the impact of whether the volunteer was gay (that is, whether the volunteer and the patient were members of the same ingroup); whether the volunteer felt *social attraction* to the patient, by which the researchers meant that the volunteers enjoyed spending time with their clients, felt respect for them, found them interesting rather than boring, and so on; and how much empathic sorrow (sympathy or pity) the volunteers felt for their patients. It turned out that social attraction was *more* strongly correlated to willingness to help than empathic sorrow was when the volunteer was not gay—that is, when the volunteer could see the patient as an "other."

The researchers were not using the concepts of allophilia or empathic joy. But social attraction, although not the same, is like allophilia and empathic joy with respect to being a positive emotion—an attraction. And it was this positive attitude toward the "other" that seems to have been more important than sympathy for the "other" in shaping a person's willingness to proactively help the "other."

This work suggests that empathic joy should play an important role in promoting positive us-and-them relations. In perhaps the most direct test of that role, a colleague and I examined the contribution of empathic sorrow to negative prejudice toward others and the contribution of empathic joy to allophilia for others We assessed the attitudes of American white high school students at predominantly white schools—measuring their levels of empathic sorrow (sympathy) and empathic joy for the members of ethnic minorities by asking them to agree or disagree with statements such as "When I learn of (X), I want to find out what is wrong and help them" and "When (members of group X) feel happy, I feel happy." We found that feeling sympathy was more strongly associated with lower levels of what we don't want in our world—prejudice—than it was with higher levels of what we *do* want in our world—allophilia.[22] Feeling empathic joy, on the other hand, was more strongly associated with higher levels of allophilia than with lower levels of prejudice.

This was only one research program, and we only studied the levels of allophilia and prejudice that were already there; we did not try to experimentally *create* allophilia or prejudice. This means we can't be sure whether higher empathic joy was causing higher allophilia or the other way around. But our research did clearly show that the experience of empathic sorrow is distinct from the experience of empathic joy and therefore should be studied—and promoted—independently of empathic sorrow. Sympathy (or the lack of it), I argue, is more central to understanding intergroup hate and hostility, while empathic joy is more central to understanding how people can really enjoy and appreciate groups other than their own. For business, political, and social leaders, this suggests that sympathy should be considered as a tool with which to reduce prejudice, mistrust, or hostility toward a particular group, while empathic joy should be considered as a tool with which to increase people's desire to live and work with members of another group.

## Sympathy's Shortcomings

While empathic sorrow (sympathy) has its merits and will always have an important role to play in us-and-them relations, it also has limitations that call into question the present focus on it in research and overreliance on it in interventions. As one research team found, "Empathy can lead to undesirable outcomes such as greater distance between groups, defensive avoidance, negative attitudes, confirmations of negative stereotypes, increased tension and hostility, hurt feelings, and lowered self-esteem."[23] Empathic sorrow can bring out well-meaning but overly sympathetic responses, such as fussing over people with disabilities to an extent that embarrasses them. Seeing a disabled person as dependent and pitiable can certainly get in the way of a real friendship or any other relationship in which people are to have equal status. Empathic joy is less prone to these overdone paternalistic reactions. It also helps us avoid another sympathy trap—thinking of (and perhaps treating) the other as a prop in one's fantasy of oneself as beneficent and generous to others, particularly to strangers.

Empathic sorrow may also be tainted by its symbiotic relationship with trouble; it cannot exist without suffering. Oscar Wilde made this observation—characteristically, in reverse: "If there was less sympathizing in the world, there would be less trouble in the world."[24] Empathic joy does not have that perverse characteristic. We should therefore temper our enthusiasm for empathic sorrow and spend more time studying and learning to apply empathic joy.

Another limitation of empathic sorrow is that it can have unintended negative effects on those with whom one sympathizes. For example, one set of studies showed that while sympathy can indicate genuine care, the recipient can experience it as implying his or her "inferiority with respect to the sympathizer."[25] This is not to say we should abandon sympathy as a human response or a tool, but rather that we need to understand it better and not take it as the only form of empathy available to us.

Sympathy can also be worn out, an experience that is sometimes referred to as *compassion fatigue* and sometimes as secondary traumatic stress disorder.[26] But recognizing empathic joy puts this problem in a new light. A nursing researcher concluded that loss of the capacity to feel empathy for clients may be "an important cause of burnout in the helping professions."[27] But look at the assumption underlying that statement: *empathy* here can only mean empathic sorrow or sympathy. And indeed, that is what the researchers had measured. Surely no one would burn out from feeling too much empathic joy. If we paid more attention to empathic joy in the helping professions, we might learn to tap a powerful force against burnout.

At its worst, sympathy may even degenerate into an appetite for human pain and suffering as a vicarious thrill, rather than as a motivation to action, as the media serve up ever more potent doses of suffering without much context. We see ever more vivid clips and glimpses of sorrow and suffering on the news, on YouTube, on the ubiquitous TV screens, on our Internet provider's home page. Such small morsels can provide little or no context, so we experience an emotional response without much real learning and generally without being given anything to do about what we're seeing.

### *The Empathy Error in Research*

A paper in the *Journal of Neuroscience* illustrates how instinctively social scientists narrow *empathy* down to *empathic sorrow* before they get down to business. The first sentence says, "Empathy refers to the ability to understand and share others' emotion and plays a key role in social behaviors." But the second says, "Perception of others in pain or distress generates empathic concerns that provide a proximate mechanism selected by evolution that motivates altruistic behaviors."[28] The academic focus on empathic sorrow has given us not only definitions and models of sympathy and studies of the antecedents of sympathy but also ever more fine-grained inquiries into such aspects of sympathy as "the role of responsibility at onset," "the role of ability to offset," "the role of stability of situation," and "the role of status controllability." We have learned a great deal about sympathy, but it's as if empathic joy is no more than a curious theoretical possibility. Perhaps the most comprehensive and influential theory of the development of empathy is that of clinical and developmental psychologist Martin Hoffman. Unsurprisingly, it is a theory of empathic distress.[29] We are creating an increasingly detailed map of one terrain, right down to the pebbles on the ground, while completely overlooking a continent.

The bias toward negative rather than positive emotions can also be seen in the way researchers study empathy—both how they seek to induce it during their experiments and how they measure it. A very typical experiment, conducted by researchers who have done influential work in the field of empathy, involves inducing empathy in the participants by having them read about a woman ravaged by AIDS, a homeless man, and a drug addict.[30] In other studies, white students were asked to empathize with accounts of African Americans being falsely accused of wrongdoing because of their race, being denied check-writing privileges, overhearing racially slanderous remarks, and other manifestations of prejudice.[31] In one study, third-grade students were divided into two groups and given either orange or green armbands. The orange-banded kids were then discriminated against all day and not praised by the teacher; next day, the roles were reversed.[32] In another study, second-graders were shown a video portraying a single mother whose children had been injured in a serious car accident and were now having trouble in school.[33]

Empathy is typically measured in such experiments by assessing the degree to which one feels "sympathetic, compassionate, soft-hearted, warm, tender and moved" or by assessing the "tendency to experience feelings of sympathy and compassion for unfortunate others" or to have "tender, concerned feelings for people less fortunate than me."[34] Participants may be asked how strongly or weakly they agree or disagree with statements such as, "When I see someone being taken advantage of, I feel kind of protective toward them" or to indicate how sorry they feel for other people "when they are having problems."[35] If the participants did have feelings of empathic joy, how would the experimenters ever know? One paper claimed to be about the more positive and "hopeful" sides of intergroup relations, yet measured empathy by having participants respond to statements such as, "I often feel very sorry for people from the other community when they are having problems" and "When I see someone from the other community being treated unfairly, I sometimes don't feel very much pity for them."[36]

This seemingly instinctive reduction of empathy to empathic sorrow may go hand in hand with another narrowing of view. Social scientists have observed that the study of minorities, which largely began with studies of groups that were numerically smaller than other groups with which they shared a community or nation, has largely shifted over the years to the narrower study of minority "victims" for whom it seems most natural to feel—and therefore most useful to generate—sympathy.[37] We will see in this chapter that, most natural or not, sympathy is neither the only possible form of empathy to feel for minorities (even victimized minorities) nor the most useful form of empathy to generate for minorities (even victimized minorities).

### Symhedonia

A sorely needed and well-executed exception to this overwhelmingly one-sided approach to empathy is the work of psychologists Edward Royzman and Paul Rozin.[38] Lacking an equivalent for the word *sympathy* to refer to a positive emotion felt in response to someone else's happiness or good fortune, they coined the word *symhedonia,* from the Greek roots meaning "together" and "pleasure," noting that their new term "combines the moral weight of sympathy with the hedonic glow of joy."[39] Symhedonia is therefore empathic joy.

Though only very recent, the symhedonia construct holds much promise and offers new insights and possibilities for leadership. For example, Royzman and Rozin found evidence suggesting that one's capacity for symhedonia can change over the course of one's life. They also concluded that symhedonia is a less common and more fragile emotional state than sympathy, speculating that the active cultural encouragement of *envy* in Western societies—to encourage ambition, competition, and consumerism—works against a very possible fuller expression of symhedonia in our world.[40]

And this is exactly what we see. A news report that a celebrity has given birth may generate interest among many of us, but not joy. Why? It seems a bit churlish not to feel happy for a neighbor, but it is quite acceptable to envy a celebrity. It is even quite acceptable to enjoy the spectacle of a celebrity's suffering as we wait in line at the checkout counter, peruse the tabloid headlines, and learn who got "dumped" and who has checked into rehab.

The finding that symhedonia is more fragile than sympathy and must be nurtured in order to be widely experienced should serve as a wake-up call. Rather than dismissing symhedonia as ephemeral and of little consequence, we need to understand it better in order to benefit more from it. Insulin is a fragile substance, easily spoiled. Even today, it is too finicky to be stored in plastic for long and must therefore be stored in glass and, further, within a certain temperature range. Yet, to hundreds of millions of people it is a life-saver, well worth the trouble it takes to manufacture, store, and inject it. Empathic joy might also be well worth some extra effort to nurture it.

There has, unfortunately, been almost no academic response to Royzman and Rozin's work. They themselves noted social science's long silence on the subject of empathic joy, looking back to the remark of Adam Smith quoted at the head of this chapter: "Two and a half centuries after [Adam] Smith, various sources continue to treat sympathy (or empathy) as a nominally neutral term . . . [But] its dominant meaning remains that of a negative emotional state anchored in and tending toward the alleviation of another's misfortune."[41]

There has been a dribble of interest in the role of empathic joy in the relationship between parents and children. Some evidence suggests experiencing empathic joy for each other seems to be associated with the promotion of a child's well-being and positive parent-child relationships.

There have also been some studies of the empathic-joy hypothesis.[42] Researchers took up the question of whether one's efforts to help a person in need or distress are motivated by a desire to relieve that person's suffering or by a self-serving desire to share vicariously in that person's joy at the relief of his or her suffering. In one study, for example, participants are told about a young woman struggling to support her younger brother and sister after their parents have been killed in a car crash; she even faces the awful possibility of having to put them up for adoption. Participants are given a chance to help this young woman; empathic joy—the joy one might feel at seeing her suffering alleviated, if only a bit—is considered as a possible explanation of who does and does not help.[43] For our purposes, it is enough to note that these studies were *not* concerned with empathic joy as a response to someone else's happiness or good fortune, other than the good fortune of being *less badly off after a tragedy*. Once again, less bad—as epitomized by "unhate"—seems to be as good as it gets.

As it happens, social science research on the development of empathy is carried out in the subdiscipline of moral development research. Very well, but why is feeling joyful for someone else who wins a victory any less moral than feeling sorrow for someone who suffers a defeat? Why would moral development research be so interested in developing the latter capacity and so uninterested in developing the former? In fact, empathic joy plays a prominent and *moral* role in Buddhist thought as *mudita*—rejoicing in others' good fortune, delighting in other people's well-being.[44] Mudita is one of Buddhism's four *brahmavihara*—"divine states" or, as we would probably call them, "virtues." We will also see in the next chapter that empathic joy stimulated by a public display of group pride can contribute to positive us-and-them relations.

## The Empathy Error in Practice

At a museum/park in the Mexican state of Hidalgo, visitors can experience a simulated migrant crossing, a grueling five-hour trek during which they walk in deep mud, balance on precarious ledges, and sprint across cornfields pursued by fake U.S. border patrol officers dressed in camouflage. A woman from Mexico City brought her family, including her twelve-year-old son, because "we get so immersed in our lives that we forget how much other people suffer."[45] Both she and the museum's creators see the benefit of empathic sorrow.

Meanwhile, in midtown Manhattan, employees of a publishing company may be attending a Diversity and Empathy seminar. Participants at one such seminar were reported to have been divided into two arbitrary groups that were then treated very differently in respect, privileges, and resources. It was a chance for them to feel bad about how bad other people are made to feel.

Thousands of programs have been designed to create empathic sorrow for all manner of "others," ranging from overweight kids to beleaguered hospital patients. The focus is overwhelmingly on sympathy—how awful it has been (or still is) to be discriminated against, ghettoized, lynched, impoverished, brutalized, made fun of, left out, disrespected, bullied, and so on. It has been argued that, as a culture, we have fallen in love with sympathy.[46] Whereas the grounds for sympathy were once extreme poverty, very severe illness, bereavement, and great natural disasters, sympathy is now extended far and wide. The *New York Times* charity drive, "The Neediest Cases," now includes drug addiction, drinking, divorce, gambling, and child abuse—problems that were not considered appropriate for public sympathy when the drive began in 1912. We buy sympathy cards for having a tough boss, growing older, or just having a bad day.[47]

Empathy programs are legion, but often not carefully conducted. Psychologists have criticized such programs for a lack of "careful consideration of the subtleties of the process or an explicit understanding of what they are trying to accomplish," observing that empathy is "widely used as a technique to improve intergroup relations, but usually without clear goals or an understanding of how it operates" and finding that, "despite the widespread use of empathy in intergroup relations programs, few programs actually measure empathy as either a mediating or outcome variable."[48] An education researcher expressed similar concerns when empathy became mandated in the United Kingdom's national educational curriculum: "Promoting empathy is the concern of a number of parts of the curriculum," he noted, but "the concept was hazy from its inception, has not been clarified by psychologists' empirical researchers and remains ambiguous as it is used in one school subject, history."[49] Another education researcher remarked of empathy that "there can be few notions so commonly employed in talking about what children need to be able to do in history, and so little examined."[50]

## The Empathy Error in Education

Perhaps nowhere is the focus on empathic sorrow more evident than in schools. In many countries around the world, teaching young people to appreciate and to like members of other social groups—be they religious, ethnic, or sexual minorities, either in the students' own nation or in other nations—is a daunting but important task. It is sometimes undertaken to promote coexistence in nations that are increasingly pluralistic. The efforts are serious because the stakes are often high: hate crimes, entrenched poverty, and—in the worst cases—violence and civil war. At other times it is undertaken for more proximal reasons, such as the desire to address a bullying incident that might have occurred. In both cases, the approach is often to teach students about the sufferings of other social groups so that the students will understand the other groups and, perhaps more importantly, empathize with them; that is, feel sorry for them.

The American educational system is steeped in empathic sorrow and sometimes goes to extremes.[51] In one middle school, for example, a social studies teacher taped the hands and feet of two students and asked them to crawl under their desks; this was to give them a more vivid impression of what it might have felt like to be transported on a slave ship.[52] The David Garcia Project at Central Michigan University provides "empathy training" to give students a greater understanding of people living with disabilities. Students wear goggles with tape on them to experience blindness, wear earplugs to experience deafness, try to button their shirts while wearing gloves stiffened with popsicle sticks to experience disabilities of the hand, or try to write and paint with a pen or brush held in the mouth to experience amputation or paralysis. This program claims to focus on "creating empathy—not sympathy—for disabled persons."[53] While I agree that living with a physical disability should be better understood, it is extreme to feed students a diet of only empathic sorrow absent empathic joy.

A story in the *New York Times* about middle school and high school empathy programs offers many details of empathic sorrow—for autistic kids, for the elderly, for classmates who don't get invited to parties—but not one detail of empathic joy.[54] One middle-school principal explained, "As a school, we've done a lot of work with human rights. But you can't have kids saving Darfur and isolating a peer in the lunchroom. It all has to go together."[55] I don't take any issue with him as far as he goes, but I don't think he goes far enough. His *all* seems to be promoting an unwillingness on the part of students to pick on the "other," but not to include more positive encounters, nor simple enjoyment of the "other" through empathy. At least, this wasn't touched on in the article, which noted that "educators [in Scarsdale] see the lessons as grooming children to be better citizens and leaders by making them think twice before engaging in the name-calling, gossip and other forms of social humiliation that usually go unpunished."[56] This seems like leadership away from what we don't want, but not leadership toward what we do want.

When I was in the third grade, we had a unit called "Empathy," which was very similar to the David Garcia Project. In our case, we got to choose our disability. We then had to tape our fingers together, sign out crutches or a wheelchair, or whatever else our chosen disability would dictate. While I cannot recall much of the experience, I do recall feeling sad that disabled people had to work so hard to do simple things I could take for granted. I suppose I also felt respect for their ability to manage such hassles and make their way in life. But nothing in the exercise triggered anything akin to seeing joy or happiness in the life of someone with a disability. And yet such joys exist— not only the joys anyone else might experience but the particular joys of overcoming an obstacle, recovering a lost ability, and being treated kindly by strangers.

Perhaps the most well-known provider of empathy interventions today is Facing History and Ourselves, an organization dedicated, according to its mission statement, "to helping teachers around the world lead their students in a critical examination of history, with particular focus on genocide and mass violence."[57] In other program materials, they describe their focus on enhancing tolerance and their ambition to "engage students of diverse backgrounds in an examination of racism, prejudice, and anti-Semitism in order to promote the development of a more humane and informed citizenry." This is no small organization; it claims to have reached some 20 million students through a network of teachers in over eighty countries. The premise underlying Facing History and Ourselves—the name itself implies a stern duty rather than anything joyful—is that "by studying the historical development and lessons of the Holocaust and other examples of genocide, students make the essential connection between history and the moral choices they confront in their own lives." But as we saw in chapter 2, exposure to genocide and mass violence will not necessarily lead to voluntary engagement with the "other." To truly become a more humane society, as Martin Luther King Jr. pointed out, not hating each other is a necessary start, but no more than a start. As I've noted throughout this book, part of being human is being curious about people and things that are different—and *enjoying* the differences.

Educators (and those of us who hire, vote for, or entrust our children to them) must be more conscious of empathic joy and try to evoke it as one way to tap the positive power of difference. This will require a significant investment. School curricula must cover not only the sufferings of particular groups but also their joys. A unit that covers the cruelties of slavery in the American South should also focus on slaves in their times of joy, creativity, and rectitude. Programs that focus equally and consistently on both empathic sorrow and empathic joy will contribute to lower levels of prejudice *and* higher levels of affection, comfort, kinship, engagement, and enthusiasm with respect to the "other." When students learn about life in the Eastern bloc, they should learn about more than the atrocities of the gulags, secret police, and purges. There is, for example, interesting evidence of the ways ordinary people used humor to put up with Communist governments, which offers a very different way to understand, appreciate, and even enjoy those "others" who lived in the former Eastern bloc countries.[58]

In this regard, I think a great opportunity was lost with then French president Nicolas Sarkozy's 2008 proposal to assign every fifth-grader to study the life of one of the more than eleven thousand children killed during the Nazi occupation of France. Sarkozy's plan met with a public outcry and was quickly abandoned, but he was onto something deep. "Nothing is more moving for a child," he explained, "than the story of a child his own age who has the same games, the same joys, and the same hopes as he but who, in the dawn of the 1940s, had the bad fortune to be defined as a Jew."[59] Note that he said "the same games, the same joys," a too rare public acknowledgment that if we are going to try to use empathy to bring different groups together, we should bring to bear the full range of empathy, not just sympathy.

On a smaller scale—but more successfully—a twelfth-grade economics teacher wanted to give her students an idea of what life had been like during the Great Depression. Most of the students, having already learned about the widespread unemployment and poverty in their American history course, characterized people's lives at that time as dull. However, they went on to conduct oral histories with people in their communities who had lived during the Depression. While some (but not all) of the interviewees remembered unemployment and lack of food, clothing, and housing, most recalled that their families had not been ruined financially and that, even with much less money than they had had before the "bust," they had continued to enjoy full lives with times of joy from entertainment and socializing.[60]

## Can We Take Empathic Joy and Sorrow Together?

Leaders who seek to use empathic joy as one way to promote positive us-and-them relations will inevitably face the question of whether the combination of empathic joy and empathic sorrow (sympathy) might be out of line. Would attention to empathic joy somehow cheapen the experience of empathic sorrow? In school, for example, would a description of enslaved people actually enjoying themselves, however briefly, betray the point of teaching students about slavery in the first place? I argue that it would not. First, if enslaved people did manage to find moments to enjoy themselves, then that's the truth, and there is—at the very least—no reason to hide it. But more than that, it reveals a truth about human beings: they are able to feel happiness and to create moments of happiness for each other, even if fleeting, in unbelievably awful circumstances. To show enslaved people doing just that is to drive home the point that they were entire human beings, of value to themselves and to each other—and potentially to so many other people—and this, in turn, is how we can measure the wrongness of their enslavement. Yet this opportunity is rarely, if ever, seized.

The white musician Johnny Otis, whom we met in chapter 1, knew very well the sufferings of African Americans. Yet, as George Lipsitz wrote in the introduction to a book Otis wrote in response to the 1965 Watts riots, "Otis had learned how to be successfully pro-Black in a society where the rewards for being anti-Black were enormous."[61] He was not simply "pro-Black" as a result of sympathy, but because he saw and felt so much joy in the company of African Americans.

In Toni Morrison's novel *Beloved*, there is an ice-skating scene in which characters whose sufferings are shown with terrible intensity are, for the time being, quite happy enjoying the cold, crisp, clear winter air, then the warmth of woolens dried by a strong fire and the taste of hot cocoa. Horrible things have happened and will happen to these characters, but for a moment, being in their heads is a pure joy. Without that moment, we would not know them as fully human. And we might not even have realized what we were missing, so accustomed are we to thinking that to really know a person or a people, it is most important to know their suffering.

Why do I feel sorrier when I find out that two friends are getting an amicable divorce than when I read in an advice column about a divorce filled with cruelty and unhappiness? I don't think it's simply because I feel sorrier for friends than for strangers, although that is clearly a factor. There is also the fact that I have personally witnessed and experienced how *happy* my married friends once were together, what a good marriage it seemed to be. It is my acquaintance with that joy that makes me aware of what has been lost. It is the past experience of empathic joy that makes me feel that loss even more keenly and that would motivate me to comfort them (or possibly even try to reconcile them) in any way I could. Without the experience of empathic joy I suspect and fear I would be far less motivated to try to comfort or help.

Even in the harshest of situations—those in which empathic sorrow will and rightly should be the dominant emotion—empathic joy may have power and import. Consider our understanding of oppression and resistance. Our vision of resistance is generally limited to its two most obviously dangerous and heroic forms—armed resistance and Gandhian nonviolent resistance. But there is also a profound resistance in simply remaining human in the face of dehumanizing powers. This has been described over and over in memoirs of the Holocaust, of life in the Communist bloc, and of many other situations of overwhelming oppression. It is at the core of such dystopian visions as George Orwell's novel *Nineteen Eighty-Four* and George Lucas's early movie *THX-1138*; in both stories, the central characters' "resistance" to an all-powerful police state includes falling in love.

Seventy years after the Holocaust, what should we feel about it? More importantly, I would say, what *can* we feel about it? Anger and sorrow, of course, but that is not all we can feel. A popular 2009 film, *Inglourious Basterds,* portrays a fictional team of Jewish-American soldiers who parachute into France and set about viciously murdering and mutilating as many German servicemen as they can. Their determination to "kick ass" certainly adds something other than pity and sympathy to the mix of cultural responses to and reflections back of the Holocaust. But we can do better than that if we look harder.

On October 16, 1940, the German Governor-General Hans Frank ordered Jews in Warsaw and its suburbs rounded up and herded into what would become the Warsaw Ghetto. According to estimates, 30 percent of the population of Warsaw would come to be crammed into 2.4 percent of the city. On November 16, the Nazis sealed off the Warsaw Ghetto with armed guards. A wall was topped with barbed wire. Jews in the Ghetto were allocated some 181 calories a day, a deliberate slow-motion mass murder by starvation. Despite this, life in the Warsaw Ghetto seems to have been socially and culturally rich. There were underground schools, hospitals, soup kitchens, orphanages, libraries, and even a symphony orchestra. Poems written in the Ghetto speak of hell, but also of birds, flowers, and seasons.[62] Emanuel Ringelblum, a historian living in another part of Warsaw who was determined to record a complete description of life in the Ghetto for future historians, wrote that "there is even humor here."[63]

The Jews in the Ghetto were able to feel many kinds of joy and we, if we are willing, can feel empathic joy with them. But should that be part of the "lesson"? We remain deeply ambivalent about complicating our portraits of those we see as victims with any emotion other than sorrow. Too ambivalent. But if programs such as Facing History and Ourselves take as their mission not only to teach history but also to promote "humane citizenship," I argue that empathic joy must be part of the formula. Empathic joy promotes allophilia, which, in turn, promotes willing, active engagement with people of groups other than one's own. If that's not humane citizenship, what is?

As a practical matter, repetitive exposure to pure empathic sorrow can cause students to limit or cut off their sympathy just to protect themselves from feeling so bad. It can also start to bore them.[64] A leavening of empathic joy may keep them engaged and prevent burnout. But folding empathic joy into the mix with sympathy must be done responsibly. With almost no social scientific studies of empathic joy, we still have much to learn about how it works and what we can do with it. Should empathic joy and empathic sorrow be included in the same lesson plan, or should they be introduced separately? How much of each and when?

Anne Frank's *Diary of a Young Girl*, her account of daily life as she, her family, and a few other Jews hid from the Nazis in the cramped hidden rooms of her father's office building, is harrowing and cannot fail to inspire sadness and pity. But she also gives us her moments of pleasure and joy; she can be both precious and precocious. She described moments of overwhelming "happiness" and "bliss"; she looks forward to—and then receives—her first kiss. The fact that she could still seek fun and look forward to joys she hoped to have in life has never worked against the worldwide and decades-long impact of her journal. Now it is for social science to figure out how and what she did to such powerful effect.

## Empathic Joy to the World

The empathy error—paying great attention to empathic sorrow and little or no attention to empathic joy—is an error because it overlooks a gift that is both natural and nurturable. Empathic joy is a crucial part of what humans are capable of feeling about each other, and it can help bring groups together in a way and to a level that sympathy alone cannot. Empathic sorrow for a group does not make people want to socialize with members of that group, to befriend them, to live in the same neighborhood with them, or to take action to increase or protect their political, social, and economic well-being. Empathic sorrow is perhaps best viewed as a window into the past and present, but it does not help us move forward toward the kinds of relations that could exist.

How can our social policies, our school programs, and our corporate cultures move beyond the empathy error? Royzman and Rozin's findings seem to me to point us part of the way. They found that empathic joy, like a flower, is fragile—but it can grow, and its growth is affected both by its environment and by human intervention.

The cards may be stacked against empathic joy to the extent that we are constantly involved in situations in which someone has more power than someone else; research has found that being in a position of power relative to others reduces the likelihood that one will take the perspective of the less powerful.[65] But other research shows that the capacity for empathy is not fixed. Can it be deliberately increased? In younger children, it can be nurtured in fairly simply ways. Simply asking questions such as "How do you think she must have felt?" or "What do you think it was like to be part of that story?" can get children to stretch their empathic capacities.

Role-playing can also be effective. Virtual-reality technology promises a revolution in empathic experience; opportunities to walk in another's shoes in virtual worlds are rapidly becoming more numerous and more fertile. We already have SPENT, an immersive online game that allows people to see how painful it is to be *spent*—broke and homeless.[66] Developed by Urban Ministries of Durham and an advertising agency, the game is meant to help advance awareness, sympathy, and, hopefully, action to aid the homeless. Surely such technology could also be used to inspire empathic joy, or at least to include it in a total experience.

In chapter 2, I discussed cross-ethnic mentoring. Companies that want to develop a deep bench of executives and managers willing to mentor members of ethnic minorities should try to harness the power of empathic joy. Most mentors feel very happy to see a younger person gain in knowledge, confidence, and success. A senior manager recalled that when his mentee received his first big job offer, "I felt as happy as if I had gotten the job offer myself."[67] Another told me that when she had mentored a newly promoted and somewhat inexperienced marketing director, "I found myself feeling so proud of her." Remembering her own mentor, she recalled: "Whenever Dick would introduce himself and his work, and then me and my work and our work together, a big smile would cross his face . . . His voice even seemed to change a bit. Just slightly louder and filled with pride."[68]

Just as mentors share in the joy of their mentees, potential mentors could share in the joy of both. A company looking to recruit minority mentors might therefore make a specific effort to allow potential mentors to experience some of that empathic joy as a way to draw them into the mentoring program.

It is well past time for researchers to study empathic joy as thoroughly as they have studied empathic sorrow. They need to investigate the factors that promote symhedonia. In the practical worlds of education, business, and government, leaders seeking to improve relations between groups need to focus both on empathic sorrow—to reduce prejudice—and empathic joy—to increase allophilia. While sympathy can help leaders lead us away from what we don't want, empathic joy will do more to help leaders lead us toward what we do want.

# SIX

# TAP THE POSITIVE POWER OF PRIDE DISPLAYS

**I**N BOSTON, where I lived for some ten years, the St. Patrick's Day parade is, among many other things, an expression of pride; attendees celebrate the major role the Irish have long played in the life of that city. There are many other ethnic groups in Boston, too. Is this a good idea?

Northwest of Boston, in Lowell, a much newer Cambodian community seeks to instill a sense of pride in a younger generation that is struggling through gang violence. But what other effects might increased Cambodian pride have on the Cambodian community and on the larger Lowell community of which it is a part?

An American political candidate, seeking to rally an audience, speaks of "the men and women who made this country great"; many in the audience swell with pride. Is this a good idea? On National Nuclear Technology Day in Iran, officials stage military displays highlighting the country's nuclear program to make citizens proud to be

Iranian. Is this a good idea? A middle school hosts a school pride day; for one day, lessons are off and seemingly apathetic students are roused to wear school colors and work on school beautification projects. Is this a good idea?

Many people feel proud of being part of a group and many leaders of groups seek to instill pride in their members. This chapter is about *pride displays,* by which I mean public acts intended to make group members feel proud of their group. But because a pride display is public, it will also affect how outsiders see the group—that is, it will affect us-and-them relations, even if that was not the intent.

Because of the widespread tendency to see improving us-and-them relations as a matter of moving from prejudice to less prejudice to—perhaps someday—no prejudice, it is easy to see pride displays as a way to build up people's pride in their own group but somewhat in defiance of the "others." Taking a two-dimensional approach to us-and-them leadership shows us that this trade-off is not always necessary and that pride displays can actually help build an "us *plus* them."

In this chapter, we will see why and how pride displays can be a valuable tool for promoting allophilia and improving us-and-them relations. We will see what particular steps leaders can take to stay on the right side of the double-edged sword of group pride.

## How Pride Displays Benefit the Proud

Pride in a group of which one is a member, whether by choice or happenstance, can provide real benefits. For example, children with positive perceptions of their own ethnic group tend to have fewer identity issues and higher self-esteem, and may have more prosocial attitudes and behavior. Other studies suggests they may also be better able to manage anger, may be at less risk of depression, and may even do better academically than children who do not have such pride in their group.[1]

Of course, the group as a whole benefits when its members are proud to be members. Both scholars and leaders have observed that promoting and displaying pride publicly can help a group advance its interests. Proud members tend to invest more resources and effort on their group's behalf. We see this at work in companies, military units, schools, communities, and congregations with high morale. This is why groups—ethnic, national, local, religious, professional, and so on—often seek to promote pride, from the college bookstore selling sweatshirts and bumper stickers and the small-town mayor giving the key to the city to a local resident who made it big to the U.S. president bestowing the Medal of Honor and a city hosting a parade when its team wins a Super Bowl. Group pride can sometimes benefit a community larger than the group itself, as when it contributes to the revitalization of a neighborhood, a decrease in crime, or an artistic movement that enriches the world. The Harlem Renaissance in the 1920s and 1930s, for example, was a complex literary, musical, artistic, and social phenomenon with a wide and long-lasting influence, but a recurrent theme was the assertion of pride in African American achievement, potential, and worthiness in the face of an overwhelmingly racist society. As writer Zora Neale Hurston put it, "Sometimes I feel discriminated against, but it does not make me angry. It merely astonishes me. How can anyone deny themselves the pleasure of my company? It's beyond me."[2]

Pride displays can help to reduce stigma, at least from the group's own point of view. We see this whenever a group seeks to cast off a name it has been given by outsiders and demands to be called by a name of its own choosing. In the United States, "Indians" chose to be called *Native Americans*; India's "untouchables" increasingly prefer to be called *Dalits*. On a much smaller scale, in the Taiwanese village of Donghe, the *Donghe Elementary School,* where 60 percent of the students are Siraya Aborigines, changed its name back to *Kabasua Elementary School,* using the original Siraya name for the town. By doing so, the school principal hopes to preserve Siraya culture in one of the few villages where it still survives.[3] It is not only racial or ethnic groups who want to have a say over what they are called. The shifts from *crippled* to *handicapped* to *disabled* to *differently abled* constitute a movement from terms that evoke empathic sorrow to terms that are more compatible with feelings of pride.

Pride displays can also help change the public definitions and categorizations of what is normal, good, or desirable in the minds of group members—and others—when group members find it impossible to fulfill the existing standards. For example, the Black Is Beautiful movement in the United States sought to redefine what is beautiful for a group whose members were never going to look like the white fashion and style icons of their day. And today, although the Afro hairstyle of that time has largely disappeared, black entertainers, models, and athletes are widely considered among the most glamorous and beautiful by African Americans, whites, Latinos, Asian Americans, Native Americans, and others.

Pride displays can draw attention to a group and its causes. Little public attention was paid to American minority cultures and identities before the civil rights movement, with the exception of negative images that legitimated inequalities. Even when the Civil Rights and Voting Rights acts of 1964 and 1965, respectively, brought greater political participation, cultural exclusion continued. In response to this cultural disenfranchisement, ethnic pride movements arose, beginning in 1966 with the Black Power movement. Black Power sought to change perceptions of African American identity and history. The movement called for African Americans to take greater pride in their race and their dignity and for all Americans to grant more recognition to African Americans' accomplishments and to their country's African American heritage. Decades earlier, while India was still a British colony, British-educated Indians began to develop an appreciation for their country's rich history and culture, which in turn contributed to the growing independence movement, both by inspiring Indians themselves with pride and by inspiring respect and admiration in some of the British.

Today, we see a movement for multiracial pride, with attendant pride displays such as the successful demand that multiracial be counted in the United States census. We see sexual orientation minorities "coming out of the closet" and demanding that their contributions be recognized, from the cultural (e.g., the arts) to the military. We see people with disabilities moving from the fringes of society to the center, demanding accessibility both literally and figuratively. For example, when the Franklin Delano Roosevelt Memorial in Washington, D.C., was being planned, some disability activists wanted it to clearly show his wheelchair—something he himself took great pains to hide—as a public display of the greatness of which people with disabilities are capable.[4]

## Pride Displays Can Work in Two Dimensions

The examples discussed above may all be good reasons for pride displays, but that doesn't mean that pride displays are automatically a good idea.

We have seen that the attitudes one can have about the members of a group other than one's own can exist along two dimensions: a hate dimension (prejudice) and a positive dimension (allophilia) of affection, comfort, kinship, engagement, and enthusiasm. So far, I have generally spoken of these attitudes as flowing *from* oneself *to* others—one's prejudice *against* members of this group, one's allophilia *for* members of that group. In this chapter, we will look at how the groups on the receiving end inspire attitudes along both dimensions; specifically, how pride displays can inspire attitudes along both dimensions.

Pride displays can alienate, anger, or frighten others; they can also inspire, invite, or delight others. And the effect is not necessarily a matter of which group has greater numbers, more power, or higher status. Majority group members can be either frightened or inspired by a display of minority group pride. Minority group members can be either frightened or inspired by a display of majority group pride. One minority group can either frighten or inspire the members of another minority group, as we sometimes see when a neighborhood's ethnic balance shifts.

## Two Types of Pride Display: Narcissistic and Justified

There is a large body of social science research on varieties of pride and the different effects of different kinds of pride.[5] For pride displays, what matters is whether a particular display is perceived as *narcissistic pride* or as *justified pride in a positive achievement*.

After the American invasion of Iraq in 2003, there was a very public display of pride. Just as victorious American soldiers were about to topple a statue of Saddam Hussein, one of them climbed up and draped the face with a U.S. flag. Even though this was largely an event staged for the media, the crowd did not like that move, seeing it as a step too far, a display of triumphalism. American commanders were quick to see the mistake and replaced the American flag with an Iraqi flag, but the image had already gone around the world, sparking anger and outrage. In this chapter on the effects of pride displays, I am not concerned with what kind of pride those soldiers were actually feeling that day, but with the kind of pride the rest of the world thought it was seeing. What may have been a genuine gesture of justified pride in liberating a country from its dictator was seen by many as a narcissistic display of American arrogance. It seemed to say, "We kicked your ass," which was true but not seen as a very great accomplishment given the imbalance in military might.[6] What right, some reasoned, did America have to brag about beating a much weaker military power and causing the deaths of many innocent people in the process?

Narcissistic pride is not necessarily bad for a group; many groups have thrived on it—at least for a while. A high school clique of girls who see themselves as superior to other girls may actually *feel* happier than those other girls. But if others perceive a group's pride as narcissistic—rightly or wrongly—that group is likely to forgo some of the feelings of kinship, comfort, and affection others might have felt for its members; it might even reap hostility, contempt, or conflict. Classmates may fear or envy the "mean girls," but rarely feel affection for them.

A news report on the "rebirth" of German pride, long in abeyance after World War II and the Holocaust, includes some examples of justified pride.[7] In the wake of the 2008–2009 world economic crisis and the more recent economic crises in Greece, Spain, Italy, and Ireland, many Germans take pride in their country's example of austerity, a pride founded on a real achievement and one that their chancellor, Angela Merkel, has expressed publicly for them. In the same report, a young German social worker expresses her feeling that her country's "rich traditions in music and literature, and its enduring emphasis on social welfare and a strong commitment to the environment, deserve more respect abroad and at home."[8] In fact, Germany pioneered health insurance, accident insurance, and old-age and invalid pensions in the 1880s, and the roster of great German writers, composers, scientists, and philosophers is remarkable.

Justified pride can also take humbler forms. Consider the 1968 strike by African American sanitation workers in Memphis. They marched with signs proclaiming "I Am a Man." They made perhaps the simplest statement of group pride possible, declaring themselves to be part of a group of which they were proud to be members—the human race—even if others did not fully acknowledge their membership. They were making a claim for themselves that was both enormous yet undeniable.

But even well-founded pride can be seen as narcissistic if the group expressing pride seems to be denying faults as well. The Beijing

Olympics in 2008 were understood by all to be a pride display, and it was widely acknowledged that China had much to be proud of, both in its long cultural history and in its recent rise to great economic and geopolitical power. The opening ceremony was spectacular. Some 4 billion viewers around the globe watched as fireworks exploded, fairies floated, and children representing China's ethnic mix paraded the flag. Many people were genuinely impressed and felt that China had earned this display of pride. But some found it narcissistic for China to mount this display while suppressing various ethnic and religious minorities and political freedom more broadly.

In sum, there are different kinds of pride with very different effects. Past studies have found, for example, that feelings of nationalistic *pride* are different and distinguishable from feelings of nationalistic *superiority* over other nations.[9] In this chapter, the important point is not that our personal experience of one kind of pride is different from our personal experience of another, but that how others will experience what they take to be our display of one kind of pride is different from how they will experience what they take to be our display of another.

## Pay Attention to How Pride Displays Affect Others

While a group may engage in pride displays largely with an eye to transforming its own members, the rest of us are watching; by definition, a pride display is out there for others to see. One way or another, others are affected. The type of pride that onlookers perceive—narcissistic or justified—is not necessarily the type of pride the group on display is actually feeling.[10] Legitimate pride may inadvertently be displayed in a narcissistic way or may be misinterpreted (innocently or maliciously) as narcissistic. Although research shows that people are rather adroit at detecting other people's narcissism, it is nevertheless possible to make mistakes about others' intentions.[11] The same is true when we look at groups; a group's public expression of genuine pride in a real accomplishment can still come across as narcissistic and undermine us-and-them relations rather than promote allophilia.

When planning a pride display, the potential for misinterpretation does not have to be the decisive factor, but neither should it be blindly ignored. Organizers of pride displays, such as pride marches, may rationally decide that the internal benefits of their action (group pride, increased activism, consciousness-raising) will be worth the costs (being seen by other groups as narcissistic). But there's no point in being taken by surprise by such reactions or in paying too high a cost for the expected benefit. Attention to how pride displays are received by other groups is particularly important if the goal is not to advance one's group at the expense of relations with other groups, but to find a way to share the world with them.

The international community faces precisely this challenge. In a world in which international cooperation is critical to solving some of the greatest challenges—from economic stability to environmental sustainability, from terrorism to nuclear proliferation—allophilia will be an essential ingredient. Reluctant cooperation—"We must hang together or, most assuredly, we will all hang separately"—will be overwhelmed by such large and complex problems. It might seem, then, that displays of group pride should take a back seat to humility in the name of diplomacy. I disagree. Displays of narcissistic pride should and must be avoided, but displays of justified pride can help promote the very allophilia we will need in order to address such difficult problems *willingly* together.

The United States is at the center of almost all such international efforts. America has always been perceived elsewhere as a proud nation. Its very founding had a certain confident swagger—a bold proclamation of independence with a still bolder assertion of universal rights. Foreigners are often puzzled or even alarmed by the prevalence of the Pledge of Allegiance and the widespread display of the national flag—not only on flagpoles but on bumper stickers, lapel pins, electric guitars, car washes, and just about anywhere else. Yet, on the whole, America is remarkably (though not uncritically or unconditionally) well-liked in many places around the world. (To discern this, one may have to look beyond the "chattering classes" and the expatriates who claim to tell us what ordinary people really think back home.)

Displays of American pride in the service of public diplomacy should not be automatically dismissed as PR or propaganda. Well-considered pride displays, based on an understanding of both dimensions of us-and-them relations, can usefully feed the allophilia that already exists and avoid feeding the anti-Americanism that also exists and that is guaranteed to get more media attention. A "Google test" at the time I was writing this chapter yielded about 1,690,000 references to "anti-Americanism," some fifty-eight times more than the 29,000 references to "pro-Americanism." There are plenty of reasons for people to feel affection, comfort, kinship, engagement, and enthusiasm with respect to the United States: real accomplishments such as forming and maintaining a constitutional democracy, allowing so many immigrants to achieve success, helping fight AIDS in Africa, inventing jazz music, and sending people to the moon.[12] But there is always a need for clarity of purpose. Is this pride display intended to reduce anti-Americanism or to increase pro-Americanism? Will the form it takes be likely to reduce anti-Americanism or to increase pro-Americanism? If the latter, is it intended to increase affection, comfort, kinship, engagement, enthusiasm, or some combination of these feelings?

It is likely that many people around the world have a mixed love/hate relationship with America. If we are concerned with those relationships, we need to understand not only why people hate us, but also why people love us and what will help that love grow. We need to recognize that, to others, we are different, but that our difference can wield a very positive power. American public diplomacy efforts to win the hearts and minds of people in other countries have so far been too haphazard and piecemeal, coming to prominence during a crisis (such as the Cold War or the Vietnam War) and fading into the background otherwise. Efforts to curb anti-Americanism neither have nor seek any serious foundation in social science. I have discussed this point in detail elsewhere.[13] Here, I will simply make the point that an important element of winning hearts and minds for America is to promote allophilia for Americans by expressing what will be seen as justifiable pride and steering clear of what will be seen as narcissistic pride. Conservatives may be too quick to express pride in some all-encompassing American greatness—sometimes called *American exceptionalism*—inherently putting everyone else on the defensive, while liberals may be too quick to deride the expression of national pride as inherently aggressive toward others. But nations become greater by aspiring to be great; and, as long as their pride is properly placed, it can be a constructive feeling, both for themselves and for others. South African pride, for example, has been an inspiration to other countries that still face the task of putting a national injustice behind them and that hope to do so with as much grace as many in South Africa did.

## How to Influence How Pride Is Perceived

Groups need not fear being proud and trying publicly to inspire pride in their members. It would be neither appropriate nor realistic for a group to be too *other-centered*—obsessed with how others see it. But neither is it in any group's interest to be actively disliked. It will pay, then, to keep an eye on how one's own group's pride comes across on the public stage, keeping in mind the precautions discussed below.

### *Be Inclusive*

When Cathy Freeman, an Australian Olympian of Aboriginal descent, won the 400-meter dash in the 2000 Sydney Olympics, she carried the Aboriginal flag—which might be seen as excluding other Australians—but she also carried the Australian flag. She had done this before, for other victories. When she first did it, after winning the 400-meter title at the Commonwealth Games in Canada in August 1994, she explained that she had not meant it as a political gesture. "I just wanted to show people that I am proud of who I am and where I come from," she said. "I represent the fact that, as an indigenous individual, there is no reason you can't be like everyone else and go out and achieve goals and dreams. That's all I wanted to represent . . . Kids are what's most important to me, and when they see someone who is strong and proud of who they are, hopefully it helps them get out the door and say, 'I'm going for that. I want to do that, be a doctor or lawyer or sprinter or whatever.'"[14]

Her gesture of pride in the heritage of her people was not without controversy. The Australian *chef de mission* at the Games officially declared it inappropriate for Freeman to carry a flag other than the Australian one. Several Australian legislators were critical, and a national debate ensued. But Australia's prime minister, Paul Keating, supported her, as did most of the Australian public.[15] It is mighty unlikely that she would have been so popular had she come out with the Aboriginal flag *instead* of the Australian flag; that might well have polarized relations between Australian Aborigines and other Australians. Freeman made her gesture in such an inclusive way that many non-Aboriginal Australians experienced it as an act of "reconciliation" rather than "rebelliousness," felt great warmth for her, and felt connected to the collective pride her achievement signified for many Aborigines.[16] While inviting all Australian into the experience of her Aboriginal pride, she also invited Aboriginals into an Australian pride that some of them had probably felt was not open or appropriate to them.

In the opposite vein, consider the rise (and, to my mind, fortunate decline) in popularity of the T-shirt slogan, "It's a Black Thing—You Wouldn't Understand." Far from inviting appreciative inquiry, this slogan precludes it—dismissively turning strangers away without even giving them a chance. The positive power of difference was distorted into a force field to keep others out. While each individual T-shirt might have been a manifestation of its owner's genuine pride in African American culture, or may just have been meant as a laugh, it could hardly help but be experienced by many onlookers as narcissistic: "There's something about us that's simply beyond you." Whether or not that something was anything to be proud of, the slogan implied that anyone who wasn't African American wasn't capable of extending any understanding beyond his or her own experience. Far from promoting connection, it warned against any impulse toward curiosity. The goal seemed to be "us *without* them."

Groups are not obliged to bend over backward to be inclusive, nor should they deny their own richness, complexity, and distinctiveness to seek inclusiveness. But a group can cherish those attributes while still leaving a door open so that others may look inside and treasure some of the things the group itself values. That can inspire people of different groups not simply to tolerate their coexistence but to desire and protect it.

### *Focus on What Is Great—Not What Is Greater*

Pride displays are more likely to evoke allophilia and less likely to appear narcissistic when they focus on what is great about a group in its own right rather than how it is better than other groups. Consider the controversial statement of then Supreme Court nominee, now Supreme Court Justice, Sonia Sotomayor: "I would hope that a wise Latina woman with the richness of her experiences would more often than not reach a better conclusion than a white male who hasn't lived that life."[17] If she had simply commented that a wise Latina would make good judicial decisions, I don't believe such a remark would have caused any uproar. But by proposing that a wise Latina would make *better* judicial decisions than a white male, she invited the accusation of narcissistic pride. This, of course, is not to say that her pride in her heritage actually is narcissistic; I have no way of knowing whether or not it is. But her display of Latina pride had the signifiers of narcissistic pride, and that's what was justifiably perceived by some. (Others, of course, were looking for anything that could be turned against her.) It seems unlikely that Sotomayor wanted to alienate non-Latinos when she made that remark, so we can take her remark as a powerful reminder of how careful one needs to be when arousing group pride.

I don't know what Lieutenant General William Boykin, then deputy undersecretary of Defense for Intelligence, had in mind when, speaking to a Christian church group about a Somali warlord, he said, "I knew that my god was bigger than his."[18] Perhaps he meant to instill pride in a religious community of which he was a member. But what he signaled to many others was narcissistic pride. To someone not of his group, his statement could hardly be taken as anything but a put-down at best and a threat at worst. Or as just absurd. How can a monotheist compare gods? It certainly couldn't serve to create affection, comfort, kinship, engagement, or enthusiasm.

### Display Pride as Pleasure, Not Just Pain

Grievances involving "us" and "them" can produce a particular kind of pride display, a defiant insistence that "you don't realize how worthy we are." This was the gist of Zora Neale Hurston's comic riposte to American racial discrimination quoted above; in effect, she was saying, "Your loss, white folks." Such a display can help build pride among members of the aggrieved group, but its effect on the "other" is as likely to be negative as positive. Are there pride displays that can be used not only to express, but also to heal such grievances?

Groups should not feel obliged to put on a happy face and ignore their real suffering, but to truly come together, something more than the suffering needs to be shared. Imagine a marriage counseling session in which each party expresses nothing but the misery the other has caused—a recipe for an uncontested divorce, at best. To save the marriage, the couple would have to acknowledge something good that had existed, something positive that is worth reviving. They would not only have to talk through their respective weaknesses, but also the qualities they find (or found) attractive in each other. In short, someone has to make the case that, despite what has gone wrong, there are good things—even great things—for the couple to again enjoy together.

## Focus on Real Accomplishments

Pride displays that emphasize specific contributions and accomplishments rather than general claims of excellence are more likely to inspire interest and admiration in others rather than offense or contempt. We can see President Obama moving from one side of the line to the other as he promotes his vision of a "green America." His displays of pride in America's undeniable history of technical invention and business development are justified, as are displays of pride in American universities. These are admired worldwide. But his displays of "pride in advance" in what America is going to do for the Green Revolution may be taken as narcissistic, at least outside the United States. Sometimes he seems to be saying that any time we get around to it, we can become the leader in the Green Revolution. Yet this revolution is already under way, and the United States has by no means been the leader. Germany, for example, is believed to be the "greenest" country.[19] Israel, not the United States, is home to the world's first solar gas-hybrid power plant. Australia, South Korea, China, Japan, Canada, and countries across the European Union, such as Italy, France, the United Kingdom, and Sweden, all have accomplishments in green technology. According to a Yale University study that weighted 149 countries on their sulfur emissions, water purity, and conservation practices, the United States ranks . . . number 39.[20] In order to tap the positive power of difference from displays of difference, there has to be a demonstrably positive difference. The United States will therefore have to *earn* its pride in this field as it has done in the past in fields such as aviation, medicine, and computer technology.

## Plan and Train

As several examples above have shown, groups need to take care to display pride without narcissism if they want to preserve (or perhaps promote) positive us-and-them relations. The need is particularly important for minority groups, for whom the stakes can be much higher. For this reason, pride displays may need to be carefully managed and the participants carefully trained. One reason the American civil rights movement was as successful as it was is that episodes that may have appeared spontaneous, naive, and driven by pure moral outrage were in fact often orchestrated and carefully designed to inspire the respect of whites for African Americans. For example, from 1947 to 1957, the Congress of Racial Equality (CORE), a key activist organization of the civil rights movement, ran monthlong nonviolence training workshops in Washington, D.C., at which participants learned both the theory and the practical skills of organizing and carrying out nonviolent resistance.[21] It took extensive training to prepare civil rights workers to weather the confrontation and violence they would encounter in the South and to maintain their impressive dignity under the most undignified and provocative circumstances. Participants in the Mississippi Freedom Summer of 1964 began with a two-week training. The Poor People's Campaign of 1968 held training programs for marchers, marshals, and even the support people.[22] All this helped the participants display a justified pride in their cause that did not turn away other Americans. In fact, it demanded their respect and admiration. In many cases, it changed people's minds and opened their hearts and sometimes it even inspired them to join the cause.

Taking a two-dimensional approach to us-and-them relations—recognizing the allophilia dimension as well as the hate dimension—gives us a much more complete and realistic picture of what can be hoped for and achieved in the relationships between different groups. Taking a similarly nuanced approach to pride displays warns us that such actions, even when intended only to mobilize the troops, can nevertheless have unintended and unwanted effects on others. Enterprising leaders can take care that pride displays are planned and carried out so as to achieve the desired effects along either dimension—reducing hate or increasing allophilia or perhaps both—while avoiding unintended effects.

# SEVEN

# LEAD BOLDLY *TOWARD*

Who is a hero? One who turns an enemy into a friend.

—Proverb from the Talmud

**W**E HAVE seen throughout this book how us-and-them leadership requires allophilia. In this chapter, I want to emphasize how allophilia requires a particular kind of us-and-them leadership. Leaders—be they formal authority figures charged with leading, or everyday people stepping up to lead from below—must lead *toward* allophilia, not only away from hate. They must do so by taking bold steps, moving beyond the roster of common us-and-them leadership approaches based on small, iterative, tit-for-tat steps.

## Leading Toward, Not Away

On February 15, 2001, Keith Orr and Martin Contreras, co-owners of a restaurant, bar, and community gathering place frequented by many gay patrons in Ann Arbor, Michigan, learned that their business was going to be the target of an anti-gay demonstration led by Fred Phelps. This disbarred attorney turned minister was notorious for picketing the funerals of people who had died of AIDS with signs such as "God Hates Fags." (When not picketing such funerals, Phelps picketed and protested outside military funerals.) Rather than organizing a counterdemonstration, Orr and Contreras initiated a quick e-mail campaign, inviting people from across the community—gay identified and not gay identified—to pledge any amount they chose *for each minute of Phelps's demonstration*. The longer Phelps picketed the bar, the more money was raised for a local gay advocacy group and community center.[1] Orr and Contreras seem to have understood intuitively that to combat hate was not enough. Rather than simply protest the picketers—which probably would not have changed anyone's attitude very much—they engaged the allophilia of local people for the gay community in their midst. Their action may even have stimulated new allophilia. Linda Lombardini, a board member of the gay community center, reported that "a father . . . brought his son into the restaurant to demonstrate to him that gay people are no different from anyone else. When he realized that we were holding a fundraiser he handed his son a ten-dollar bill to give to me."[2] In Orr's words, their response to Phelps's demonstration gave people "a constructive way to combat a destructive person."[3]

This was an example of *leading toward*. Instead of engaging the hate dimension and trying to fight it to a draw, Orr and Contreras intuitively engaged the allophilia dimension—in this case by encouraging proactive engagement and support—and built community. They focused their energies on what they wanted—a community in which difference is respected and diverse groups are actively supported—rather than on what they didn't want—the us-against-them world of Phelps. They did not suddenly create all the goodwill on which they were able to draw (although they may have helped to create it over the years), they mobilized it. They gave a latent attitude a specific mission. As a result, that attitude became action. Leaders who give people a way to act on a positive attitude can thus reinforce the attitude itself, as people experience the fact that it is real, that it works, that it feels good to be this way.

## The Role of Formal Authority

Orr and Contreras's action also shows that leadership can come from many different points in a community, whether that community is Ann Arbor, Michigan, or the world. Certainly, large-scale us-and-them conflicts are, at least in part, the responsibility of those groups' formal leaders. But when leaders fail to act successfully—or fail to act at all—individuals can address the problem themselves by taking the advice of top-five hit song from 1969: "Come on, people, smile on your brother. Everybody get together, try to love one another right now."[4]

I want to be clear that when I recognize a role for many different sources of leadership, I do not wish to let formal leaders off the hook. Although leadership from the ground up is possible, formal leaders have a critical role to play. Even if they are not the ones who usher in change, their leadership will be needed to make change *sustainable*. We have recently witnessed bottom-up revolutions in Tunisia, Egypt, and Libya, but what happens from now on will largely depend on new, more responsible systems coming into place. Formal leaders— including the military—will need to lead, and lead in new ways, for positive change to result. The American civil rights movement—a large-scale turning of us-and-them relations—was neither wholly bottom-up nor wholly top-down. It tapped existing positive feelings and attitudes among both African Americans and whites—feelings and attitudes that, as we have seen, are natural and nurturable. But it was very well led at both the national and local levels. Rosa Parks's refusal to move to the back of the bus was a planned act of civil disobedience— some aspects of it were deliberately staged.[5] Nevertheless, it stood for genuinely common feelings and summoned up genuinely spontaneous responses from many ordinary people who joined the bus boycott, which in turn was carefully managed by civil rights leaders at various levels.

While the need for formal leaders to promote allophilia on a large scale might strike you as common sense, it is supported by research, too. For example, study after study has examined if and when interacting with someone from another group in positive ways can change one's attitude toward that group as a whole. Unfortunately, the studies often find that one will develop a more positive attitude toward that particular person, but not necessarily toward others from that person's group.[6] That is, contact may spark an individual friendship, but probably not broader allophilia. We *subtype* that person: "Yes, I like him, but he's not really one of *them*." In fact, the new acquaintance is often taken to be an exception who therefore confirms one's negative attitude toward the group in general; the exception that proves the rule.

In fact, not only has the contact research found that positive contact often will not generalize, but it has also found that the conditions under which contact is most likely to generalize are very specific: personal contact is consistently more likely to produce a lasting improvement in an individual's attitude toward an "other" (a group, that is) when there is approval for the change in attitude from someone in a position of authority.[7] So, while there is clearly a role for all of us, there is—as I mentioned in chapter 4—a particularly important and effective role for our formal leaders, who can influence the conditions in which we live and make contact with the "other." Allophilia cannot be left to develop organically without support from formal leaders; that process won't be fruitful enough to create the kinds of pluralistic communities that many people wish to see. As I have said throughout this book, the positive power of difference is natural, but it needs to be nurtured. Not only must leaders resist playing groups against each other, but they must also break out of one-dimensional thinking about us-and-them relations and lead in both dimensions.

If formal authority figures are to lead on issues of difference, then policy makers, scholars, and the leaders themselves will need a new way of thinking about the problems they address. Researchers too often come up with what might be called "Martha Stewart" recipes for positive relations—rather exacting and elaborate recipes that work perfectly in the television studio (or, in the case of social science research, in a laboratory experiment) but are very hard to pull off at home. Formal leaders in the world will need strategies that are a little more "Rachael Ray"—easier to achieve in everyday life under everyday conditions.

Yet grassroots leaders, working on the ground, are often guilty of a version of the "Martha Stewart" approach when they circumscribe their efforts in small, well-controlled interventions. Even if you can create environments in which people work collaboratively and appreciate each other as individuals, they still go back into a world of people who are from other groups and whom they have not had a chance to get to know individually. For example, many wonderful programs have brought Jewish Israeli and Muslim Arab children to summer camps in idyllic settings in the United States for positive experiences with each other. Likewise, many corporate retreats have brought fractious managers together for a facilitated experience in a peaceful setting, away from the distractions and the usual triggers of interpersonal and interdepartmental conflict. But the children and the managers go back home or back to work and the changes in attitude that were achieved in highly controlled environments do not last and do not extend to all those other "others."

In contrast, Nazia Masrawa, the mayor of the Arab Israeli town of Kfar Qara, and Chaim Gaash, mayor of the nearby Jewish town of Pardes Hanna, are attempting to use contact to improve some very poor us-and-them relations but they are running the experiment in quite the opposite way—by keeping the contact well within the real world rather than in a protected incubator. Masrawa acknowledges, "Every day there is enough tension in our lives to begin a war" and that "We will never agree on the history, or on politics."[8] Instead, he and Gaash focus on immediate problems—not those between their two communities, but rather those shared by both. For example, a women's group decided to deal with problems facing girls and young women, such as eating disorders. Teenagers decided to create productive afterschool activities and retirees decided to create recreational activities for elderly men.[9]

Both scholars and practitioners of positive intergroup relations are going to have to engage the "other" far more broadly and systematically if they want to go beyond powerful experiments—whether done in the lab or in a summer camp—to actually transform the world.

## Bold Steps *Toward*

The Keith Orr and Martin Contreras case, besides exemplifying the need to lead toward allophilia, exemplifies the specific way to do it that is the focus of this chapter: leading by taking bold steps. As we will see, bold steps in us-and-them relations have been avoided or abandoned in many leadership circles, undermining the quality of our leaders not just in the area of us-and-them relations but also in many other areas of public leadership.

When we look through history to see how leaders have actually moved their followers beyond hate, we sometimes find them sidestepping the typical orderly progression of small, incremental diplomatic steps taken to reduce hostility between nations. Instead, they take surprising and bold steps forward. Those steps may not lead in a clearly foreseeable way to a particular desired result, but they seem suddenly to transform the whole situation, bringing new possibilities within reach. Yitzhak Rabin's involvement in and signing of the Oslo Accords in 1993 was just such a bold step, as was Nelson Mandela's open forgiveness of his and his people's white oppressors upon his release from prison in 1990 and as president of South Africa through 1999. Neither of these actions was the next careful step in a gradual process. Mandela, in particular, seemed ready and committed to turn an enemy into a friend as quickly as possible.

Social science research sheds some light on this phenomenon. A classic psychological study, for example, found that the formation of friendships among first-year college students in the same dorm depended not only on what two students happened to have in common but on the mere (or should we say *more powerful?*) fact that they were in the same place together.[10] Similarity may attract, but in any case, people tend to befriend their neighbors. And on the level of international politics, we have seen how powerful a mere visit by one world leader to an "enemy" country can be. Richard Nixon's 1972 visit to Beijing was such a move, as was Anwar Sadat's 1977 visit to Jerusalem. China and the United States were no more similar after Nixon's visit than they had been before, yet by knocking on China's door, so to speak, Nixon made it seem as if the two peoples at least lived in the same neighborhood.

Obviously, such bold steps were not all equally successful. Such steps open up new possibilities, but they do not guarantee success. Leaders need to act boldly, but not erratically. Both Nixon's and Sadat's visits were surprises to the public, and neither was the logical next step in a process of mutual reciprocation. But each was the product of much preparation (although, interestingly, the agendas of both visits were more open-ended than is typical for a diplomatic mission). It is also important to note that bold steps, while very likely to be symbolic, must go beyond symbolism if they are to achieve any of the potential they seem to create. They must surprise and delight us, but they must also create a framework for further practical action.

There has been some very interesting research bearing on bold steps and their surprise factor. Many social science experiments have made use of the *Prisoner's Dilemma,* a structured game in which each of two players (who may be either real people or computer programs simulating real players) has strong incentives both to cooperate with the other for mutual benefit and to betray the other for individual benefit. For example, two players may take turns offering each other part of a sum of money. Neither pure selfishness nor absolute generosity works out very well in the long run.

The study of the Prisoner's Dilemma, including the competitions between computers running different strategies, seemed to show that the strategy most beneficial to both players was tit for tat; that is, matching the other player's move with a measured move of equal generosity or selfishness. North Korea launches a missile; the South Koreans and Americans conduct a joint naval exercise the next week. *Tit for Tat* was in fact the name of a strategy devised by political scientist Robert Axelrod. The strategy was to start with one cooperative move and, from then on, simply echo the opponent's moves. Such findings were quickly and widely applied to the practice of real-world negotiation; tit for tat is what we typically see in international diplomacy. According to tit-for-tat reasoning, us-and-them leadership moves should be small, inherently conservative, and incremental.

The Tit for Tat strategy has cast a very broad shadow, deeply influencing the training of political and business leaders. But it is missing something very important. In the late 1980s, Polish mathematician Martin Nowak devised a Prisoner's Dilemma strategy called *Generous.* A player (human or computer) will mostly play tit for tat, but every so often—and unpredictably—will ignore a selfish move by the opponent, coming back with a *generous* move rather than responding in kind. These acts of simulated "forgiveness" are effective in breaking a cycle of retaliation, but because they are unpredictable, the opponent cannot game them so as to play the program for a sucker. Generous has been found to outperform Tit for Tat!

The implications for leadership are huge. Bold steps—not predictable from one's own or the opponent's past behavior—open up new possibilities for what *could be* rather than just an endless extension or gradual improvement, through diplomatic tit for tat, of what has always been. In a sense, the bold leader says, "My next move is not based on what you have just done. Obviously, we are not happy with each other or we wouldn't be here negotiating. But there are possibilities beyond either continuing or stopping particular behaviors. And if, after all this time, we find we can neither continue what we have been doing nor simply stop what we have been doing, then it's time to take a different path altogether." (That is, in effect, to add a second dimension to our us-and-them relations.)

The Prisoner's Dilemma tournaments have something else to teach us. Both Tit for Tat and Generous have been contest winners, yet both the inventors, Axelrod and Nowak, have taken care to emphasize that the best strategy depends on what other strategies are in the competition. Thus, there is a need for what-if thinking: one cannot simply try to devise the all-purpose *best* strategy, but must ask, "What if this or that happens? What would the best strategy be?" Going further, one must ask, "What new things *could happen* if we used this or that new kind of strategy?" This is just the kind of what-if thinking that practitioners need to apply to the practice of us-and-them relations and that scientists need to apply to the science of us-and-them relations.

A bold step forward can be institutional. John F. Kennedy, by founding the Peace Corps in 1961, sent thousands of U.S. citizens around the world. Each Peace Corps volunteer made his or her own bold move toward the "other" and, by this means, Kennedy touched in a positive way many more places than he could possibly have visited himself as president. His vision for the Peace Corps was not at all an obvious next step for the United States at that time. Peace Corps volunteers were not going to deter the Red Army. The proposal sparked considerable suspicion and controversy. And although the Peace Corps has promoted goodwill between Americans and the people of other nations while helping a bit in global development, it has actually been a very small program. There were only fifteen thousand volunteers in service at its peak in 1966 and the number dwindled to fewer than five thousand for most of the 1980s.[11] Yet it still looms large in the national imagination and often finds favor on *both* sides of the aisle. Why? I believe it is due to its bold appeal to our better selves, to our capacity for curiosity, appreciation, and engagement with respect to "others"—an appeal to our common good rather than simply to our common interests.

Are we developing leaders capable of such bold moves? As I pointed out in chapter 4, the institutions charged with developing our formal political leaders are law schools and, to a lesser extent, policy schools, both of which tend to instill—in fact, to drill in—the tit-for-tat or negotiation model of us-and-them leadership. This model bases future steps largely on past steps, which can be effective for achieving limited goals but is hardly a basis for transformative change. Training in this model teaches leaders to understand their options by looking back rather than forward. Of greater concern, it teaches that leaders should take others' interests into account as a more efficient way to advance their *own* group's interests—an approach unlikely to lead to the transformation of us-and-them relations. People behave quite differently when their engagement with others is based on caring about them, admiring them, or feeling related to them and comfortable with them; that is, when it is based on the positive power of difference. John Kennedy, who many considered the most inspirational government leader in his generation, did not have a law degree. Perhaps his lack of legal and diplomatic training was his greatest asset.

In my opinion, negotiation-based, tit-for-tat strategies are not really leadership at all. I may not be alone. As *New York Times* columnist Thomas Friedman put it, "What is missing today in so many places: leaders who surprise us by rising above their histories, their constituencies, their pollsters, their circumstances—and just do the right things."[12] We have embraced models of leadership that at best minimize the negative consequences for the leader and for his or her group, yet we know that real leadership calls for great risk and sacrifice, not only—as politicians love to encourage us—on the part of the people, but also on the part of the leaders themselves.

I would also remind the social science research community that we have our own chance to take some bold steps; that is, to increasingly conduct what-if science, guided—though never blinded—by the desire to make a better world. Just as Nelson Mandela had the guts to stay rooted in his own group while stepping out beyond it—for the sake of South Africa's blacks *plus* whites—social scientists can show their own kind of courage by stepping beyond their usual subject matter and studying scientifically what Mandela did and how others might be able to do something like it.

What are the bold steps that leaders can take, moving beyond usual leadership methods in order to transform us and them—and even us *versus* them—into us *plus* them?

### Bold Step 1: Use Accountability to Avoid the Ingroup/Outgroup Leadership Trade-off

Leaders, like physicians, should endeavor to do no harm. This in itself can be a bold step beyond the ordinary practice of leadership. In chapter 4, I discussed the *ingroup/outgroup leadership trade-off* that leaders too often make, stirring up hostility or rivalry with another group in order to solidify their standing in their own group.[13] One of the least spectacular but most effective bold steps any leader can take toward better us-and-them relations is simply to avoid making this traditional trade-off.

For leaders seeking to avoid the ingroup/outgroup leadership trade-off, a two-dimensional model of us-and-them relations is essential. It allows—in fact, it requires—the leader to distinguish between actions that will primarily increase or decrease hostility to an "other" and actions that will primarily increase or decrease allophilia toward an "other."[14] Generally, some actions from each category will be in order, but neither should be expected to produce the results appropriate to the other.

Even so, the trade-off can be surprisingly hard to avoid. Some of the very things that can help a leader promote strong cohesion in his or her own group can also exacerbate conflicts with other groups unless the leader pays careful attention to avoiding this possibility. It is no accident that revving up a team effort is often called "rallying the troops"—and in the end, what are troops for but to fight?

One practical way for leaders to avoid the ingroup/outgroup leadership trade-off is suggested by the accountability networks that can be so helpful for people doing battle with frustrating or self-destructive habits and addictions. Leaders should make specific commitments to specific parties to do specific things that promote allophilia. For example, a leader can publicly commit to meet regularly with members of the "other" group or to appoint members of the "other" group to decision-making bodies. A CEO should commit himself or herself to really learning about conditions to which employees object and demonstrating that he or she has done so by meeting with employee representatives and showing that knowledge, even if he or she doesn't agree with their requests or demands. As I write this, two opponents for a Massachusetts seat in the U.S. Senate, Republican Scott Brown and Democrat Elizabeth Warren, have committed themselves publicly to an attempt to discourage third-party negative campaign ads directed at each other.[15] The mayor of a city with an uneasy mix of ethnic groups should commit to showing acceptance of them not just by turning up at local festivals but by advocating for policies that would benefit these groups with educational, business, or housing opportunities—as long as those advantages are not achieved at each other's expense. Leaders should commit themselves to acts of common decency toward the "other," as we saw recently when U.S. warships rescued Iranian fishermen in the Persian Gulf three times in the space of a month, at a time when there was more than the usual level of tension between the American and Iranian governments.[16]

Leaders may also be able to use the phenomenon known as *positive interdependence,* which occurs when a group can succeed in its joint task only if its members succeed individually. This has mainly been put to use in classrooms, where teachers can deliberately create assignments or projects characterized by positive interdependence. Most leaders in other fields don't have that kind of control over their followers and constituents and are not so free to decide what tasks need to be accomplished. Nevertheless, leaders can sometimes take advantage of naturally occurring positive interdependence to promote allophilia amongst groups. For example, trade agreements and mutual defense/security agreements can embody genuine positive independence and therefore offer an opportunity for people to develop a positive attitude toward a different group. Of course, such agreements can also be one-sided or exploitive, as when one country needs investment and another country "needs" cheap labor and a place to conduct environmentally destructive manufacturing. Such interdependence can hardly be a springboard for allophilia. Neither can the kind of *negative* interdependence described by former U.S. National Security Advisor Zbigniew Brzezinski: "[F]or the foreseeable future, we know and the Chinese know that, if one hurts the other, one will suffer oneself."[17] Brzezinski sees this interdependence as a hopeful deterrent to large-scale conflict, and that may be so, but it is not a foundation for positive us-and-them relations.

I would call it real leadership to use trade agreements and mutual defense/security agreements to build positive interdependence and not just to maximize each country's own interests. Agreements founded on positive interdependence are likely to be more useful and longer lasting.

Business teams can have positive interdependence, and business leaders should take advantage of that to build positive us-and-them relations. In many organizations, for example, the IT function is seen by everyone else as an "other," owing both to its specialized skills and to the fact that it seems independent of whatever business the company is in. Some companies, however, are careful to involve IT personnel in various sales, marketing, and even manufacturing activities, so that the IT people gain a better sense of the business on which their jobs depend and other employees gain a better sense of how IT can help them do their own jobs. To make this work, the leader needs to make sure team members fully understand their collective purpose and not only their own roles. The leader also needs to explicitly recognize and reward successful teamwork, specifically as it happens and not just in a general way at the end. In other words, while positive interdependence will not in itself bring about allophilia, it can provide an occasion for other allophilia-building efforts to have a greater chance of success.

Interdependence is going to be increasingly common in us-and-them situations—whether promoting an international response to an international threat, designing a new product, or forming a committee to buy new playground equipment—simply because the world is becoming more and more interconnected. That interdependence might be negative—that is, when one participant can only win if others lose—but it can also be positive. Leaders should harness genuine instances of positive interdependence to help them tap the positive power of difference and not simply try to overcome the negative power of difference.

One key to accountability, no matter what particular approach is taken, is measurement. A leader cannot be accountable unless he or she has a way to know—and to demonstrate to others—whether things are getting better or worse. As described in chapter 1, governments and organizations often measure and track negative relations, monitoring such things as discrimination complaints and hate crimes. But as we then saw in chapter 2, one cannot observe well the progress of positive attitudes by measuring a decline in negative attitudes. Instead, one must track the actions taken in order to promote allophilia and the short-term and long-term responses to them. Those responses can be measured through attitude surveys, actions taken by various groups, the Allophilia Scale, and so on.

While there is no end of historical examples of the ingroup/outgroup leadership trade-off in action—often bringing about just the results the leader hoped for, at least in the short term—there is also a growing body of research finding that the trade-off may not even be necessary in order to bring about those results. The discussion in chapter 3 showed that, contrary to what has long been the received wisdom, increasing a group's enthusiasm for itself does *not* have to be accompanied by an increase in negative feelings toward any other group.[18] In fact, a group's aggressive hostility toward other groups seems to be more a product of factors other than the group's positive feelings toward itself.[19] In many cases, ingroup favoritism means that the group will indeed, given the chance, provide itself with more benefits than it will provide to some other group, but it does not mean that the group will actively punish members of the other group.[20] One team of social psychologists has found repeatedly that people *won't* favor their ingroup if it means having to punish an outgroup; they will *only* favor their ingroup in situations in which they are also favoring (but less strongly) the outgroup![21]

### *Bold Step 2: Demonstrate Acceptance*

Social scientists use the term *perceived acceptance* to refer to the extent to which one believes that one's group is accepted by some other group. My study of Arab and Jewish citizens of Israel (referred to in chapter 2) gives us a glimpse of how a bold step of acceptance could nurture the positive power of difference. My colleagues and I found that, for each group of Israelis—Jewish and Arab citizens—feeling accepted by the other group is critical to feeling goodwill toward that group, which in turn is critical to being willing to act in support of that group. What's more, each group has different criteria for feeling accepted. Arab citizens are likely to feel accepted by the Jewish population if they feel that their Jewish neighbors support closing gaps in government spending for education, health, welfare, and infrastructure in the Arab sector. Jewish citizens are likely to feel accepted by the Arab population if they feel that their Arab neighbors are committed to Israel's long-term economic and political security and well-being. Each side, failing to feel accepted, will have less allophilia toward the other side and feel less inclined to act in support of the other side. Here are the makings of a vicious cycle—each group feeling less liked and then acting in ways that make it more disliked.

But here, too, are the makings of a virtuous cycle. The Arab and Jewish citizens my colleagues and I studied have quite specific and actionable ideas of what genuine acceptance would be like. Steps toward the fulfillment of those visions would lead to positive outcomes that the mere absence of hate and prejudice could never bring about. Here again, leaders can take the steps described earlier:

- Talk to the "other"—not just about their problems, but about the people themselves and their lives.

- Find ways to show affection for the "other"—not just acceptance, tolerance, or "willingness to deal."

- Advocate for the "other" when there is a chance to do so out of goodwill, not simply as tit for tat.

- Take any and every opportunity to show common decency toward the "other."

National leaders, of course, have more power than ordinary citizens to address a group's criteria for feeling accepted. A national leader also has the power to take a brave step that will symbolize that acceptance on behalf of his or her group, perhaps even more than the group actually feels it. In this way, the leader can lead both groups at once, leading the other group to feel more accepted and his or her own group to feel more accepting.

It's easy for a leader to miss an opportunity to show acceptance. Jordan's Queen Rania coauthored a heartwarming children's book, *The Sandwich Swap,* about getting to know others—a vision of openness, engagement, and acceptance. Boosted by a powerful publisher, Disney/Hyperion, interviews with no less than Oprah Winfrey and Barbara Walters, and even a reading at the United Nations, the book quickly reached the *New York Times* best-seller list. Yet Queen Rania passed up a chance for a brave step forward, in a part of the world that so desperately needs leaders willing to make them, when she declined to have a Hebrew edition published.[22]

### Bold Step 3: Hold Governments Accountable for Coexistence

Coexistence is a critical global issue. Most countries have significant minority populations. Worldwide migration continues to make many communities and nations more demographically diverse than ever. For example, one-fifth of the people now living in Germany are immigrants or of immigrant background.[23] Yet at the same time, different groups are often very segregated, not only in where they live but in how, when, and where they are likely to have any contact with the "other." And more and more nations are joining the watch list of divided societies— places in which difference is playing out along the negative dimensions and us-and-them relations are at risk of erupting violently into us-*versus*-them relations, threatening safety, prosperity, and democratic rule in that country and sometimes in neighboring countries.

With the stakes so high, political leaders and policymakers might be expected to make us-and-them relations a top priority, but for the most part, they do not. Many countries have a minister dedicated to advancing minority groups' interests. But, as we saw in chapter 4, advancing the interests of constituent groups is not the same thing as advancing coexistence and the collective good. I know of no country—failing, divided, or otherwise—that has seriously tasked and funded a minister for coexistence, by whatever name, or that tracks any kind of social cohesion index along with such commonly tracked indicators of a country's well-being as gross domestic product, consumer confidence, and crime rate.

This is not to say that governments haven't done anything at all. But the steps they have taken so far are only tiny steps, creating agencies and programs that have too few resources and staff and that command too little of the attention of those with the greatest political power. Australia, for example, has a government initiative called Living in Harmony, which uses several strategies—including funded community projects, competitive grants, a partnership program, and a public information strategy—"to encourage all Australians to contribute to and build upon Australia's social cohesion. The program has a particular emphasis on the promotion of Australian values and mutual obligation."[24] But this is more a program of public awareness than an investment of resources. Perhaps the most serious, disciplined, and sustained effort is Northern Ireland's Shared Future initiative, which goes well beyond ad campaigns. One particularly clever policy is to ask all public departments—from parks to roads to utilities—for impact statements on how their current projects are expected either to advance coexistence among sectarian groups, to undermine that coexistence, or not to affect it all. Over time, this repeated consciousness that coexistence is something we can make or unmake in everyday decisions and actions should strengthen the collective will to build community. Another important quality of the Shared Futures initiative is that it spreads responsibility for thinking about coexistence around. A common problem of organizational diversity efforts is that they are pigeonholed in an office of diversity. Logically, how can *coexistence* be one small department's job?

Why are approaches like this so rare, even as more and more communities have the diversity that calls for such efforts? Why such timid responses around the world to so serious a challenge? First, political systems are set up mainly to broker deals and distribute (or deny) benefits to various groups, each with its lobbies, activists, and spokespeople. Second, political leaders resist making coexistence initiatives a political priority because many of the specific issues linked with coexistence, such as school curricula, official language policy, religious beliefs, and civil rights, are political hot potatoes that the leaders would rather finesse than solve. Third, few public-sector leaders have been educated or trained to manage coexistence. Most prefer to leave the task of improving relations between communities to the "third sector" of religious and other nonprofit and nongovernmental organizations, rather than claiming the work as their own responsibility. But the third sector, though it often does amazing work, operates with limited resources and, frankly, without formal accountability. Fourth, governments are often moved to address coexistence only when a crisis looms or has already arrived. Such responses are too little and too late. Fifth, as we have seen all along, leaders and policymakers are blinded by a one-dimensional model of us-and-them relations that only encourages them to reduce intolerance and hate.

We can explain why governments don't get more involved, but in the end, we must change this. Governments need to take a much more proactive, coherent, and rigorous approach to coexistence, with programs and policies that actively promote positive feelings and positive actions between the members of different groups. That is, as well as fighting prejudice, they need a strategy to actively and distinctly promote allophilia. They need to assign responsibility and accountability to specific leaders with the authority, staff, and resources to carry out the strategy. These leaders will need to take some bold steps outside the usual methods of leadership. They will need to focus on achieving the common good rather than on balancing common interests. They will need to resist the temptation to leave coexistence largely in the hands of religious leaders and NGOs. They will need to treat coexistence as the urgent matter it is, even when there is no ugly crisis forcing the issue.

Another bold step toward making government accountable for coexistence would be to ground coexistence programs in rigorous social science and a commitment to measurement and assessment through which a program's impact can be tested and improved. The fact that coexistence programs have a moral purpose does not in any way imply that they should not take full advantage of scientific rigor. As mentioned above, there should be benchmarks for success or failure and mechanisms for responding as the situation improves, degrades, or just changes over time. Care should be taken to measure what we want—allophilia—not merely what we don't want—hate crimes, housing segregation, and so on. Bravo to Bhutan, described in chapter 2, for breaking free of the common approach to measuring progress and national success in purely economic terms such as GDP. All these steps would make it more likely that the coexistence effort would be taken seriously and that progress would be made.

Today's efforts do not meet these criteria. For example, the UN's Alliance of Civilizations is undertaking an important coexistence mission to "mobilize concerted efforts to promote cross-cultural relations among diverse nations and communities."[25] But its efforts lack both the rigor and the leadership to be considered a real initiative.[26] Looking at the websites of other UN programs—such as that of the United Nations Development Programme—charged with reducing poverty, increasing literacy, creating jobs, enhancing technical cooperation between industrialized and non-industrialized nations, and so on, one finds laudable attention paid to the scientific research underlying their efforts as well as to methodologies, metrics, and results. But on the Alliance of

Civilizations website, you will find no attention to social science or to metrics but plenty of attention to speeches and conferences.[27] Why not treat the challenge of coexistence as seriously and professionally as we treat the challenges of illiteracy and economic development?

The science brought to bear on coexistence, like the science brought to bear on illiteracy and economic development, should to a large extent be what-if science. I have made the point throughout this book that we need not only a social science of *what is* and *what has been,* but also a forward-looking social science of *what-if.* This would lead to policies, programs, and practices with the power to bring what-if to pass. Both social scientists and the policymakers who make use of their findings need to make a bold decision to step outside their current reluctance to engage in science driven by moral purpose. As we have already seen, there is no reason value-driven science cannot be pure and powerful science.

Another problem may be that the commonly used term *social cohesion* tends to imply something mutually useful—an avoidance of trouble, often because everyone's economic well-being has been so damaged by past us-and-them conflicts. Enemies look at the ruin of their own and their children's prospects and finally say, "We have had enough of fighting," meaning, "You are still our enemy, but we have had enough of fighting you." Perhaps the better concept would be *social harmony.* The musical image reminds us that well-harmonized voices and instruments are not merely *useful,* they are *beautiful,* something to be desired for its own sake. A well-harmonized community would be both useful and beautiful.

### Bold Step 4: Move from Affinity for "Us" to Allophilia for "Them"

We have a lot of data showing that diversity is problematic. Under some conditions, it can bring conflict, decrease group outputs, and make political decisions difficult or impossible. These are the data that get much of the media attention. But we have two reasons not to throw in the towel. First, there is the *fact* of diversity. It's here and it cannot be assimilated away. Second, there is the *potential* of diversity. As we saw in chapter 4, achieving that potential is a lot easier said than done. But difficult is not impossible. There are many difficult things we are still trying to do despite many years of failure. Finding a cure for Alzheimer's disease or AIDS has proven very difficult, but very few think we should simply quit. Scientists have been trying to harness the energy of nuclear fusion—not in a bomb, but rather in a stable state that generates safer and cleaner power. They have not succeeded, but neither have they all given up. And keep in mind that, in all these cases, there has been progress, but only through steady effort. The challenges of diversity are real, but the effort to understand "us *versus* them" should not crowd out a bold effort to understand "us *plus* them" and make it a reality.

One practical step for work organizations is to use affinity groups as a springboard to allophilia. Many corporate diversity initiatives, for example, include (and fund) affinity networks. Within an industry or a particular company, members of a particular group—Latinos or women or disabled people or gays and lesbians—get together to discuss and address issues that affect their particular group and to offer each other support. This is fine as far as it goes, but it does little or nothing to promote allophilia. Companies and organizations that fund affinity groups could direct that some portion of a group's funding be used to address the quality of that group's relations with *other* groups. In other words, funding would come with a requirement to build not only a stronger "us" but also a stronger "us plus them."

The same goes for college campuses. There, we can often find an African American group, a Catholic group, a Republican group, and many more. What if their funding applications included questions about how their proposed activities would not only enrich their own communities but would also connect their communities to the broader community and enrich the *entire* community? Campus centers for intercultural relations, or the campus multicultural house, do seek this end, but too often speak only to the very few who self-select by joining. For broader change, the constituent groups themselves, and not just a spanning group, need to be recruited into the work and made accountable.

Government branches and agencies of course have their own missions, but they can also be gently directed—as with the Shared Future initiative—to issue impact statements explaining how their activities would impact relations among the different communities that make up the political whole, whether county, city or nation. For example, how will a park's placement encourage its use by multiple communities? Will a highway divide some ethnic neighborhoods even as it connects others?

### Bold Step 5: Win Hearts and Minds, Not Just Bellies

The term *winning hearts and minds* has been in use at least since the 1950s, yet this indispensible approach to international relations is far from being an established strategy. As I have discussed at length elsewhere, a model of us-and-them relations that includes allophilia makes clear that winning hearts and minds is a fundamental leadership task.[28]

American allophilia for England, the "mother country," was a decisive benefit during World War II. Allophilia for America has brought an untold number of immigrants who, collectively, have made a tremendous contribution to its economic and cultural successes. But these examples show that allophilia cannot be turned on and off at need. Winning hearts and minds is therefore a crucial form of national security and a crucial diplomatic resource—something we may need and should be able to rely on at any time. Governments need to pursue it as standard operating procedure, not as one aspect of crisis management. But to do that, they need to know a lot more about how it works.

It would therefore be a bold act of leadership to support practical and interdisciplinary research on the basic processes and pathways by which hearts and minds are won, on the efficacy and ethics of government efforts to win hearts and minds, and on how to distinguish between our gut reactions to such efforts and our reasoned objections to them. Winning hearts and minds has to be done not only effectively but also responsibly. As we will see later in this chapter, an effort to win hearts and minds can easily cross the line to become propaganda—or at least be seen as propaganda—when the effort is highly centralized.

A national leader interested in making use of the positive power of difference must complement economic aid to other countries with attention to the higher-level needs of their people, such as love and belonging, esteem, and self-actualization.[29] It is important to use the emerging science on allophilia and related work to define more precisely the goals of winning hearts and minds and, in turn, to evaluate more rigorously which methods will increase affection, engagement, kinship, comfort, and enthusiasm. Gratitude for food or protection is not the same as allophilia. Focusing only on others' material interests, without also considering hearts and minds, won't even guarantee that the people we have helped won't later hate us for injuries to their self-esteem and self-actualization.

### Bold Step 6: Connect the World for Good

Is social networking leading us to a worldwide community more attentive to the collective good and more able to achieve it? That is certainly a possibility, but it is not a given. Web-enabled connectivity now crosses all gaps—ethnic, national, religious, linguistic, and socioeconomic—and every day, new uses are being found for it. So far, though, most of those uses are relatively trivial time-wasters: posting photos of parties, following celebrities' inane tweets, or letting the world know you're settling down to watch the game. But the more social science learns about the full range of possibilities for us-and-them relations, the more we can do with our ever-expanding and ever-improving information technology to bring those possibilities about.

Too many people believe that social networking technology will lead us to some positive goal or desirable end state that is inherent in the technology itself. It is leaders who must do the leading, and if one kind of leader does not offer a particular kind of leadership, other kinds of leaders will offer other kinds of leadership. Right now, the social networking technologies and applications are—despite the do-good narratives created by their company CEOs—overwhelmingly organized to prioritize profit first, and transform society *in desirable ways* second, if at all. Often, the desire to transform society in a dramatic way overshadows any desire to transform it in a socially desirable way. We like to believe the story we are being told that positive social change is somehow a by-product of commercial business developing new technologies and new apps—what I call the *Facebook fallacy*. In fact, investors—who are part of the equation from the very earliest of days of these enterprises—are looking for the greatest possible return on their investment, which is why Facebook, for all the good it might do and sometimes does do, is first and foremost a giant online billboard. When Facebook filed for an initial public offering on February 1, 2012, observers noted that "its value will be determined by whether it can leverage [users' personal data] to attract advertisers" and that it "has only just begun to scratch the surface of making money off those hundreds of millions of people getting on Facebook every day."[30] Facebook itself attributes its revenue growth to its ability to let marketers "show their ads to a subset of our users based on demographic factors . . . and specific interests that they have chosen to share with us on Facebook."[31] Whatever founder Mark Zuckerberg may have had in mind, shareholders motivated by advertising profits are about to become co-owners of the enterprise. It would be a bold step in business leadership to use this technology for serious efforts to nurture the positive power of difference.

For example, in chapter 6, I mentioned the persistent mix of pro- and anti-American attitudes around the world and how various displays of American pride can shift attitudes one way or the other. Now, let's consider how technology might be used to help public diplomacy promote allophilia for the United States—to win hearts and minds. The world faces problems such as international terrorism, climate change, nuclear proliferation, and global economic vulnerability, each requiring American involvement and benefiting from American leadership. But the United States cannot simply call the shots; it needs the engaged and willing partnerships of other countries. And as should be abundantly clear by now, stamping out anti-Americanism is not at all the same thing as nurturing engaged and willing partnerships—and is not enough.

Public diplomacy efforts could benefit from social science research, as other branches of the government—including the military—have often done. Senior leaders at the Department of State understand the importance of more effective public diplomacy, but much of their limited and decreasing Congressional funding remains tied to centralized and out-of-date pre-Internet approaches. Scientific findings on allophilia—its causes and effects—might well help the public diplomacy community to get over its own inertia and to win greater funding from Congress. There are fledgling efforts, but they are underfunded and often lack theoretical backing from social scientists.

Many of the diplomats who would theoretically be responsible for initiating and carrying out a shift in approach may not be up to the task, themselves unversed in technology. And as pointed out in chapter 4, they were not trained in us-plus-them relations. In 2003, for example, the Department of State launched *Hi* magazine, aimed at winning the hearts and minds of Middle Eastern and Muslim youth. But *Hi* magazine was a flop—publication was suspended after just two and a half years. What went wrong? *Hi* did not seem to have achieved any popularity with its intended audience, partly because it was a light and superficial effort—simply put, too lame.[32] Today, we need to reach that same audience more than ever. Can the U.S. government try again and do any better? Centralized approaches like *Hi* will probably not make much of a hit; rightly or wrongly, they will smell to many like propaganda. But we now have the social networking technology to do something much more likely to evoke deeper levels of comfort, kinship, and admiration—in essence, allophilia.

In the Internet age, citizens of countries around the globe can already engage directly, cheaply, and often enjoyably with each other. We have the hardware platforms (growing global Internet access through computers, smartphones, and other handheld devices). We have expanding software platforms (Facebook, Twitter, Skype, and others). Together they form the technology platform for connecting people by the thousands or millions—yet individually. Foreign and domestic enemies are already using Internet platforms quite effectively to spread prejudice and hatred. Instead of using the technology simply to avoid losing the battle against prejudice and hate, our public diplomacy should be using it to win hearts and minds.

It would take only modest funds to enable ordinary Americans to connect directly to people in other countries through social networking media—what I call *citizen-to-citizen diplomacy 2.0* or *C2C 2.0*. When the New York Philharmonic performed in North Korea in 2008, it was only a hundred or so musicians entertaining a very select audience. Even if broadcast to a wider North Korean audience, the concert was literally and figuratively a staged event, not likely to win many hearts and minds. In many other parts of the world, however, we could achieve a much greater effect by letting anyone with an Internet connection sit in—virtually—on local American concerts, sports events, city council meetings, school plays, and so on. Imagine an ordinary American taking a group of ordinary Saudis or Russians or Colombians on an interactive visit to the local pizza parlor, where they could chat with the staff and customers and maybe order up some pizzas to be delivered to a local senior center—a gift from some distant "friends." This is already possible, so the time to do it is now. High schools, senior centers, service clubs such as Kiwanis and the Lions, and many other organizations could be assisted, through investments from the government, to establish very enhanced pen-pal programs with their counterparts around the globe. C2C 2.0 can work because what is ordinary in one place becomes extraordinary in its ability to pique curiosity and spark allophilia somewhere else. Not every contact will be positive, but the overall picture will show the diversity and dynamism of the American people, the American landscape, and the institutions of American society. Direct experience of ordinary Americans' bona fide pride in these things will help win hearts and minds. And language need not be a barrier. Many people around the world already know English and, while real-time video translators remain on the horizon, there are already excellent text-based translators.

Going a step further (but still well this side of science fiction), imagine virtual interactive visitor centers and their potential to open up worlds their visitors may never see firsthand. Not everyone has a chance to get on a plane to visit the United States. But the United States can certainly create moveable green (e.g., solar-powered) interactive visitor centers, roughly the size of a movable modular house, that would travel around in other countries—public art kiosks of a sort. Inside, visitors could be linked interactively to kiosks in the United States so that the traveling visitor center in, say, Bolivia would become a virtual visitor center in Times Square, on the Mall in Washington, on a main street in Omaha, or on the beach in Hawaii. Webcams would show the local scene and there would be interactive access to all sorts of other views and information—and to meet American citizens who stop in a linked kiosk to say hello.

Of course, the United States needn't always be the destination. Imagine, for instance, a Lebanese Christian walking into a kiosk about the size of phone booth and being virtually transported to a Muslim neighborhood where she might never think of going in person—a neighborhood only five miles from her home. She sees the food, she hears (and maybe even joins) a conversation in a café. Where more formal argument and leadership have failed, a feat of interactive technology (not beyond what already exists) can make the case for coexistence. Such a material contribution to allophilia—and therefore peace—in the Middle East alone would be well worth the investment.

Right now, not only is information technology being used largely for frivolous purposes, but we seem to be moving toward an electronic narrowing rather than a widening of people's interest in and understanding of "others." We are seeing the increasing use of both manual and automatic filters to *eliminate* information—especially news— that conflicts with whatever a user already thinks or believes and narrows his or her exposure to other experiences and other understandings of the world. One observer has noted that features such as "If you liked . . . " on sites such as amazon.com appear to be introducing you to something new while in fact reinforcing (as well as their constantly evolving algorithms allow) what you are *already* comfortable with.[33] In a refreshing response, a website called LibraryThing offers the "UnSuggester," which takes the "If you liked . . . " premise and turns it on its head. It analyzes the 50 million books LibraryThing members have recorded as owned or read and comes back with books *least likely* to share a library with the book you suggest."[34] Imagine a search engine that knows you want Rush Limbaugh and gives him to you—but along with Ralph Nader! This service would give you what you want and enough else to *broaden* and *deepen* your perspective. Thanks to a clever use of a search algorithm, you would get a broader view of various "others."

Finally, imagine you are young person anywhere in the world who wants to learn English but has no affordable and accessible way to do so. No problem—you log onto a website and there you have a free and entertaining multimedia English language tutor. You can even connect to it through a cell phone, so you could study a bit of English while you're on the subway. Frankly, I find it shocking that American libraries struggle to find enough volunteers to teach recent immigrants English; it is so clearly in our national interest to have an excellent and globally available website available free for learning American English and, as a result, learning more about the American people. One young American, Jessica Beinecke, having become fluent in Mandarin Chinese, created her own online program called OMG! Meiyu, which means (translating both the American text lingo and the Chinese) "Oh my God! American English." Her animated presentation of American slang has been watched over 7 million times on YouTube and is followed by over 200,000 people on the Chinese equivalent of Twitter. She has a Chinese fan club of over 4,000 members.[35] It certainly appears that her lessons are an invitation to join the fun of being an American—or, in the language of allophilia, to feel comfort, kinship, and engagement with Americans—and are being taken that way by many young Chinese. This is a far cry from the ill-fated *Hi,* and the director of Voice of America seems to see the us-and-them potential: "What Jessica is doing is going to be something that I think you'll see more people doing here, which is reaching out to the younger generation in different countries and communicating with them."[36]

I'm sure anyone reading this can come up with his or her own ideas. The possibilities are limitless, and the benefits would be tremendous. Many of the same strategies could be used by other countries and could also be used to connect different religious faiths, or suburban and urban populations, or any of the many diversities that make up our world. It is particularly encouraging that there are so many things that could be done by NGOs or even by entrepreneurial—or just clever—private citizens.

There is much to be learned about how to get people to do things that are good for them and others. There has been valuable research on how to get young people to begin saving for retirement, how to get patients to follow medical instructions, how to get everyone to take better care of their own long-term health. This research could help developers, whether government or private, make allophilia-oriented apps that, ideally, people find easier to use than to avoid and that are fun to use. Since the purpose is to promote positive us-and-them attitudes, these apps should be engineered to generate feelings of affection, comfort, kinship, engagement, enthusiasm—and let's add curiosity and admiration.

Governments should certainly use their resources to carry out some of these ideas, building and maintaining allophilia as a regular vital function of foreign policy rather than as a Band-Aid response to a crisis. These techniques and others like them could be the international relations equivalent of the healthy diet and exercise that reduce the likelihood of an ambulance ride to the emergency room. All of the suggestions made in this chapter can be put into action all over the world all the time, unless banned by another government. And even then, clever citizens often find ways around the censors' firewalls as they seek to break down us-and-them walls.

## *Bold Step 7: Practice Positive Us-and-Them Religious Leadership*

Religious and spiritual leaders have an important role in nurturing the positive power of difference, but it is not the role they may typically take upon themselves. Religious leaders often call for the peace and compassion that are central to their faiths, or they are sought out by NGOs as representatives of peace and compassion. Yet religious leaders have sometimes been major contributors to hate and prejudice, either through acts of commission or omission. Religious leaders have tolerated and even fomented conflicts between Jews and Muslims in the Middle East, Orthodox Serbs and Catholic Croats in Bosnia, Catholics and Protestants in Northern Ireland, and Hindus and Muslims in India.

Religious leaders who truly want to break the cycles of hatred, segregation, and violence in their communities or countries have to do more than encourage their followers not to behave badly toward the "other." As we have seen, that is not good enough. Those leaders must positively *engage* the "other" and lead their followers to do the same. The brotherly love needs to extend out from the congregation—but not too far out. Many faith leaders encourage understanding and kindness for all humanity or rally their followers to the aid of a distant "other" suffering some disaster, but neither are those enough. The understanding, kindness, and willingness to help must extend, in word and deed, very specifically to those "others" that a particular faith community does not currently love but with whom it does currently share a neighborhood or a country. A new generation of leaders seems to be putting the interfaith message front and center. The Interfaith Youth Core [*sic*] (IFYC), for example, offers a fairly universalist message—"What if people of all faiths and traditions worked together to promote the common good for all?"—but its members are expected to do this through engagement with and service to specific others.[37] This can mean standing up for an "other" that is under attack. When Fred Phelps—whom we met at the beginning of this chapter—arrived to picket on Stanford's campus, a Hindu member of IFYC helped organize a campuswide response, particularly in support of Stanford's gay and lesbian community—the usual objects of Phelps's hatred—and the Jewish community, since Phelps had been expected to stage his picket near the campus Hillel.[38]

Many political and other secular leaders will also need to move outside their usual style of leadership. In addition to invoking their own faith to mobilize voters, they will need to work with—and sometimes through—religious communities to nurture allophilia in their civil communities. In doing so, they cannot simply defer to religious leaders in matters of religious "us plus them." To the extent that they look to religious leaders for help and provide those leaders with platforms and resources, they must also hold them accountable for making concrete contributions across faiths, not just within their own faith communities.

Some of the bravest steps in interfaith leadership will have to be taken by followers. They will have to demand that their leaders do not demonize the "other" and, perhaps more importantly, that their leaders do not treat the "other" as simply an "other"—a group of people not to be hated but not to be engaged all that much, either. Followers like this will demand that their leaders show active respect toward the "other" because they themselves are curious about and willing to engage this "other," even while staying faithful to their own group and religion. In short, it might be the followers who lead their leaders toward what the followers want. This may already be happening in the United States, as some religious and political leaders seem to be realizing that their congregants and constituents are no longer interested in treating the members of other religious groups or the agnostics and the atheists in their communities as outgroups, but rather as nothing less than fellow citizens and brothers and sisters. Karol Wojtyla, the future Pope John Paul II, grew up in a Poland in which Catholic leaders encouraged their parishioners to boycott Jewish businesses. A Jewish friend recalled Wojtyla denouncing his own religious leaders' prejudice even as a young man, and he not only denounced anti-Semitism but worked to counteract it when he became a powerful religious leader himself.[39]

Rabbi Jonathan Sacks's book, *The Dignity of Differences*—a response to Samuel Huntington's article, "The Clash of Civilizations?"—comes close to recognizing the allophilia dimension in interfaith relations. Sacks asks, "Can we hear the voice of G-d in a language, a sensibility, a culture not our own?" Surely hearing the voice of G-d in another group's faith and practices would include some affection, comfort, kinship, engagement, and enthusiasm for that group. Sacks also recognizes the need for us-and-them leadership. He reasons, "If religion is not part of a solution, it will certainly be part of the problem."[40] I disagree with him strongly, however, when he poses coexistence as simply a moral question. If we are to realize our full social potential, the question is not simply, "Can we live together?" (that is, can we reconcile our moral codes to allow, if not require, the positive engagement of the "other"?)—the question addressed by Sacks—but *How* can we live together?" This second question is actually a set of scientific questions, such as, "In what conditions are we inclined to want to live together?" "Who among us are most willing to live together?" "What makes those people tick?" My argument is that, in a world of globalization and increasing contact with "others," we should be interested in coexistence not only as a moral possibility and a moral good, but also as a practical, everyday, secular problem that can be tackled by taking not only our theology but our social science in new directions.

## Us Plus Them: The Natural Needs to Be Nurtured

As each incremental us-plus-them win becomes part of our social infrastructure, we will also need scientifically grounded methods of maintaining it. In the United States, we are in a painful process of learning that the social infrastructure (such as primary school education and primary health care) can no more maintain itself without investment than the physical infrastructure (such as bridges and roads) can. Positive difference, too, requires maintenance and continual investment. For one thing, the mix of groups is certain to change over time. New groups will arrive or arise who are not part of the common "us"; distinct new bonds of allophilia will have to be forged. Such maintenance, like the maintenance of physical and social infrastructure, actually requires bold leadership, if only because maintenance is typically so unexciting and easy to neglect.

The Cordoba caliphate in Spain (929–1031 CE) is often invoked as a golden age of religious tolerance. As one journalist summarized it,

"Once upon a time long ago in a place on the edge of the known world, Muslims, Jews, and Christians lived together in peace and created a vibrant, extraordinary civilization."[41] Cordoba was both an economic success and an intellectual center where there was not only tolerance but eager exchange between different religious and cultural groups. This society was partly a result of historical happenstance, but it was also a deliberate creation. It was not perfect; there was still discrimination and worse. Nor, in the end, could it survive merely on its own goodness. As early as 976, tolerance began to decline under a fading Cordoba caliphate and then under other Muslim regimes, coming to an end altogether under Catholic rule. In 1492, Jews were forced either to convert to Roman Catholicism or leave Spain, and in 1501, Muslims were forced into the same choice. The Spanish Inquisition would follow.

From this extraordinary episode of history, we can learn something about what sort of us-and-them relations are possible, but also something about how much they depend on context and on the continuous efforts of leaders willing to keep leading *toward,* who understand that positive us-and-them relations are always natural—they are part of our human repertoire—but always need to be nurtured. It is important for a school to respond to a hate crime, for a company to recruit and develop minority managers, for a government to attempt healing after a civil war. But it is in some ways a bolder step to devote resources and high-level attention to maintaining those gains and building on them day in and day out, remaining committed to reaching the positive and not just escaping the negative, even when no one is paying that much attention and there is not much glory to be earned.

## Our Next Turn

As the world gets smaller, we lose the chance to coexist by virtue of sheer separation. But as the science of relations between groups moves ahead, it offers us more realistic assurances than we have ever had that the incredible diversity of modern societies can be a boon rather than a ticking time bomb. As new, more positive forms of social relations are studied and promoted, hate will not disappear. But it will cede its undeserved place at the center of how we think about us-and-them relations and how we try to shape them.

What does it require to get there?

Turning.

Turning from looking back to looking forward.

Turning from the task of understanding hate and how it can be reduced to the task of understanding affection, comfort, kinship, engagement, and enthusiasm and how they can be nurtured.

Practicing the heroism of turning an enemy into a friend.

Turning from what went wrong in the past and why to what we can do much better in the future and how.

Turning to science to understand a wider range of possibilities for different groups to live and work together and turning to scientifically founded policies, practices, and programs with the power to revolutionize not only how well we live but how well we live together.

# NOTES

## Chapter One

1. I originally wrote this sentence as: "You're not like me, but what fun it is!"—as if the two should be expected to be mutually exclusive, a perhaps telling example of the persistence with which difference is equated with negativity. This was a potent reminder to me of the power of any juxtaposition of "us" and "them" to suggest negativity and conflict.

2. Al Lewis, "Just Shut Up and Do Your Job," *Denver Post,* December 2, 2007, http://www.denverpost.com/business/ci_7606898?source=bb.

3. In 2007, the EU Centre on Monitoring Xenophobia and Racism was renamed the European Union Agency for Fundamental Rights and given an expanded scope.

4. http://www.ofmdfmni.gov.uk/index/equality/community-relations/a-shared-future-strategy.htm.

5. See Todd L. Pittinsky and Stefanie Simon, "Intergroup Leadership," *Leadership Quarterly* 18, no. 6 (2007): 586–605.

6. Organization for Security and Co-Operation, http://www.osce.org/hcnm.

7. See for example, Rush Dozier, *Why We Hate* (New York: McGraw-Hill, 2003); Jack Levin and Gordana Rabrenovic, *Why We Hate* (New York: Prometheus Books, 2004); Aaron T. Beck, *Prisoners of Hate: The Cognitive Basis of Anger, Hostility, and Violence* (New York: Harper Perennial, 2000); C. V. Murali, *Prisoners of Hate* (New Delhi, India: Pustak Mahal, 2010); Yehezkel Hameiri, *Prisoners of Hate: The Story of Israelis in Syrian Jails* (Jerusalem: Transaction Publishers, 1969); Neil Kressel, *Mass Hate: The Global Rise of Genocide and Terror* (Boulder, CO: Westview Press, 2002); Bob Harris, *Who Hates Whom: Well-Armed Fanatics, Intractable Conflicts, and Various Things Blowing Up: A Woefully Incomplete Guide* (New York: Three Rivers Press, 2007); Philip Perlmutter, *Legacy of Hate: A Short History of Ethnic, Religious, and Racial Prejudice in America* (New York: M.E. Sharpe Inc., 1999); Jack Levin and Jack McDevitt, *Hate Crimes Revisited: America's War Against Those Who Are Different* (New York: Basic Books, 2002); Caryl Stern-LaRosa and Ellen Hofheimer Bettmann, *Hate Hurts: How Children Learn and Unlearn Prejudice* (New York: Scholastic Inc., 2000).

8. See, for example, Stephen C. Wright et al., "The Extended Contact Effect: Knowledge of Cross-Group Friendships and Prejudice," *Journal of Personality and Social Psychology* 73 (1997): 73–90; Gordon Allport, *The Nature of Prejudice*

(Cambridge, MA: Addison-Wesley, 1954); and Thomas Pettigrew and Linda Tropp, "A Meta-analytic Test of Intergroup Contact Theory," *Journal of Personality and Social Psychology* 90, no. 5 (2006): 751–783.

9. Philip Rose, *You Can't Do That on Broadway! A Raisin in the Sun and Other Theatrical Improbabilities* (New York: Proscenium Publishers, 2001).

10. Johnny Otis, *Listen to the Lambs* (Minneapolis: University of Minnesota Press, 2009), xl.

11. Irwin Katz and R. Glen Hass, "Racial Ambivalence and American Value Conflict: Correlational and Priming Studies of Dual Cognitive Structures," *Journal of Personality and Society Psychology* 55, no. 6 (1988): 893–905.

12. John J. Woodmansee and Stuart W. Cook, "Dimensions of Verbal Racial Attitude: Their Identification and Measurement," *Journal of Personality and Social Psychology* 7 (1967): 240–250.

13. Alexander M. Czopp and Margo J. Monteith, "Thinking Well of African Americans: Measuring Complimentary Stereotypes and Negative Prejudice," *Basic and Applied Social Psychology* 28, no. 3 (2006): 233–250.

14. Jennifer Fehr and Kai Sassenberg, "Willing and Able: How Internal Motivation Can Help to Overcome Prejudice" (poster presented at the European Association of Experimental Social Psychology, 15th General Meeting, Opatija, Croatia, June 2008).

15. Allport, *The Nature of Prejudice,* 425–426.

16. Samuel Huntington, "The Clash of Civilizations," *Foreign Affairs* 72, no. 3 (1993): 25.

17. Ibid., 22–49.

18. http://bangordailynews.com/2009/05/13/politics/census-maine-oldest-whitest-state-in-nation/.

19. Katie Zezima, "A Lone Man's Stunt Raises Broader Issues," *New York Times,* September 5, 2006, http://www.nytimes.com/2006/09/05/us/05maine.html?_r=2&ref=us&oref; Pam Belluck, "Mixed Welcome as Somalis Settle in a Maine City," *New York Times,* October 16, 2002, http://www.nytimes.com/learning/teachers/featured_articles/20021016wednesday.html.

20. Susan Taylor Martin, "A Collision of Cultures Leads to Building Bridges in Maine," *St. Petersburg* (Florida) *Times,* March 13, 2005, http://www.sptimes.com/2005/03/13/Worldandnation/A_collision_of_cultur.shtml.

21. Martin Luther King Jr., "Beyond Vietnam: A Time to Break Silence," speech delivered on April 4, 1967, at a meeting of Clergy and Laity Concerned at Riverside Church in New York City.

22. James Tobin, *Essays in Economics* (Cambridge, MA: MIT Press, 1982).

23. *Linguistic groups:* Bernd Heine and Derek Nurse, "Introduction," in *African Languages: An Introduction,* ed. Bernd Heine and Derek Nurse (Cambridge, UK: Cambridge University Press, 2000), 1–10; *ethnic groups:* Jeff Blair, "Ethnic and National Identity in Africa," World Affairs Council and FIUTS, accessed September 12, 2010, http://www.world-affairs.org/globalclassroom/curriculum/EthnicNational IdentityInAfrica.pdf.

24. Patricia G. Devine and Kristin A. Vasquez, "The Rocky Road to Positive Inter-group Relations," in *Confronting Racism: The Problem and the Response,* ed. Jennifer L. Eberhardt and Susan T. Fiske (Thousand Oaks, CA: Sage Publications, Inc., 1998).

25. "Prejudice, Everyday Bigotry and Hate Crimes Are Target of NCBI Training at USF," *University of South Florida News,* March 26, 2008, http://news.usf.edu/article/templates/?a=601.

## Chapter Two

1. "Why Do Turkish People Hate Arab [*sic*]?" website, http://answers.yahoo.com/question/index?qid=20070713044155AAZoi2j.

2. Todd L. Pittinsky, Jennifer J. Ratcliff, and Laura A. Maruskin, *Coexistence in Israel: A National Study* (Cambridge, MA: Harvard Kennedy School, Center for Public Leadership, 2008).

3. Ibid.

4. Hand in Hand website, http://www.handinhandk12.org.

5. Tania Tam et al., "The Mediational Role of Intergroup Emotions and Empathy in Contact Between Catholics and Protestants in Northern Ireland" (unpublished manuscript).

6. Owen Hargie and David Dickson, "Putting It All Together: Central Themes from Researching the Troubles," in *Researching the Troubles: Social Science Perspectives on the Northern Ireland Conflict* (Edinburgh: Mainstream Press, 2003), 289–306.

7. Bernadette C. Hayes, Ian McAllister, and Lizanne Dowds, "In Search of the Middle Ground: Integrated Education and Northern Ireland Politics," *Research Update* no. 42 (January 2006), http://www.ark.ac.uk/publications/updates/update 42.pdf.

8. Kate Hairsine, "Munich Exhibition Uncovers Europe's Historical Fascination with the Orient," *Deutsche Welle* (English ed.) online, January 2, 2011, http://www.dw.de/dw/article/0,,6424448,00.html.

9. Ibid.

10. Roland Kelts, *Japanamerica: How Japanese Pop Culture Has Invaded the US* (New York: Palgrave Macmillan, 2006).

11. Bruce Clarke, *Twice a Stranger: The Mass Expulsions That Forged Modern Greece and Turkey* (Cambridge, MA: Harvard University Press, 2006).

12. Elisa Tamarkin, *Anglophilia: Deference, Devotion, and Antebellum America* (Chicago: University of Chicago Press, 2008).

13. Gordon Allport, *The Nature of Prejudice* (Cambridge, MA: Addison-Wesley, 1954), 42.

14. Teaching Tolerance, http://www.tolerance.org/about.

15. "Unhate," Benetton website, http://unhate.benetton.com/foundation/.

16. John T. Cacioppo and Gary G. Berntson, "Relationship Between Attitudes and Evaluative Space: A Critical Review, with Emphasis on the Separability of Positive and Negative Substrates," *Psychological Review* 115, no. 3 (1994): 401–423; Gregory A. Bigley and Jone L. Pearce, "Straining for Shared Meaning in Organization Science: Problems of Trust and Distrust," *Academy of Management Review* 23, no. 3 (1998): 393–404.

17. Nehemiah Jordan, "The Asymmetry of 'Liking' and 'Disliking,'" *Public Opinion Quarterly* 29 (Summer 1965): 315–325.

18. Barbara L. Fredrickson, "The Role of Positive Emotions in Positive Psychology: The Broaden-and-Build Theory of Positive Emotions," *American Psychologist* 56, no. 3 (2001): 218–226; Barbara L. Fredrickson, "What Good Are Positive Emotions?" *Review of General Psychology* 2, no. 3 (1998): 300–319.

19. See, for example, Peter Salovey et al., "Emotional States and Physical Health," *American Psychologist* 55, no. 1 (2000): 110–121; Jeremy W. Pettit et al., "Are Happier People Healthier? The Specific Role of Positive Affect in Predicting Self-Reported Health Symptoms," *Journal of Research in Personality* 35 (2001): 521–536; Deborah D. Danner, David A. Snowdon, and Wallace V. Friesen, "Positive Emotion in Early Life and Longevity: Findings from the Nun Study," *Journal of Personality and Social Psychology* 80 (2001): 804–813; LeeAnne Harker and Dacher Keltner, "Expressions of Positive Emotion in Women's College Yearbook Pictures and Their Relationship to Personality and Life Outcomes Across Adulthood," *Journal of Personality and Social Psychology* 80, no. 1 (2001): 112–124.

20. Vincent Nowlis and Helen H. Nowlis, "The Description and Analysis of Mood," *Annals of the New York Academy of Sciences* 65, no. 4 (1956): 345–355; Uli Schimmack, "Response Latencies of Pleasure and Displeasure Ratings: Further Evidence for Mixed Feelings," *Cognition and Emotion* 19, no. 5 (2005): 671–691.

21. Janet W. Schofield, "School Desegregation and Intergroup Relations: A Review of the Research," *Review of Research in Education* 17 (1991): 335–409.

22. Ibid.

23. Martin Patchen, Gerhard Hofmann, and James D. Davidson, "Interracial Perceptions Among High School Students," *Sociometry* 39, no 4 (1976): 341–354.

24. Cacioppo and Berntson, "Relationship Between Attitudes and Evaluative Space."

25. Miriam J. Rodin, "Liking and Disliking: Sketch of an Alternative View," *Journal of Personality and Social Psychology* 4, no. 3 (1978): 473–478.

26. John T. Cacioppo, Wendi L. Gardner, and Gary G. Berntson, "Beyond Bipolar Conceptualizations and Measures: The Case of Attitudes and Evaluative Space," *Personality and Social Psychology Review* 1, no. 1 (1997): 3–25; Charles E. Osgood, George J. Suci, and Percy H. Tannenbaum, *The Measurement of Meaning* (Urbana, IL: University of Illinois Press, 1957); Russel F. Green and Marvin R. Goldfried, "On the Bipolarity of Semantic Space," *Psychological Monographs: General and Applied* 79, no. 6 (1965): 1–31; Jordan, "The Asymmetry of 'Liking' and 'Disliking.'" In the realm of us-and-them relations, see Todd L. Pittinsky, Seth A. Rosenthal, and R. Matthew Montoya, "Liking Is Not the Opposite of Disliking: The Functional Separability of Positive and Negative Attitudes Toward Minority Groups," *Cultural Diversity and Ethnic Minority Psychology* 17, no. 2 (April 2011): 134–143; Colin Ho and Jay W. Jackson, "Attitudes Towards Asian Americans: Theory and Measurement," *Journal of Applied Social Psychology* 31, no. 8 (2001): 1553–1581; Tam et al., "The Mediational Role."

27. Pittinsky, Rosenthal, and Montoya, "Liking Is Not the Opposite of Disliking"; Todd L. Pittinsky, Seth A. Rosenthal, and R. Matthew Montoya, "Measuring Positive Attitudes Toward Outgroups: Development and Validation of the Allophilia Scale," in *Moving Beyond Prejudice Reduction: Pathways to Positive Intergroup Relations,*

Notes 211

ed. Linda Tropp and Robyn Mallett (Washington, DC: American Psychological Association, 2011), 41–60.

28. Kurt Lewin, *Field Theory in Social Science: Selected Theoretical Papers*, ed. Dorwin Cartwright (New York: Harper & Row, 1951).

29. Tam et al., "The Mediational Role."

30. Pittinsky, Rosenthal, and Montoya, "Liking Is Not the Opposite of Disliking."

31. Ibid.

32. Ibid.

33. Todd L. Pittinsky and R. Matthew Montoya, "Is Valuing Equality Enough? Equality Values, Allophilia, and Social Policy Support for Multiracial Individuals," *Journal of Social Issues* 65, no. 1 (2009): 151–163.

34. David A. Thomas, "The Truth About Mentoring Minorities: Race Matters," *Harvard Business Review*, April 2001, 99–107.

35. Pittinsky and Montoya, "Is Valuing Equality Enough?"

36. Pittinsky, Rosenthal, and Montoya, "Measuring Positive Attitudes."

37. These examples were first presented in Todd L. Pittinsky, Laura M. Bacon, and Loren Gary, "Beyond Tolerance," *Tikkun*, March–April 2007, 31–35.

38. DeWayne Wickham, *Bill Clinton and Black America* (New York: Ballantine Books, 2002).

39. Ibid., 71.

40. Ibid., 52.

41. Ibid., 40.

42. Toni Morrison, "Clinton as the First Black President," *New Yorker*, October 1998.

43. For an example of research on universal orientations, see Stephen T. Phillips and Robert C. Ziller, "Toward a Theory and Measure of the Nature of Non-Prejudice," *Journal of Personality and Social Psychology* 72, no. 2 (February 1997): 420–434; for an example of research on the altruistic personality, see Gustavo Carlo et al., "The Altruistic Personality: In What Contexts Is It Apparent?" *Journal of Personality and Social Psychology* 61, no. 3 (1991): 450–458; Pittinsky, Rosenthal, and Montoya, "Liking Is Not the Opposite of Disliking."

44. Hélène Mulholland and Nicholas Watt, "David Cameron Defends Plans for Well-being Index," *The Guardian*, November 25, 2010, http://www.guardian.co.uk/politics/2010/nov/25/david-cameron-defends-wellbeing-index.

45. Pittinsky, Rosenthal, and Montoya, "Measuring Positive Attitudes."

46. S. Alfieri and E. Marta, "Positive Attitudes Toward the Outgroup: Adaptation and Validation of the Allophilia Scale," *Testing, Psychometrics, Methodology in Applied Psychology* 18, no. 2 (2011): 99–116.

47. Ibid.

## Chapter Three

1. Barbara Bradley Hagerty, "New College Teaches Young American Muslims," *Morning Edition*, National Public Radio, September 8, 2010.

2. "Value of Diversity Training Tough to Measure," *Talk of the Nation*, National Public Radio, March 9, 2010, http://www.npr.org/templates/story/story.php?storyId=124495770.

3. Bernadette Park and Charles M. Judd, "Rethinking the Link Between Categorization and Prejudice Within the Social Cognition Perspective," *Personality and Social Psychology Review* 9, no. 2 (2005): 108–130.

4. Ibid.

5. Anthony G. Greenwald, Debbie E. McGhee, and Jordan L. K. Schwartz, "Measuring Individual Differences in Implicit Cognition: The Implicit Association Test," *Journal of Personality and Social Psychology* 74, no. 6 (1998): 1464–1480.

6. *Project Implicit,* https://implicit.harvard.edu/implicit/.

7. "Left for Dead: The Gay Man Who Befriended His Attacker," *The Oprah Winfrey Show,* January 1, 2006.

8. Jesse Erwin, "The IAT: How and When It Works," *Observer* 20, no. 11 (2007), http://www.psychologicalscience.org/observer/getArticle.cfm?id=2270.

9. Ibid.

10. Hart Blanton et al., "Strong Claims and Weak Evidence: Reassessing the Predictive Validity of the Race IAT," *Journal of Applied Psychology* 94, no. 3 (2009): 567–582.

11. Chris Berdik, "Invisible Bias," *Boston Globe,* December 19, 2004.

12. Brian A. Nosek et al., "Pervasiveness and Correlates of Implicit Attitudes and Stereotypes," *European Review of Social Psychology* 18, no. 1 (2007): 36–88.

13. Jaihyun Park, Karla Felix, and Grace Lee, "Implicit Attitudes Toward Arab Muslims and the Moderating Effects of Social Information," *Basic and Applied Social Psychology* 29, no. 1 (2007): 35–45.

14. Research results from ibid.

15. Robert F. Bornstein, "Exposure and Affect: Overview and Meta-analysis of Research, 1968–1987," *Psychological Bulletin* 106, no 2. (1989): 265–289; Robert Zajonc, "The Attitudinal Effects of Mere Exposure," *Journal of Personality and Social Psychology* 9, no. 2 (1968): 1–27.

16. Nilanjana Dasgupta and Anthony G. Greenwald, "On the Malleability of Automatic Attitudes: Combating Automatic Prejudice with Images of Admired and Disliked Individuals," *Journal of Personality and Social Psychology* 81, no. 5 (2001): 800–814.

17. Andrew Karpinski and James L. Hilton, "Attitudes and the Implicit Association Test," *Journal of Personality and Social Psychology* 81, no. 5 (2001): 774–788.

18. Sarah F. Brosnan and Frans B. M. de Waal, "Monkeys Reject Unequal Pay," *Nature* 425 (2003): 297–299.

19. Robert M. Sapolsky, "Peace Among Primates," *Greater Good,* Fall 2007, http://greatergood.berkeley.edu/article/item/peace_among_primates.

20. Ibid.

21. John T. Jost, "Outgroup Favoritism and the Theory of System Justification: An Experimental Paradigm for Investigating the Effects of Socio-Economic Success on Stereotype Content," in *Cognitive Social Psychology: The Princeton Symposium on the Legacy and Future of Social Cognition,* ed. Gordon B. Moskowitz (Mahwah, NJ: Erlbaum, 2001), 89–102.

22. John J. Woodmansee and Stuart W. Cook, "Dimensions of Verbal Racial Attitude: Their Identification and Measurement," *Journal of Personality and Social Psychology* 7 (1967): 240–250.

23. Susan T. Fiske et al., "A Model of (Often Mixed) Stereotype Content: Competence and Warmth Respectively Follow from Status and Competition," *Journal of Personality and Social Psychology* 82, no. 6 (2002): 878–902; Amy J. C. Cuddy, Susan T. Fiske, and Peter Glick, "The BIAS Map: Behaviors from Intergroup Affect and Stereotypes," *Journal of Personality and Social Psychology* 92, no. 4 (2007): 631–648.

24. Fiske et al., "A Model of (Often Mixed) Stereotype Content"; Amy J. C. Cuddy, Michael I. Norton, and Susan T. Fiske, "This Old Stereotype: The Stubbornness and Pervasiveness of the Elderly Stereotype," *Journal of Social Issues* 61, no. 2 (2005): 265–283.

25. Cuddy, Fiske, and Glick, "The BIAS Map."

26. Findings for these groups in, respectively, Cuddy, Norton, and Fiske, "This Old Stereotype"; Monica H. Lin, Virginia S. Y. Kwan, Anna Cheung, and Susan T. Fiske, "Stereotype Content Model Explains Prejudice for an Envied Outgroup: Scale of Anti-Asian American Stereotypes," *Personality and Social Psychology Bulletin* 31, no. 1 (2005): 34–47; and Peter Glick, "Sacrificial Lambs Dressed in Wolves' Clothing: Envious Prejudice, Ideology, and the Scapegoating of Jews," in *Understanding Genocide: The Social Psychology of the Holocaust,* ed. Leonard S. Newman and Ralph Erber (Oxford/New York: Oxford University Press, 2002), 113–142.

27. Susan T. Fiske, Jun Xu, Amy C. Cuddy and Peter Glick, "(Dis)Respecting Versus (Dis)Liking: Status and Interdependence Predict Ambivalent Stereotypes of Competence and Warmth," *Journal of Social Issues* 55, no. 3 (1999): 473–489.

28. Mark Gerzon, "Reaching Across the Aisle: Innovations for Cross-Party Cultural Collaboration" in *Crossing the Divide: Intergroup Leadership in a World of Difference,* ed. Todd L. Pittinsky (Boston: Harvard Business School Press, 2009), 203–218.

29. James D. Fearon and David D. Laitin, "Explaining Interethnic Co-Operation," *American Political Science Review* 90, no. 4 (1996): 715–735.

30. Henri Tajfel et al., "Social Categorization and Intergroup Behaviour," *European Journal of Social Psychology* 1, no. 2 (1971): 149–178.

31. Henri Tajfel and John C. Turner, "An Integrative Theory of Intergroup Conflict," in *The Social Psychology of Intergroup Relations,* ed. S. Worchel and W. G. Austin (Monterey, CA: Brooks-Cole, 1979), 33–47.

32. Murray Horwitz and Jacob M. Rabbie, "Individuality and Membership in the Intergroup System," in *Social Identity and Intergroup Relations,* ed. Henri Tajfel (Cambridge, UK: Cambridge University Press, 1982), 241–274; Henri Tajfel, "Experiments in Intergroup Discrimination," *Scientific American* 223, no. 5 (1970): 96–102; Tim Wildschut, Chester A. Insko, and Lowell Gaertner, "Intragroup Social Influence and Intergroup Competition," *Journal of Personality and Social Psychology* 82, no. 6 (2002): 975–992.

33. Horwitz and Rabbie, "Individuality and Membership in the Intergroup System"; Jacob M. Rabbie and Hein F. M. Lodewijkx, "Conflict and Aggression: An Individual-Group Continuum," in *Advances in Group Processes,* vol. 11, ed. B. Markovsky, J. O'Brien, and K. Heimer (Greenwich, CT: JAI Press, 1994): 139–174.

34. R. M. Montoya and T. L. Pittinsky, "The Norm of Group Interest and Adherence to Group Norms," *Group Processes & Intergroup Relations,* invited revision.

35. R. Matthew Montoya and Todd L. Pittinsky, "The Norm of Group Interest and Attitudes in the Intergroup Context," unpublished manuscript.

36. Amélie Mummendey and Sabine Otten, "Positive-Negative Asymmetry in Social Discrimination," *European Review of Social Psychology* 9 (1998): 107–143.

37. Marilynn Brewer, "The Psychology of Prejudice: Ingroup Love or Outgroup Hate?" *Journal of Social Issues* 55, no. 3 (1999): 430–444.

38. Sigmund Freud, *Group Psychology and the Analysis of the Ego* (London: Hogarth Press, 1921); Muzafer Sherif et al., *Intergroup Conflict and Cooperation: The Robbers Cave Experiment* (Norman, OK: University of Oklahoma Book Exchange, 1961); John Thibaut, "An Experimental Study of the Cohesiveness of Underprivileged Groups," *Human Relations* 3, no. 3 (1950): 251–278; Albert Pepitone and Robert Kleiner, "The Effects of Threat and Frustration on Group Cohesiveness," *Journal of Abnormal Social Psychology* 54, no. 2 (1957): 192–199.

39. Steve Hinkle and Rupert Brown, "Intergroup Comparisons and Social Identity: Some Links and Lacunae," in *Social Identity Theory: Constructive and Critical Advances*, ed. Dominic Abrams and Michael A. Hogg (New York: Springer, 1990), 48–70.

40. James L. Gibson, "Do Strong Group Identities Fuel Intolerance? Evidence from the South African Case," *Political Psychology* 27, no. 5 (2006): 665–705.

41. Montoya and Pittinsky, "The Norm of Group Interest and Adherence to Group Norms."

42. Darren Davis and Ronald Brown, "The Antipathy of Black Nationalism: Behavioral and Attitudinal Implications of an African-American Ideology," *American Journal of Political Science* 46, no. 2 (2002): 239–252; James Sidanius et al., "Ethnic Enclaves and the Dynamics of Social Identity on the College Campus: The Good, the Bad, and the Ugly," *Journal of Personality and Social Psychology* 87, no. 1 (2004): 96–110.

43. Elizabeth Cashdan, "Ethnocentrism and Xenophobia: A Cross-Cultural Study," *Current Anthropology* 42, no. 5 (2001): 760–764.

44. Daniel M. Posner, "The Political Salience of Cultural Difference: Why Chewas and Tumbukas Are Allies in Zambia and Adversaries in Malawi," *American Political Science Review* 98, no. 4 (November 2004): 529–545.

45. For the opposing view—that cultural differences are at the root of many of the world's conflicts—see Samuel P. Huntington, "The Clash of Civilizations?" *Foreign Affairs* 72, no. 3 (1993): 22–49; Ted R. Gurr, *Peoples Versus States: Minorities at Risk in the New Century* (Washington, DC: United States Institute of Peace, 2000); Donald Horowitz, *Ethnic Groups in Conflict* (Berkeley/Los Angeles: University of California Press, 1985); Donald Horowitz, *The Deadly Ethnic Riot* (Berkeley/Los Angeles: University of California Press, 2001); Samuel P. Huntington, *Political Order in Changing Societies* (New Haven, CT: Yale University Press, 1968).

46. Steven Erlanger, "In Gaza, Hamas's Insults to Jews Complicate Peace," *New York Times,* April 1, 2008, http://www.nytimes.com/2008/04/01/world/middleeast/01hamas.html.

47. Po Bronson and Ashley Merryman, "See Baby Discriminate," *Newsweek,* September 5, 2009, http://www.newsweek.com/2009/09/04/see-baby-discriminate.html.

48. Solomon Asch, "Studies of Independence and Conformity: A Minority of One Against a Unanimous Majority," *Psychological Monographs* 70, no. 9 (1956): 1–70.

49. Ian Dishart Suttie, *The Origins of Love and Hate* (London: Free Association Books, 1935; repr. 1988).

50. *Ambivalent racism:* Irwin Katz, Joyce Wackenhut, and R. Glen Hass, "Racial Ambivalence, Value Duality, and Behavior," in *Prejudice Discrimination and Racism: Theory and Research,* ed. John F. Dovidio and Samuel L. Gaertner (New York: Academic Press, 1986); *aversive racism:* Joel Kovel, *White Racism: A Psychohistory* (New York: Random House, 1970); *symbolic racism:* D. O. Sears, "Symbolic Racism," in *Eliminating Racism: Profiles in Controversy,* ed. Phyllis Katz and Dalmas A. Taylor (New York: Plenum Press, 1988); *modern racism:* John B. McConahay, "Modern Racism, Ambivalence, and the Modern Racism Scale," in *Prejudice, Discrimination, and Racism,* ed. John F. Dovidio and Samuel L. Gaertner (New York: Academic Press, 1986); *racial resentment:* Donald R. Kinder and Lynn M. Sanders, *Divided by Color* (Chicago: University of Chicago Press, 1996); *implicit racism:* this is a commonly used name for findings from implicit association tests (IATs); see, for example, the use of the term in the *Wikipedia* entry for the Implicit Association Test: http://en.wikipedia.org/wiki/Implicit_Association_Test.

## Chapter Four

1. Marlene Mackie, "Arriving at 'Truth' by Definition: The Case of Stereotype Inaccuracy," *Social Problems* 20, no. 4 (1973): 431–447.

2. Marc Macey, "A Decade After Massacres, Rwanda Outlaws Ethnicity," *New York Times,* April 9, 2004.

3. Debbe Kennedy, "How to Put Our Differences to Work," *Leader to Leader,* no. 52 (Spring 2009): 49–55.

4. Alice M. Isen, "Toward Understanding the Role of Affect in Cognition," in *Handbook of Social Cognition,* ed. Robert S. Wyer Jr. and Thomas K. Srull (Hillsdale, NJ: Lawrence Erlbaum Associates, 1984), 174–236; Alice M. Isen, "A Role for Neuropsychology in Understanding the Facilitating Influence of Positive Affect on Social Behavior and Cognitive Processes," chap. 38 in *Handbook of Positive Psychology,* ed. C. R. Snyder and Shane J. Lopez (Oxford/New York: Oxford University Press, 2002), 528–540; Barbara L. Fredrickson, "The Value of Positive Emotions," *American Scientist* 91, no. 4 (2003): 330–335; Barbara Fredrickson and Thomas Joiner, "Positive Emotions Trigger Upward Spirals Toward Emotional Well-Being," *Psychological Science* 13, no. 2 (2002): 172–175.

5. Lee Jussim et al., "Prejudice, Stereotypes, and Labeling Effects: Sources of Bias in Person Perception," *Journal of Personality and Social Psychology* 68, no. 2 (1995): 228–246.

6. Todd L. Pittinsky, Seth A. Rosenthal, and R. Matthew Montoya, "Liking Is Not the Opposite of Disliking: The Functional Separability of Positive and Negative Attitudes Toward Minority Groups," *Cultural Diversity and Ethnic Minority Psychology* 17, no. 2 (April 2011): 134–143; Todd L. Pittinsky, Seth A. Rosenthal, and R. Matthew Montoya, "Measuring Positive Attitudes Toward Outgroups: Development and Validation of the Allophilia Scale," in *Moving Beyond Prejudice Reduction: Pathways to Positive Intergroup Relations,* ed. Linda Tropp and Robyn Mallett (Washington, DC: American Psychological Association, 2011), 41–60.

7. Barnaby Rogerson, "Fighters for the Family," review of *Levant: Splendour and Catastrophe on the Mediterranean,* by Philip Mansel, *Times Literary Supplement,* April 29, 2011, 7.

8. For one example of a common practice, see Glenn S. Pate, "Research on Prejudice Education," *Educational Leadership* 38, no. 4 (1981): 288–291.

9. Elizabeth Levy Paluck, "Diversity Training and Intergroup Contact: A Call to Action Research," *Journal of Social Issues* 62, no. 3 (2006): 439–451; Elizabeth L. Paluck and Donald P. Green, "Prejudice Reduction: What Works? A Critical Look at Evidence from the Field and the Laboratory," *Annual Review of Psychology* 60 (2009): 339–367; Walter G. Stephan and Cookie White Stephan, *Improving Intergroup Relations* (Thousand Oaks, CA: Sage Publications, 2001); Carolyn Wiethoff, "Motivation to Learn and Diversity Training: Application of the Theory of Planned Behavior," *Human Resource Development Quarterly* 15, no. 3 (2004): 263–278.

10. Cindy Lindsay, "Things That Go Wrong in Diversity Training: Conceptualization and Change with Ethnic Identity Models," *Journal of Organizational Change Management* 7, no. 6 (1994): 18–33.

11. Nico H. Frijda, Peter Kuipers, and Elisabeth ter Schure, "Relations Among Emotion, Appraisal, and Emotional Action Readiness," *Journal of Personality and Social Psychology* 57, no. 2 (1989): 212–222; Taya R. Cohen et al., "Introducing the GASP Scale: A New Measure of Guilt and Shame Proneness," *Journal of Personality and Social Psychology* 100, no. 5 (2011): 947–966.

12. See, respectively, Paul Restucca, "Looking for Greater Results; Studies Show Training Often Fails to Change Minority Hiring Mix," *Boston Herald*, April 14, 2008; Barbara Kessler, "A Case Study in Diversity: An Awareness-Training Course Reveals the Complexity of Bridging Difference," *Dallas Morning News*, April 25, 1994.

13. See, for example, Penny Lunt, "Should You Do Diversity Training?" *ABA Banking Journal* 86 (1994): 53–55; Patricia L. Nemetz and Sandra L. Christensen, "The Challenge of Cultural Diversity: Harnessing a Diversity of Views to Understand Multiculturalism," *Academy of Management Review* 21, no. 2 (1996): 434–462.

14. William Beaver, "Let's Stop Diversity Training and Start Managing for Diversity," *Industrial Management*, July–August 1995, 7.

15. Todd L. Pittinsky, "A Two-Dimensional Theory of Intergroup Leadership: The Case of National Diversity," *American Psychologist* 65, no. 3 (2010): 194–200.

16. See, for example, ibid.; Todd L. Pittinsky and Stefanie Simon, "Intergroup Leadership," *Leadership Quarterly* 18, no. 6 (2007): 586–605; Todd L. Pittinsky, ed., *Crossing the Divide: Intergroup Leadership in a World of Difference* (Boston: Harvard Business School Press, 2009).

17. Marilynn B. Brewer and Norman Miller, "Beyond the Contact Hypothesis: Theoretical Perspectives on Desegregation," in *Contact and Conflict in Intergroup Encounters*, ed. Miles Hewstone and Rupert J. Brown (Oxford, UK: Blackwell, 1984), 281–302.

18. Samuel L. Gaertner et al., "Reducing Intergroup Bias: The Benefits of Recategorization," *Journal of Personality and Social Psychology* 57, no. 2 (1989): 239–249.

19. Matthew J. Hornsey and Michael A. Hogg, "Assimilation and Diversity: An Integrative Model of Subgroup Relations," *Personality and Social Psychology Review* 4, no. 2 (2000): 143–156.

20. Muzafer Sherif, "Superordinate Goals in the Reduction of Intergroup Conflict," *American Journal of Sociology* 63, no. 4 (1958): 349–356.

21. Barack Obama, "Remarks by the President on a New Beginning," white house.gov, http://www.whitehouse.gov/the_press_office/Remarks-by-the-President-at-Cairo-University-6-04-09/.

22. Poppy McLeod, Sharon Lobel, and Taylor Cox, "Ethnic Diversity and Creativity in Small Groups," *Small Group Research* 2, no. 27 (1996): 248–264.

23. Robert Putnam, "E Pluribus Unum: Diversity and Community in the Twenty-first Century: The 2006 Johan Skytte Prize Lecture," *Scandinavian Political Studies* 30, no. 2 (2007): 137–174.

24. Michael Jonas, "The Downside of Diversity: A Harvard Political Scientist Finds That Diversity Hurts Civic Life," *Boston Globe,* August 5, 2007.

25. William E. Cross Jr. and Linda Strauss, "The Everyday Functions of African American Identity," in *Prejudice: The Target's Perspective,* ed. Janet K. Swim and Charles Stangor (San Diego, CA: Academic Press, 1998), 267–279; Nancy A. Gonzales and Ana Mari Cauce, "Ethnic Identity and Multicultural Competence: Dilemma and Challenges for Minority Youth," in *Toward a Common Destiny: Improving Race and Ethnic Relations in America,* ed. Willis D. Hawley and Anthony W. Jackson (San Francisco: Jossey-Bass, 1995), 131–162.

26. Todd L. Pittinsky, "Allophilia: A Cornerstone for Citizenship Education in Pluralistic Countries," *Citizenship Teaching and Learning* 6, no. 2 (March 2011): 175–187.

27. Thomas F. Pettigrew and Linda Tropp, "A Meta-Analytic Test of Intergroup Contact Theory," *Journal of Personality and Social Psychology* 90 (2006): 751–783.

28. International Bureau of the American Republics, "Notable Address by President Wilson," *Bulletin of the Pan American Union* 37 (1913): 685.

29. Sam Dillon, "Foreign Languages Fade in Class—Except Chinese," *New York Times,* January 20, 2010, http://www.nytimes.com/2010/01/21/education/21chinese.html.

30. http://www.thecommentator.com/article/167/the_eurozone_germany_crisis_opportunity?print=true.

31. Chana Joffe-Walt, "During the Holidays, Greeks Discuss Country's Future," National Public Radio, http://www.npr.org/2011/12/22/144149761/during-the-holidays-greeks-discuss-countrys-future.

32. Robert M. Sapolsky, "A Natural History of Peace," *Foreign Affairs* 85, no. 1 (2006): 104–120.

33. Summary of "A Natural History of Peace," by Robert M. Sapolsky, *Foreign Affairs,* January–February 2006, http://www.foreignaffairs.com/articles/61382/robert-m-sapolsky/a-natural-history-of-peace.

34. "New Baboon," *Radiolab,* WNYC, October 2, 2009, http://beta.radiolab.org/2009/oct/19/new-baboon/.

## Chapter Five

1. Senegal's constitution provides for freedom of religion, and the government generally respects this right in practice. See Bureau of Democracy, Human Rights, and Labor, "Senegal," *International Religious Freedom Report 2006,* http://www.state.gov/g/drl/rls/irf/2006/71321.htm.

2. Edward Harris, "Muslim Christmas in Senegal," Associated Press, December 24, 2005, http://www.foxnews.com/story/0,2933,179678,00.html.

3. Ibid.

4. Helle Mathiasen, "Empathy and Sympathy: Voices from Literature," *American Journal of Cardiology* 97, no. 12 (2006): 1789–1790.

5. Changming Duan and Clara E. Hill, "The Current State of Empathy Research," *Journal of Counseling Psychology* 43, no. 3 (1996): 261–274; Krystina A. Finlay and Walter G. Stephan, "Improving Intergroup Relations: The Effects of Empathy on Racial Attitudes," *Journal of Applied Social Psychology* 30, no. 8 (2000): 1720–1737; Zipora Shechtman and Ola Basheer, "Normative Beliefs Supporting Aggression of Arab Children in an Inter-Group Conflict," *Aggressive Behavior* 31 (2005): 1–12.

6. Edward B. Royzman and Paul Rozin, "Limits of Symhedonia: The Differential Role of Prior Emotional Attachment in Sympathy and Sympathetic Joy," *Emotion* 6, no. 1 (February 2006): 82.

7. Jane Lazarre, *Beyond the Whiteness of Whiteness: Memoir of a White Mother of Black Sons* (Durham, NC: Duke University Press, 1996): 4.

8. C. Daniel Batson et al., "Empathic Joy and the Empathy–Altruism Hypothesis," *Journal of Personality and Social Psychology* 61, no. 3 (September 1991): 413–426.

9. Irwin Katz, Joyce Wackenhut, and R. Glen Hass, "Racial Ambivalence, Value Duality, and Behavior," in *Prejudice, Discrimination, and Racism: Theory and Research,* ed. John F. Dovidio and Samuel L. Gaertner (New York: Academic Press, 1986), 35–59.

10. Alexander M. Czopp and Margo J. Monteith, "Thinking Well of African Americans: Measuring Complimentary Stereotypes and Negative Prejudice," *Basic and Applied Social Psychology* 28, no. 3 (2006): 233–250.

11. Donna Eisenstadt et al., "Dissonance and Prejudice: Personal Costs, Choice, and Change in Attitudes and Racial Beliefs Following Counter-Attitudinal Advocacy That Benefits a Minority," *Basic and Applied Social Psychology* 7 (2005): 127–141.

12. Theodore Ribot, as quoted by Stephen D. Reicher, "The Determination of Collective Behaviour," in *Social Identity and Intergroup Relations,* ed. Henri Tajfel (Cambridge, UK: Cambridge University Press, 1982), 63–64.

13. Jon E. Roeckelein, *Elsevier's Dictionary of Psychological Theories* (Amsterdam: Elsevier, 2006), 190.

14. Todd L. Pittinsky and R. Matthew Montoya, "Symhedonia in Intergroup Relations: The Relationship of Empathic Joy to Prejudice and Allophilia," *Psicologia Sociale* 3 (2009): 347–364.

15. Ibid.

16. David Hume, *A Treatise of Human Nature* (London: Everyman, 1751; rprt. 1911).

17. For example, one researcher found that positive and negative emotions independently predicted evaluations of minority groups; see Anton J. Dijker, "Emotional Reactions to Ethnic Minorities," *European Journal of Social Psychology* 17, no. 3 (1987): 305–325.

18. Tania Tam et al., "The Mediational Role of Intergroup Emotions and Empathy in Contact Between Catholics and Protestants in Northern Ireland" (unpublished manuscript).

19. Ibid.; *Coexistence in Israel: A National Study* (Cambridge, MA: Harvard Kennedy School, Center for Public Leadership, 2008).

20. Barbara L. Fredrickson, "The Role of Positive Emotions in Positive Psychology: The Broaden-and-Build Theory of Positive Emotions," *American Psychologist* 56, no. 3 (2001): 218–226; Barbara L. Fredrickson, "What Good Are Positive Emotions?" *Review of General Psychology* 2, no. 3 (1998): 300–319; Barbara Fredrickson and Christine Branigan, "Positive Emotions Broaden the Scope of Attention and Thought-Action Repertoires," *Cognition and Emotion* 19, no. 3 (2005): 313–332.

21. Stefan Stürmer, Mark Snyder, and Allen Omoto, "Prosocial Emotions and Helping: The Moderating Role of Group Membership," *Journal of Personality and Social Psychology* 88, no. 3 (2005): 532–546.

22. Pittinsky and Montoya, "Symhedonia in Intergroup Relations."

23. Walter G. Stephan and Krystina Finlay, "The Role of Empathy in Improving Intergroup Relations," *Journal of Social Issues* 55, no. 4 (1999): 729–743.

24. Oscar Wilde, *The Plays of Oscar Wilde* (Ware, UK: Wordsworth Classics, 2000), 330.

25. Bruce Blaine, Jennifer Crocker, and Brenda Major, "The Unintended Negative Consequences of Sympathy for the Stigmatized," *Journal of Applied Social Psychology* 25, no. 10 (May 1995): 889–905.

26. Charles R. Figley, *Compassion Fatigue: Coping with Secondary Traumatic Stress Disorder in Those Who Treat the Traumatized* (New York: Brunner/Mazel, 1995), 232–248.

27. Carol A. Williams, "Empathy and Burnout in Male and Female Helping Professions," *Research in Nursing and Health* 12 (1989): 169–178.

28. Xiaojing Xu et al., "Do You Feel My Pain? Racial Group Membership Modulates Empathic Neural Responses," *Journal of Neuroscience* 29, no. 26 (July, 2009): 8525–8529.

29. Martin L. Hoffman, *Empathy and Moral Development: Implications for Caring and Justice* (Cambridge, UK: Cambridge University Press, 2000).

30. C. Daniel Batson et al., "Empathy, Attitudes, and Action: Can Feeling for a Member of a Stigmatized Group Motivate One to Help the Group?" *Personality and Social Psychology Bulletin* 28, no. 12 (2002): 1656–1666.

31. Finlay and Stephan, "Improving Intergroup Relations."

32. Michael J. Weiner and Frances E. Wright, "Effects of Undergoing Arbitrary Discrimination Upon Subsequent Attitudes Toward a Minority Group," *Journal of Applied Social Psychology* 3, no. 1 (January 1973): 94–102.

33. Nancy Eisenberg et al., "Relation of Sympathy and Personal Distress to Prosocial Behavior: A Multimethod Study," *Journal of Personality and Social Psychology* 57, no. 1 (July 1989): 55–66.

34. C. Daniel Batson et al., "Similarity and Nurturance: Two Possible Sources of Empathy for Strangers," *Basic and Applied Social Psychology* 27 (2005): 15–25; Mark H. Davis, *Empathy: A Social Psychological Approach* (Boulder, CO: Westview Press, 1994), 57; Mark H. Davis, "A Multidimensional Approach to Individual Differences in Empathy," *JSAS Catalogue of Selected Documents in Psychology* 10, no. 4 (1980): 1–17.

35. Davis, *Empathy*, 56.

36. Tania Tam et al., "Postconflict Reconciliation: Intergroup Forgiveness and Implicit Biases in Northern Ireland," *Journal of Social Issues* 64, no. 2 (June 2008): 303–320.

37. Serge Moscovici and Juan A. Pérez, "A Study of Minorities as Victims," *European Journal of Social Psychology* 37, no. 4 (July–August, 1972): 725–746.

38. Royzman and Rozin, "Limits of Symhedonia."

39. Ibid., 82.

40. Ibid.

41. Ibid.

42. Batson et al., "Empathic Joy and the Empathy–Altruism Hypothesis."

43. C. Daniel Batson, Shannon Early, and Giovanni Salvarani, "Perspective Taking: Imagining How Another Feels Versus Imagining How You Would Feel," *Personality and Social Psychology Bulletin* 23, no. 7 (1997): 741–758.

44. Thich Nhat Hanh, *The Heart of the Buddha's Teaching: Transforming Suffering into Peace, Joy, and Liberation* (Berkeley, CA: Parallax Press, 1998).

45. Sara Miller Llana, "Mexicans Cross 'the Border'—at a Theme Park," *Christian Science Monitor,* February 21, 2007, http://www.csmonitor.com/2007/0221/p01s04-woam.html.

46. Candace Clark, *Sympathy and Misery* (Chicago: University of Chicago Press, 1997).

47. Ibid.

48. Stephan and Finlay, "The Role of Empathy in Improving Intergroup Relations," 738, 740, and 732.

49. Peter Knight, "Empathy: Concept, Confusion and Consequences in a National Curriculum," *Oxford Review of Education* 15, no. 1 (1989): 41–53.

50. Peter J. Lee, quoted in Susan D. Dion and Michael Dion, *Braiding Histories: Learning from Aboriginal Peoples' Experiences and Perspective* (Vancouver, BC: UBC Press, 1998), 125.

51. O. L. Davis Jr., "In Pursuit of Historical Empathy," in *Historical Empathy and Perspective Taking in the Social Studies,* ed. O. L. Davis Jr., Elizabeth Anne Yeager, and Stuart J. Foster (Lanham, MD: Rowman and Littlefield, 2001).

52. Tony Aiello, "Teacher Under Fire for Misguided Slavery Lesson," WCBSTV, December 5, 2008, http://wcbstv.com/watercooler/slavery.haverstraw.middle.2.880370.html.

53. http://brandellvolunteercenter36844.orgsync.com/org/cmuvolunteercenter/davidgarcia.

54. Winnie Hu, "Gossip Girls and Boys Get Lessons in Empathy," *New York Times,* April 5, 2009.

55. Ibid.

56. Ibid.

57. http://en.wikipedia.org/wiki/Facing_History_and_Ourselves.

58. Peter Beckmann, *Whispered Anecdotes: Humor from Behind the Iron Curtain* (Boulder, CO: Golem Press, 1969); Ben Lewis, "Hammer & Tickle," *Prospect,* May 20, 2006. http://www.prospectmagazine.co.uk/2006/05/communist-jokes/.

59. Elaine Sciolino, "By Making Holocaust Personal to Pupils, Sarkozy Stirs Anger," *New York Times,* February 16, 2008, http://www.nytimes.com/2008/02/16/world/europe/16france.html.

60. Davis, "In Pursuit of Historical Empathy."

61. Introduction by George Lipsitz to Johnny Otis, *Listen to the Lambs* (Minneapolis: University of Minnesota Press, 2009), xxi.

62. Emanuel Ringelblum, "Poetry in Hell," trans. Sarah Moskovitz, http://poetryinhell.org.

63. Yad Vashem, "'Let the World Read and Know': The Oneg Shabbat Archives," The Holocaust Martyrs' and Heroes' Remembrance Authority, http://www1.yadvashem.org/yv/en/exhibitions/ringelbum/ringelblum.asp.

64. Marty T. Glynn, Geoffrey Bock, and Karen C. Cohn, *American Youth and the Holocaust: A Study of Four Major Holocaust Curricula* (New York: National Jewish Resource Center, 1982).

65. Adam Galinsky et al., "Power and Perspectives Not Taken," *Psychological Science* 17, no. 12 (2006): 1068–1074.

66. "Play SPENT," Urban Ministries of Durham website, http://www.umdurham.org/spent.html.

67. Personal communication, February 1, 2012.

68. Ibid.

## Chapter Six

1. *Anger management:* Howard C. Stevenson, "Managing Anger: Protective, Proactive, or Adaptive Racial Socialization Identity Profiles and African-American Manhood Development," *Journal of Prevention and Intervention in the Community* 16, no. 1–2 (1997): 35–61; *lowered depression risk:* Jelani Mandara et al., "The Effects of Changes in Racial Identity and Self-Esteem on Changes in African American Adolescents' Mental Health," *Child Development* 80, no. 6 (2009): 1660–1675; *academic success:* Emilie Phillips Smith, Jacqueline Atkins, and Christian M. Connell, "Family, School, and Community Influences upon Ethnic Attitudes and Relationships to Academic Outcomes," *American Journal of Community Psychology* 32, no. 1–2 (2003): 159–173; Tabbye M. Chavous et al., "Racial Identity and Academic Attainment Among African American Adolescents," *Child Development* 74, no. 4 (2003): 1076–1090.

2. Zora Neale Hurston, "How It Feels to Be Colored Me," *The World Tomorrow,* May 1928.

3. Lok-Sin Loa, "Dongshan Township School Readopts Its Old Aborigine Name," *Taipei Times,* July 24, 2010, http://www.taipeitimes.com/News/taiwan/archives/2010/07/24/2003478691.

4. Not all activists for people with disabilities agreed; some felt it might be seen as a deliberate play for sympathy, others feel the monument should reflect the fact that Franklin Delano Roosevelt himself made great efforts to hide his disability. In the end, only a small bit of the wheelchair is visible—from the back of the statue.

5. The idea that pride takes different forms and that these different forms can be either good or problematic has a rich tradition in different disciplines. It can be seen in social science research showing that the experience of pride comes in "two flavors," the consequences of which can be either positive behaviors and outcomes or more negative outcomes, such as aggression, hostility, and conflict. For different approaches on

the "two flavors" of pride, see J. L. Tracy and C. Prehn, "Arrogant or Self-confident? The Use of Contextual Knowledge to Differentiate Hubristic and Authentic Pride from a Single Nonverbal Expression," *Cognition & Emotion* 26 (2012): 14–24; B. J. Bushman and R. F. Baumeister, "Threatened Egotism, Narcissism, Self-Esteem, and Direct and Displaced Aggression: Does Self-Love or Self-Hate Lead to Violence?" *Journal of Personality and Social Psychology* 75, no. 1 (1998): 219–229; W. Keith Campbell, "Narcissism and Romantic Attraction," *Journal of Personality and Social Psychology* 77, no. 6 (1999): 1254–1270; Carol. C. Morf and Frederick Rhodewalt, "Unraveling the Paradoxes of Narcissism: A Dynamic Self-Regulatory Processing Model," *Psychological Inquiry* 12, no. 4 (2001): 177–196; Delroy L. Paulhus et al., "Two Replicable Suppressor Situations in Personality Research," *Multivariate Behavioral Research* 39, no. 2 (2004): 303–328. In this chapter, I consider not the kinds of pride we experience ourselves, but rather two kinds of pride we can *attribute* to others; see J. J. Ratcliff, T. L. Pittinsky, and S. Simon, "The Contrasting Influence of Perceived Hubristic- and Authentic-Pride on Intergroup Relations," poster presentation at the tenth annual meeting of the Society for Personality and Social Psychology, Tampa, FL, February 2009.

6. Tom Ashbrook, "Iraq After the Drawdown," *On Point,* August 24, 2010, http://www.onpointradio.org/2010/08/iraq-after-the-drawdown.

7. Nicholas Kulish, "German Identity, Long Dormant, Reasserts Itself," *New York Times,* September 11, 2010, http://www.nytimes.com/2010/09/11/world/europe/11germany.html.

8. Ibid.

9. Seymour Feshbach, "Nationalism, Patriotism, and Aggression: A Clarification of Functional Differences," in *Aggressive Behavior: Current Perspectives,* ed. L. Rowell Huesmann (New York: Putnam, 1994), 275–291; Rick Kosterman and Seymour Feshbach, "Towards a Measure of Patriotic and Nationalistic Attitudes," *Political Psychology* 10 (1989): 257–274.

10. There is a related question: whether we are more likely to interpret something as narcissistic when exhibited by a member of a group we don't like. The dislike might precede the perception of narcissism, rather than resulting from it. As with many relations in the social sciences, these two are likely intertwined; we are more likely to dislike groups we perceive as collectively narcissistic (such as "Wall Street bankers") and when we dislike a group, an act that might otherwise have been seen as simply prideful may be instead be perceived as narcissistic.

11. Laura E. Buffardi and W. Keith Campbell, "Narcissism and Social Networking Websites," *Personality and Social Psychology Bulletin* 34 (2008): 1303–1324.

12. The reader may be wondering if allophilia applies in a case like this. Isn't negativity or positivity really displayed toward the American government or American leadership rather than toward the American people? Actually, the three are much more intertwined than is commonly recognized. During the invasion of Iraq, for example, we often heard from pundits around the globe that people in their countries like Americans; it's America—that is, the actions of the American government or of American businesses—that they strongly dislike. This sounds reasonable but is scientifically dubious; it is not clear that our brains maintain such rigid distinctions. There is experimental evidence, for example, that negative feelings about a leader (a nation's

president, for example) will engender negative feelings about the leader's followers—the rest of us. See Todd L. Pittinsky et al., "How and When Leader Behavior Affects Intergroup Liking: Affect, Approval, and Allophilia," in *Research on Managing Groups and Teams: Affect and Groups*, ed. Elizabeth A. Mannix, Margaret A. Neale, and Cameron Anderson (Oxford, UK: Elsevier Science Press, 2007): 125–144. In addition, as an applied example of how the actions of a nation reflect back on perceptions of the national collective, consider a headline in the London's *Daily Mirror* after the election of President George W. Bush: "How Can 59,054,087 People Be So Dumb?" November 4, 2004.

13. Todd L. Pittinsky, "Winning Hearts and Minds: From Slogan to Leadership Strategy," in *Rethinking Leadership and "Whole of Government" National Security Reform: Problems, Progress, and Prospects*, ed. Joseph R. Cerami and Jeffrey A. Engel (Carlisle, PA: Strategic Studies Institute, U.S. Army War College, 2010), 165–186.

14. Christopher Clarey, "Cathy Freeman Is Sprinting with the Torch of Aboriginal Pride," http://www.nytimes.com/specials/olympics/cntdown/0505oly-run-aussie-sprinter.html.

15. Larry Rivera, "Australia's Aboriginal Olympians: Cathy Freeman, Nova Peris-Kneebone," *New York Times*, May 5, 1996, http://www.nytimes.com/specials/olympics/cntdown/0505oly-run-aussie-sprinter.html.

16. "A Tribute to Cathy Freeman," *Wandoo Didgeridoo*, http://www.wadidge.com.au/didgeridoo-news/cathyfreeman.html.

17. Charlie Savage, "A Judge's View of Judging Is on the Record," *New York Times*, May 14, 2009, http://www.nytimes.com/2009/05/15/us/15judge.html.

18. Michael Kinsley, "The Religious Superiority Complex," *Time*, October 27, 2003, http://www.time.com/time/magazine/article/0,9171,1101031103-526503,00.html.

19. Stefan Theil, "No Country Is More 'Green by Design,'" *Newsweek*, June 28, 2008, http://www.newsweek.com/2008/06/28/no-country-is-more-green-by-design.html.

20. "The World's Greenest Countries," *Newsweek*, http://www.newsweek.com/2008/01/22/the-world-s-greenest-countries.html.

21. Joanne Sheehan, "Decades of Nonviolence Training: Practicing Nonviolence," *Nonviolent Activist*, July–August 1998, http://www.warresisters.org/nva0798-4.htm.

22. Ibid.

## Chapter Seven

1. Keith Orr, "Fred Phelps Press Release," http://www.autbar.com/fred_phelps_press_release.htm.

2. Ibid.

3. Ibid.

4. Chester (Chet) William Powers Jr., "Let's Get Together" [also recorded as "Get Together"].

5. Peter Applebome, "Our Towns; The Man Behind Rosa Parks," *New York Times*, December 7, 2005, http://query.nytimes.com/gst/fullpage.html?res=9903E7DE1031F934A35751C1A9639C8B63&pagewanted=all.

6. Marilynn Brewer, Valerie Dull, and Layton Lui, "Perceptions of the Elderly: Stereotypes as Prototypes," *Journal of Personality and Social Psychology* 41, no. 4

(1981): 656–670; Shelley E. Taylor, "A Categorization Approach to Stereotyping," in *Cognitive Processes in Stereotyping and Intergroup Behavior,* ed. David L. Hamilton (Hillsdale, NJ: Lawrence Erlbaum, 1981), 83–114; David L. Hamilton and Jim S. Sherman, "Stereotypes," in *Handbook of Social Cognition,* 2nd ed., ed. Robert S. Wyer Jr. and Thomas K. Srull (Hillsdale, NJ: Erlbaum, 1994), 1–68.

7. Gordon Allport, *The Nature of Prejudice* (Cambridge, MA: Addison-Wesley, 1954); Thomas Pettigrew and Linda Tropp, "A Meta-analytic Test of Intergroup Contact Theory," *Journal of Personality and Social Psychology* 90, no. 5 (2006): 751–783.

8. Gary Rosenblatt, "Baby Steps Toward Arab-Jewish Cooperation," *Jewish Week,* July 5, 2011, http://www.thejewishweek.com/editorial_opinion/gary_rosenblatt/baby_steps_toward_arab_jewish_cooperation; Dan Fleshler, "Defiant Dreamers of Arab-Jewish Coexistence," *Huffington Post,* June 22, 2011, http://www.huffingtonpost.com/dan-fleshler/defiant-dreamers-of-coexistence_b_880199.html.

9. Fleshler, "Defiant Dreamers of Arab-Jewish Coexistence."

10. Leon Festinger, Stanley Schachter, and Kurt Back, *Social Pressures in Informal Groups* (Cambridge, MA: MIT Press, 1948).

11. Lex Rieffel, "Reconsidering the Peace Corps: Volunteering, Global Governance, U.S. Politics, International Organizations, Civil Society," *Brookings Policy Brief Series #127,* The Brookings Institution, December 2003, http://www.brookings.edu/papers/2003/12globalgovernance_rieffel.aspx.

12. Thomas L. Friedman, "Surprise, Surprise, Surprise," *New York Times,* August 21, 2010, http://www.nytimes.com/2010/08/22/opinion/22friedman.html.

13. Todd L. Pittinsky and Stefanie Simon, "Intergroup Leadership," *Leadership Quarterly* 18, no. 6 (2007): 586–605; Todd L. Pittinsky, ed., *Crossing the Divide: Intergroup Leadership in a World of Difference* (Boston: Harvard Business School Press, 2009).

14. As noted in chapter 2, it is not a complete separation of factors that affect positive attitudes toward the "other" and factors that affect negative attitudes toward the "other." Factors that are most important in increasing positive attitudes are likely to have some effect on reducing negative attitudes as well, though not as much.

15. Associated Press, "Sen. Scott Brown, Elizabeth Warren Agree to Curb Attack Ads," *Boston Herald,* January 23, 2012, http://bostonherald.com/news/us_politics/view.bg?articleid=1398120.

16. J. David Goodman, "U.S. Navy Says It Assists Third Iranian Crew in Distress," *New York Times,* January 19, 2012, http://www.nytimes.com/2012/01/20/world/middleeast/united-states-navy-says-it-assists-third-iranian-crew-in-distress.html.

17. Zbigniew Brzezinski, interview by Judy Woodruff, "Brzezinski: U.S. Should Work With Russia, Turkey to Solve Global Problems," *PBS NewsHour,* National Public Radio, February 8, 2012, http://www.pbs.org/newshour/bb/business/jan-june12/brzezinski_02-08.html.

18. Marilynn B. Brewer, "In-Group Bias in the Minimal Intergroup Situation: A Cognitive-Motivational Analysis," *Psychological Bulletin* 86, no. 2 (1979): 307–324; John C. Turner, "Social Categorization and Social Discrimination in the Minimal Group Paradigm," in *Differentiation Between Social Groups: Studies in the Social Psy-*

*chology of Intergroup Relations,* ed. Henri Tajfel (London: Academic, 1978): 235–250; Marilynn Brewer, "The Psychology of Prejudice: Ingroup Love or Outgroup Hate?" *Journal of Social Issues* 55, no. 3 (1999): 429–444.

19. Naomi Struch and Shalom H. Schwartz, "Intergroup Aggression: Its Predictors and Distinctness from In-Group Bias," *Journal of Personality and Social Psychology* 56, no. 3 (March 1989): 364–373.

20. Marilynn Brewer and Robert J. Brown, "Intergroup Relations," in *Handbook of Social Psychology,* 4th ed., eds. Daniel T. Gilbert, Susan T. Fiske, and Gardner Lindzey (New York: Oxford University Press, 1998), 554–594.

21. Amélie Mummendey et al., "Categorization Is Not Enough: Intergroup Discrimination in Negative Outcome Allocations," *Journal of Experimental Social Psychology* 28 (1992): 125–144.

22. Maya Sela, "Jordan's Queen Rania Rejects Offer to Publish Hebrew Edition of Her Children's Book," *Haaretz,* July 14, 2010, http://www.haaretz.com/misc/article-print-page/jordan-s-queen-rania-rejects-offer-to-publish-hebrew-edition-of-her-children-s-book-1.301791.

23. Nicholas Kulish, "German Identity, Long Dormant, Reasserts Itself," *New York Times,* September 11, 2010, http://www.nytimes.com/2010/09/11/world/europe/11germany.html.

24. "Diversity and Social Cohesion Program: Everyone Belongs" (Belconnen, Australia: Department of Immigration and Citizenship, 2010), http://www.harmony.gov.au.

25. http://www.unaoc.org/repository/implementation_plan.pdf.

26. Claudia Rosett, "The U.N.'s 'Alliance of Civilizations,'" *Forbes,* March 26, 2009, http://www.forbes.com/2009/03/25/alliance-of-civilizations-opinions-columnists-obama-un.html.

27. Home page of United Nations Alliance of Civilizations website, http://www.unaoc.org, accessed October 30, 2010; Wikipedia contributors, "Alliance of Civilizations," *Wikipedia, the Free Encyclopedia,* http://en.wikipedia.org/wiki/Alliance_of_Civilizations.

28. Todd L. Pittinsky, "Winning Hearts and Minds: From Slogan to Leadership Strategy," in *Rethinking Leadership and 'Whole of Government' National Security Reform: Problems, Progress, and Prospects,* ed. Joseph R. Cerami and Jeffrey A. Engel (Carlisle, PA: Strategic Studies Institute, U.S. Army War College, 2010), 165–186.

29. Abraham A. Maslow, "Theory of Human Motivation," *Psychological Review* 50, no. 4 (1943): 370–396.

30. Somini Sengupta and Evelyn M. Rusli, "Personal Data's Value? Facebook Set to Find Out," *New York Times,* February 1, 2012; Shayndi Raice, "Facebook Sets Historic IPO," *Wall Street Journal,* February 1, 2012.

31. Quoted in Raice, "Facebook Sets Historic IPO."

32. Alex Soble, "The Business Brand of America," *Yale Globalist,* 2009, http://tyglobalist.org/index.php/20090404186/Focus/The-Business-of-Brand-America.html.

33. Aaron Retica, "Homophily," *New York Times Magazine,* December 10, 2006, http://www.nytimes.com/2006/12/10/magazine/10Section2a.t-4.html.

34. "UnSuggester," LibraryThing website, http://www.librarything.com/unsuggester/2608.

35. Jessica Beinecke, interview with Hari Sreenivasan, "'OMG! Meiyu' Introduces China to American Slang, Idioms and Jay-Z," *PBS NewsHour,* February 10, 2012, http://www.pbs.org/newshour/bb/world/jan-june12/omg_02-10.html.

36. As it happens, Beinecke works at Voice of America, but OMG! Mieyu is not a VOA production; quotation is from Jessica Beinecke, interview.

37. "About the Movement," Interfaith Youth Core [*sic*] website, http://www.ifyc.org/about-movement, accessed February 11, 2012.

38. "Interfaith Leaders," Interfaith Youth Core [*sic*] website, http://www.ifyc.org/interfaith-leaders, accessed January 2012; Ruthie Arbeiter, "Stanford Shares the Love," *Stanford Review,* February 5, 2010, http://stanfordreview.org/article/stanford-shares-the-love/. Hillel is a worldwide Jewish campus organization.

39. Douglas Martin, "Jerzy Kluger, John Paul's Jewish Confidant, Dies at 90," *New York Times,* January 7, 2012, http://www.nytimes.com/2012/01/08/world/europe/jerzy-kluger-pope-john-paul-iis-jewish-confidant-dies-at-90.html. Martin is citing Jonathan Kwitny, *Man of the Century: The Life and Times of John Paul II* (New York: Henry Holt, 1997).

40. Jonathan Sacks, *The Dignity of Difference: How to Avoid the Clash of Civilizations* (London: Continuum, 2009), 9.

41. Jane Lapman, "Religious Tolerance Before It Was Hip," *Christian Science Monitor,* July 25, 2002, http://www.csmonitor.com/2002/0725/p15s02-bogn.html.

# INDEX

# ABOUT THE AUTHOR

**TODD L. PITTINSKY** is associate professor of technology and society at SUNY Stony Brook. He was previously associate professor of public policy at the Harvard Kennedy School, where he served as research director for Harvard's Center for Public Leadership. In 2001, he launched the Allophilia Project (www.allophilia.org) to understand and advance the positive attitudes people can have for groups other than their own; that is, attitudes that go beyond tolerance to proactive engagement, enthusiasm, support, and enjoyment. Pittinsky is the coauthor of *Working Fathers: New Strategies for Balancing Work and Family,* editor of *Crossing the Divide: Intergroup Leadership in a World of Difference,* and coeditor of *Restoring Trust in Organizations and Leaders: Enduring Challenges and Emerging Answers.* Published widely in scholarly journals, his work has also been profiled in *The Economist* and the *Boston Globe* and has been cited in *Science,* the *Washington Post,* and the *Wall Street Journal* and on National Public Radio. He received his BA in psychology from Yale and his PhD jointly from Harvard's Graduate School of Arts and Science and Harvard Business School. Pittinsky has worked for leading technology companies, including Netscape and Opsware, and consults to organizations in the for-profit, nonprofit, and government sectors. Pittinsky can be reached at todd@pittinsky.com.